T0294643

The Art of Access

The Art of Access

A Practical Guide for
Museum Accessibility

Heather Pressman and Danielle Schulz

ROWMAN & LITTLEFIELD
Lanham • Boulder • New York • London

Published by Rowman & Littlefield
An imprint of The Rowman & Littlefield Publishing Group, Inc.
4501 Forbes Boulevard, Suite 200, Lanham, Maryland 20706
www.rowman.com

6 Tinworth Street, London SE11 5AL, United Kingdom

British Library Cataloguing in Publication Information Available

Library of Congress Cataloging-in-Publication Data

Names: Pressman, Heather, 1980- author. | Schulz, Danielle, 1984- author.
Title: The art of access : a practical guide for museum accessibility /
  Heather Pressman and Danielle Schulz.
Description: Lanham : Rowman & Littlefield, [2021] | Includes
  bibliographical references and index.
Identifiers: LCCN 2020052936 (print) | LCCN 2020052937 (ebook) | ISBN
  9781538130506 (cloth) | ISBN 9781538130513 (paperback) | ISBN
  9781538130520 (epub)
Subjects: LCSH: Museums and people with disabilities—United States. |
  Museum buildings—Barrier-free design—United States. | Museums—Social
  aspects—United States.
Classification: LCC AM160 .P74 2021 (print) | LCC AM160 (ebook) | DDC
  069/.170973—dc23
LC record available at https://lccn.loc.gov/2020052936
LC ebook record available at https://lccn.loc.gov/2020052937

This book is dedicated to everyone
who is "different, not less."

Contents

Acknowledgments

This book would not have been possible without the help, support, and expertise of many people. We would like to thank the founding members of the Art of Access Alliance Denver: Misha Fraser, Robin Gallite, Regan Linton, Damon McLeese, and Lisa Rigsby Peterson. A very special thank you to Regan for sharing her very personal story with us and our readers.

We would like to thank Emily O'Hara, curator of exhibit design at the Detroit Zoo, for graciously sharing her exhibition design knowledge and experience with us. A portion of chapter 10 is based on a session we presented alongside her at the American Alliance of Museums Annual Meeting in 2018. Not being exhibit designers, we are greatly indebted to Emily for her assistance and guidance with this chapter.

Thank you to Max and Rebecca Miller for allowing us to share Max's words that illustrate how museum programs for people with disabilities really do make a difference and have an impact.

Many thanks to Brian "Be" Bernard for sharing his unique approach of connecting people of all abilities through his fun and interactive creative practice.

Thanks to Caroline Braden, Cecile Puretz, and Lynn Walsh for sharing their stories of the access communities of practice they helped to start in cities across the country.

We would like to thank the following organizations and individuals who gave us permission to use their images in this book: American Alliance of Museums; Brian Bernard; Boston Children's Museum; Dallas Museum of Art;

Darren Wilson of UXcentric; Denver Art Museum; Flint Hills Design; Norman Hathaway; Institute for Human Centered Design and the New England ADA Center; Miami Dade Department of Cultural Affairs; Missouri Botanic Gardens; René Moffatt; Museo tattile di pittura Antica e moderna Anteros; Museum of Science, Boston; Museum of Science and Industry, Chicago; National Endowment for the Arts; Rodrigo Nuno and HistoryMiami Museum, National Museum of American History; Rubin Museum of Art; Pentagram Design Studio; Shedd Aquarium; Smithsonian National Museum of American History; and Vizcaya House and Gardens.

Good faith efforts were made to contact and obtain permission for images used in this book. Should the rights owner come forth, we shall obtain permission and include appropriate permissions wording in future printings of this book.

Thank you to Rowman & Littlefield for the opportunity to contribute to this important work and field of study. A special thanks to our editor Charles Harmon and his staff for helping guide us through the process.

Thank you to Betty Siegel for continuing to inspire those around you and for making the world a more accessible and beautiful place.

Finally, we would like to thank our families, especially our husbands, for all their love and support while we worked on this labor of love. This book could not have happened without you.

Preface

Picture in your mind a small painting about twelve by eighteen inches in size. In the foreground there is a man with a big hat. He is also wearing clothing that resembles a coat or shirt. You can only see him from the shoulders up and he is in profile. He has a large hawk-like nose and a fairly prominent chin. In the background it looks like the countryside. How does your understanding, or the picture in your mind, change when you learn that the color of his hat and clothes are cardinal red? That he takes up most of the foreground of the picture? That he has black hair? Up until this point your understanding of this painting has been entirely based upon the information we have decided to give you. We have limited your access to the meaning of this artwork by controlling the information you receive. Too often this is the reality for someone with a disability when engaging with a museum. This type of gatekeeping of information is translated by an outside person. Thankfully, there are procedures and approaches that address this unequal access to information.

Here is a story about Jamie, who was born blind. In 2004, Jamie spent the year studying in Italy. She was working on her PhD in music history and improving her Italian. While in Italy she learned about the Istituto Francesco Cavazza, an institute for the blind in Bologna. At the institute some local artists created tactile plaster versions of famous paintings, such as Botticelli's **Venus,** to engage visitors with low or no vision. Institute volunteers, some even the artists themselves, would guide visitors through the tactile plaster paintings they created. Jamie attended several of these volunteer-led sessions, some of which included an art making component. During one of these sessions, the volunteer artist guided Jamie's hands around the painting, enabling her to create a picture of the artwork in her mind. The volunteer led Jamie's hands over the Duke of Urbino's large hat, down his aquiline nose, and across his prominent chin. Jamie was guided along the river, starting at the source where it sprawls out across the middle ground behind the Duke, and following its course as it slowly disappears into the background of the Tuscan country-side. During this experience of tracing foreground to background, the volunteer said to Jamie, "This is what people mean when they are talking about perspective." It was in that moment that a light bulb went off—at the age of forty, Jamie finally understood what perspective was. This experience of accessing the artistic elements of famous paintings through tactile plaster paintings and volunteer-led guidance afforded Jamie the opportunity to experience visual art in a new and accessible way. A way that unlocked understanding of a fundamental concept that many sighted people take for granted: perspective.

Figure P.1. *Federico da Montefeltro* by Piero della Francesca.
Source: Le Gallerie degli Uffizi

Figure P.2. Bas relief plaster version of *Federico da Montefeltro.*
Source: Museo tattile di pittura Antica e moderna Anteros

WHAT ARE INCLUSION, DIVERSITY, EQUITY, AND ACCESSIBILITY?

Jamie's story illustrates the magic that can take place when an individual is able to fully access museum experiences on their own terms in an inclusive environment. All too often the inclusion of diverse perspectives, such as Jamie's, is not the norm in cultural organizations, as there are systemic inequalities against entire segments of the population based on ability, gender identity, race, socioeconomic status, and more. Yet, spurred by questions of relevance and social value, many museums are now developing policies and practices that promote diversity, encourage equity, and cultivate an accessible and inclusive environment where experiences like Jamie's can indeed become the norm. But what exactly does it mean to be an accessible and inclusive museum?

The concepts of accessibility and inclusion are not new. Over the past six decades or so there has been an expanding emphasis on dismantling barriers to access and on engaging a much broader range of visitors. Thanks to years of advocacy and social justice work from dedicated community advocates, museums are being called upon to demonstrate their responsiveness and relevance to their communities through inclusive practices. The American Alliance of Museums (AAM) joined its strength and support to this ongoing endeavor by naming diversity, equity, accessibility, and inclusion as a chief focus of its 2016–2020 strategic plan.[1] The impetus to prioritize this work stemmed from an impassioned keynote speech from Dr. Johnnetta Betsch Cole at the 2015 AAM annual meeting, where she called for museums to be "of social value by not only inspiring but creating change around one of the most critical issues of our time—the issue of diversity."[2] Building upon foundational advocacy work completed by the Diversity Professional Network (DivCom), AAM convened the Working Group on Diversity, Equity, Accessibility, and Inclusion (DEAI) in spring 2017, composed of twenty museum professionals committed to diversity and inclusion and representing a variety of disciplines, perspectives, and areas of expertise. The group met over a period of six months to investigate effective components of inclusive museum practices and furnish working definitions of these foundational terms for the field.

AAM's definitions help contribute to the shared language of this work, shedding light on what we actually mean when we say the words "diversity," "equity," "accessibility," and "inclusion." That being said these are still working definitions, intended to be put into practice, handled, and then adjusted to fit the needs of the user. Language, words, and labels constantly shift and change over time. However, as eloquently stated by the DEAI working group, "Debate on definitions must not hinder progress."[3] The debate around these terms, and consequently the dynamic nature of DEAI work, can be uncomfortable at first, as there is always fear of the unknown and of making a mistake, particularly when the stakes are high (as they inevitably are with this work). It is for this very reason that many organizations simply avoid the situation entirely, making the case that if they do not have the expertise on-staff (i.e., a diversity or accessibility coordinator) they cannot perform access and inclusion work to a certain standard and therefore should not approach it

DIVERSITY, EQUITY, ACCESSIBILITY, AND INCLUSION DEFINITIONS

DIVERSITY

Diversity is all the ways that people are different and the same at the individual and group levels. Even when people appear the same, they are different. Organizational diversity requires examining and questioning the makeup of a group to ensure that multiple perspectives are represented.

EQUITY

Equity is the fair and just treatment of all members of a community. Equity requires commitment to strategic priorities, resources, respect, and civility, as well as ongoing action and assessment of progress toward achieving specified goals.

ACCESSIBILITY

Accessibility is giving equitable access to everyone along the continuum of human ability and experience. Accessibility encompasses the broader meanings of compliance and refers to how organizations make space for the characteristics that each person brings.

INCLUSION

Inclusion refers to the intentional, ongoing effort to ensure that diverse individuals fully participate in all aspects of organizational work, including decision-making processes.

It also refers to the ways that diverse participants are valued as respected members of an organization and/or community.

American Alliance of Museums

Figure P.3. Diversity, Equity, Accessibility, and Inclusion definitions from the American Alliance of Museums.
Source: American Alliance of Museums

at all. While these apprehensions should be acknowledged, this fear of the unknown should not outweigh the fundamental and sustainable value this type of work can afford to **all** museums. The AAM Working Group found DEAI principles to be the "bedrocks of ethical and morally courageous museum work," that when followed, can "signal how the field can remain relevant to an ever-diversifying US population."[4] Inclusion is fundamental to the viability of museums, and as a result, something which every organization can and should take on.

There is a palpable energy around this work at the moment. The recommendations provided by AAM's DEAI Working Group, as well as the framework included in this book, are coming at a time when many in the sector are ready to commit to this work. Some institutions are putting a public stake in the ground around access and inclusion and actively aligning their strategic mission and core values to DEAI principles (such as the Minneapolis Institute of Art),[5] while others are just dipping an exploratory toe into the world of equitable museum work. Regardless of where you or your organization fall along this spectrum, know that you are in good company.

ABOUT THIS BOOK

DEAI is a huge field in and of itself and as a result we could not hope to tackle it all in one book. Instead, within these pages we are going to focus on the letter "A," which is concentrating on accessibility (giving equitable access to everyone along the continuum of human ability and experience). The idea for this book was borne out of a conversation among colleagues working in the field of cultural accessibility about how to design workshops that would benefit and support museum colleagues—especially those just starting out—to engage in accessibility work. When it came to best practices for promoting access and inclusion in museums, we found an information desert to a certain extent; knowledge and resources were scattered and hard to find for those just getting started and unsure of where to look. Furthermore, when valuable resources were found, there was not an easy way to share with others. We saw many of the same questions around accessibility practices popping up on AAM, DivCom, and other such forums time and again. Much of the knowledge-sharing that did exist came through direct channels, with colleagues sharing best practices over phone calls, through emails, and in-between bites at lunches. While this is a great way to build relationships, in reality it continues to just localize the information-sharing and is only a Band-Aid to the larger issue. Obviously, there is a thirst for this type of knowledge, yet very few methods exist to properly share the work to a wider network. We knew that cities like New York and Chicago, and areas like New England and the Bay Area, had consortiums that afforded professional development opportunities and shared resources for people living in those regions.[6] But that left us, in the Mountain Plains Region, with little to no available platforms to give and receive this information. So we decided to find avenues that were available to us.

This seed of an idea—providing easily actionable accessibility steps—grew into regional and national conference presentations. While we were thrilled to be supporting people, first in our own backyard and then around the country, a frustration remained—there lacked any comprehensive, consolidated resources that we could recommend to people on how to get started making a museum accessible and inclusive. Instead, we were sending people away with a hodgepodge of internet links and suggestions for other people and places to contact (that list, albeit a bit more comprehensive, is included in appendix A). There are indeed many wonderful books out there about audience-specific access, but they do not cover the basics of getting started with general museum accessibility. Since there was not one comprehensive "how to" guide for accessible museums available, we decided to write one!

The purpose of this book is to serve as a tool in your journey to making your museum more accessible and welcoming. Disability is on the rise, with an aging population and an increase in the diagnosis of cognitive disabilities among the young. According to the 2010 census, nearly 20 percent of Americans have a disability and current estimates indicate that close to 25 percent of the population has a disability of some kind or another.[7] That means that one out of every four members in your community has a disability (whether visible or not). If your museum is excluding 25 percent of your community, whether intentionally or not, this is problematic and potentially illegal. This book applies to everyone in the museum field and every type of museum (cultural organizations too!). So who should read it? Anyone who has an interest or role in accessibility and inclusion, including educators, exhibition designers and developers, CEOs and directors, folks in marketing and communication, development staff. In short, **everyone**! If you are asking yourself, "Why do I need to make my museum more accessible? What does that even mean?" Then this book is for you!

This book will cover a variety of ideas, actions, and steps that you and your museum can take to becoming more accessible and inclusive.

In chapter 1, we will discuss the history of disability as a human rights concern, including a brief history of the Section 504 Rehabilitation Act of 1973 and the Americans with Disabilities Act (ADA), which was signed into law in 1990.

Disability Impacts
ALL of US

COMMUNITIES   HEALTH   ACCESS

61 million adults in the United States live with a disability

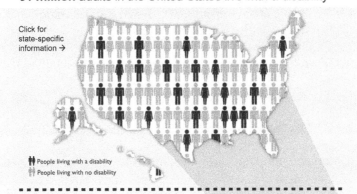

Click for
state-specific
information →

People living with a disability
People living with no disability

26% of adults in the United States have some type of disability

(1 in 4)

The percentage of people living with disabilities is highest in the South

Percentage of adults with functional disability types

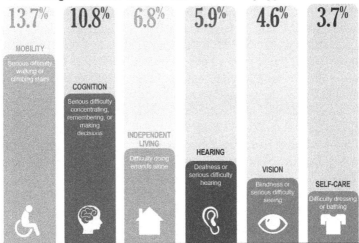

13.7%
MOBILITY
Serious difficulty walking or climbing stairs

10.8%
COGNITION
Serious difficulty concentrating, remembering, or making decisions

6.8%
INDEPENDENT LIVING
Difficulty doing errands alone

5.9%
HEARING
Deafness or serious difficulty hearing

4.6%
VISION
Blindness or serious difficulty seeing

3.7%
SELF-CARE
Difficulty dressing or bathing

Figure P.4. Centers for Disease Control and Prevention Disability Impact infographic.
Source: Centers for Disease Control and Prevention

Chapters 2 and 3 focus on partnerships, which will help make your accessible museum successful. Both community and organizational partnerships are key to the success of any accessibility and inclusion initiative.

Chapter 4 will cover the first hurdle for many people—how to physically get into your building. This chapter will explore both physical and environmental access.

Chapter 5 will look at the way museums design and present information to visitors, supporting cognitive access to spaces.

Chapter 6 covers sensory access considerations.

Chapter 7 examines ways of addressing digital accessibility needs and requirements.

Chapter 8 looks at financial access, an element of accessibility that is often overlooked.

Chapter 9 is all about language and communication. How do the words we use get interpreted?

Chapter 10 will discuss inclusive exhibitions and programming, including content, design, and even comfort, among many other things.

Chapter 11 is focused on professional development and employee training.

Chapter 12 sets you on the road to being a welcoming museum.

There are three appendices that provide available resources, define important terms, and layout questions to get started.

In these pages we shine a light on successful methods of inclusive design from the field, create a space for conversation, and demystify the perceived barriers (be they financial, cultural, or systematic) that trick museums into thinking they cannot undertake accessibility work. You may be saying, "Where do I start? What if I have zero budget and staff for this?" No matter how big or small your museum is, you can use most, if not all, the suggestions in this book. Some recommendations will take more time than others, and some will take money. You will find guidelines, stories, and examples that aim to help you and your museum become more strategic and intentional in welcoming visitors of all abilities and experiences. We offer practical and actionable steps that museums of any size can take to create the infrastructure needed for an accessible and inclusive organization. For example, one simple step we took in this book is to use **bold**, rather than *italics*, to emphasize points because it is more accessible to read by individuals with dyslexia. By the end of the book, you will understand what is legally required of museums in terms of accessibility and you will be able to create a plan to move your museum forward toward being a more accessible and welcoming institution in your community. Everyone needs support to get started, and we hope to provide the road map that enables you to take that first step.

NOTES

1. American Alliance of Museums, **Facing Change: Insights from the American Alliance of Museums' Diversity, Equity, Accessibility, and Inclusion Working Group** (Arlington, VA: American Alliance of Museums, 2018), 1. https://www.aam-us.org/wp-content/uploads/2018/04/AAM-DEAI-Working-Group-Full-Report-2018.pdf.

2. American Alliance of Museums, **Facing Change**, 1.

3. American Alliance of Museums, **Facing Change**, 8.

4. American Alliance of Museums, **Facing Change**, 4.

5. The Minneapolis Institute of Art considers inclusion and accessibility "to be a driver of institutional excellence" and they actively seek out diversity of participation, thought, and action. "Inclusion, Diversity, Accessibility and Inclusion Policy," Minneapolis Institute of Art, accessed January 31, 2019, https://new.artsmia.org/about/diversity-and-inclusion-policy/.

6. The Museum Access Consortium in New York, Chicago Cultural Accessibility Consortium, Cultural Access New England, and Bay Area Arts Access Collective.

7. "CDC: 1 in 4 US adults live with a disability," Centers for Disease Control and Prevention, last modified August 16, 2018, https://www.cdc.gov/media/releases/2018/p0816-disability.html.

Chapter One

Different, Not Less

Essential Background

Before diving into the many resources and information available to assist you in making access an integral part of your organization, it is important to first understand the history of accessibility as a human rights concern and recognize the reasons why full inclusion is essential. People with disabilities have battled against decades of ingrained prejudices and false assumptions to establish their rights. "You cannot discuss accessibility in a vacuum. You need context," asserts Betty Siegel, director of VSA and Accessibility at The John F. Kennedy Center for the Performing Arts, in her widespread and spirited presentations about cultural access.[1] The many barriers facing people with disabilities begin with attitudes—attitudes often rooted in misunderstandings and misinformation about what it is like to live with a disability. There are many different kinds of disabilities. In addition to physical, developmental, and cognitive impacts, disability can also include invisible, emotional, social, and educational challenges. Disability is quite complex, and every person is unique; no two people who identify as having the same disability will have the completely same life experiences. Misunderstandings about the experiences of people with disabilities frequently stem from deep-seated and widespread assumptions. Within these pages we will call attention to the misinformed presumptions and models of the past that have created today's stereotypes. We will then examine how they have evolved our contemporary understandings to inform the legislation that protects and promotes the rights and opportunities for individuals with disabilities. Only with this foundational information in hand can we better advocate for and support the investment of time, money, and action for all museums and cultural institutions to remove barriers from their facilities, design accessible exhibitions and programs, and provide effective communication for their museum visitors.

THE MODELS OF DISABILITY

The disability experience has changed throughout time; it has been perceived differently during distinct historical periods and by various cultures.[2]
In Western civilization, disability in the twentieth century has primarily
been defined by a medical model, which characterizes disability as being
the result of a physical (or biological) condition that causes clear disadvan-
tages and limitations to the person. This model situates disability within the
individual, and focuses on ways to cure, manage, or alter a person's illness
or disability through treatment by way of therapy, rehabilitation, or remedia-
tion. The **medical model of disability**, with its emphasis on individuals with
disabilities as the source of the problem, has led to the widespread practice
of defining people by their condition or their perceived limitations (and the
accompanying stereotypes that come along with it). Through this lens, rehabilitation programs and other health-care interventions have been viewed as
the principal means to rectify the perceived problems confronting those with
disabilities. Say we have a friend named Sally. Sally is a wheelchair user.
She decides to visit her town's art museum, the entrance of which has a flight
of ten stairs, but no ramp. Under the medical model, the limitation and barrier to entering the building belongs to Sally—it is her problem that she uses
a wheelchair and if she wants to visit the museum, she must make medical
strides to remedy her situation.

In the past, people and organizations working within the medical model
attempted to "cure" disabilities through medical means in order to improve
a person's functioning, and thus to "allow disabled persons a more 'normal'
life."[3] The onus to change was put upon the person. The medical model of
disability compelled people with disabilities to adapt to environments in the
quest for abstract normalcy. This emphasis not only led to a general misun-
derstanding of the disability experience, but it victimized people with disabilities and effectively ignored the environmental and social contributions
to disability. In order to expand the public perception of disability as being
more than a person's functional limitation, society needed to consider the full
experience of disability—including individual needs and aspirations—and
seriously review the environmental factors that create barriers, which are
themselves the real limitations.

A conceptual and cultural shift toward understanding disability through
the lens of social justice occurred in the latter part of the twentieth century
with the passage of both the Rehabilitation Act of 1973 and the Americans
with Disabilities Act of 1990 (ADA) (both laws are described in more detail
below). These landmark laws addressed the physical and societal barriers facing individuals with disabilities. The Rehabilitation Act of 1973 focused on

the removal of architectural, transportation, and employment barriers[4] while the ADA required "reasonable accommodations" for people with disabilities in public locations.[5] These acts brought public awareness to the environmental and attitudinal issues confronting disability communities. Following the passage of these two acts, academics began promoting the **social model of disability**, depicting disability as a by-product of the interaction **between** an individual and their environment. From this social model, the idea of disabling environments emerged; a setting can contain the physical or attitudinal barrier that restricts someone from participating in an activity or space. In our example with Sally, the social model recognizes that it is the building and its stairs that are the issue; these pose the barrier to Sally's participation in the museum. It is the disabling environment that needs to be fixed, not Sally or other mobility device users. Adding a ramp to the museum entrance would not only allow entry for wheelchair users like Sally, but would also create easier access for people with strollers, people temporarily on crutches, deliveries with carts/dollies, toddlers just learning to walk, and more.

The philosophies and strategies of the medical and social models of disability are vastly different. The medical model looks to fix or correct the person with a disability, thus enabling them to engage with the world. The social model looks to remove environmental barriers and create access through universal design, accommodations, and inclusive environments. The social model changes the role of the person with a disability from the patient—an object of intervention, or a research subject—into a community member, customer, patron, partner, and museum guest. The term "social model" was first coined in 1982 by Mike Oliver,[6] disability rights activist and Britain's first professor of disability studies. As he put it, "Models are ways of translating ideas into practice and the idea underpinning the individual [medical] model was that of personal tragedy, while the idea behind the social model was that of externally imposed restriction."[7] Under the outdated medical model, disability was the diagnosis or medical "problem" of an individual. Under the social model disability is a social and environmental issue around access and inclusion.[8] Rather than being a problem in this newer social model, disability is a result of the experience a person has while intersecting with the environment.

The social model of disability was developed because the traditional medical model did not respectfully illustrate people's personal experiences with disability, nor did it work toward developing more inclusive ways of living. The social model of disability helps to illustrate the social and environmental barriers that make life more challenging for people with disabilities. Removing these barriers provides more choice, equality, control, and independence, and this includes visiting museums and other cultural organizations. It is vital that cultural organizations look at disability through the social model and ensure their facilities, programs, websites, and exhibitions do not become yet another environmental constraint or barrier to visiting and are indeed accessible.

In 2001, the World Health Organization (WHO), working in collaboration with members of different disability communities, publicly established a more progressive, intersectional definition of disability based on social models and human rights.[9] With this new model, referred to as the **biopsychosocial model**, the WHO defined disability as an umbrella term covering three components: impairments, considered an issue in body function or structure; activity limitations, viewed as difficulties encountered by an individual in executing a task or action; and participation restrictions, determined to be problems experienced by an individual involved in life situations.[10] The WHO considers disability to be more than a health problem; it views disability as "a complex phenomenon, reflecting the interaction between features of a person's body and features of the society in which he or she lives. Overcoming the difficulties faced by people with disabilities requires interventions to remove environmental and social barriers."[11] Barriers can be physical (think steps, not ramps), or they can be attitudinal (assumptions that people with disabilities are unable to do certain things). Disability, therefore, is caused by society rather than by a person's impairment or difference. The social and biopsychosocial models look at ways of removing barriers that restrict life choices for people with disabilities. By removing social and environmental barriers, people with disabilities have full choice and control over their own lives.

A BRIEF HISTORY OF DISABILITY RIGHTS

Since the mid-1900s, people with disabilities have fought against negative attitudes and oppression, they have battled "centuries of biased assumptions, harmful stereotypes and irrational fears" for recognition of disability as a fundamental aspect of the human experience.[12] During the first half of the twentieth century, disability was viewed through the medical model, and considered something abnormal—often shameful—that needed to be medically cured. Wounded and disabled World War I veterans returning from overseas brought awareness to disability issues as they pressured the US government to provide rehabilitation and vocational training in exchange for their service.[13] While this brought attention to disability in one area, across the board people with disabilities remained marginalized in society, at times even institutionalized for rehabilitation, and their everyday experiences were largely overlooked. Transportation, housing, and public facilities remained inaccessible through the 1960s.

The disability rights movement in the United States can be traced back to the 1960s, taking shape at the same time the civil rights movement was forming. Similar to civil rights activists, disability advocates demanded equal treatment, equal opportunity, and equal access in society. They argued that the unjust stigma and social discrimination surrounding disability "needlessly harms and restricts the lives of those with disabilities and results in economic disparities, social isolation, and oppression."[14] Activists lobbied for actions to address the physical and social barriers facing the disability community. Representative Charles Vanik and Senator Hubert Humphrey (later vice president under Lyndon Johnson and whose grandson had Down syndrome), tried unsuccessfully to introduce bills to amend the Civil Rights Act of 1964 to include disability. In 1968, Congress passed the Architectural Barriers Act which stated that "all future public buildings and those buildings significantly altered with federal funds needed to be accessible to all citizens."[15] While this legislation set the stage for further activism, it had no enforcement arm attached to it, therefore limiting its effectiveness. The law was also limited in its scope: it only applied to public buildings, not public transportation, recreational facilities, housing, or privately owned commercial spaces. It took until the early 1970s for members of Congress to argue that civil rights antidiscrimination laws should include language about people with disabilities in addition to prohibiting discrimination on the basis of sex, religion, and race. Two monumental laws addressing antidiscrimination and equal rights passed during this decade and dramatically changed the lives of people with disabilities: the Rehabilitation Act of 1973, which addressed equal access by removal of architectural, employment, and transportation barriers, and in 1975 the Education for All Handicapped Children Act (now the Individuals with Disabilities Education Act [IDEA]), guaranteeing equal access to public education for children with disabilities.

Signed in September 1973, the Rehabilitation Act was the first major effort from the US government to support equal access for people with disabilities and is considered the first disability civil rights law to be enacted in the United States. Within the act are seven titles that address the barriers facing individuals with disabilities:[16]

- Title I outlines Vocational Rehabilitation Services, including evaluation standards and performance indicators.
- Title II covers Research and Training, launching research agencies such as the National Institute on Disability, Independent Living, and Rehabilitation.

- Title III is Professional Development and Special Projects and Demonstrations, speaking to training programs.
- Title IV established the National Council on Disability.
- Title V covers Rights and Advocacy, encompassing employment, protection, and nondiscrimination.
- Title VI outlines Employment Opportunities for Individuals with Disabilities, discussing availability of services.
- Title VII reports on Independent Living Services and Centers for Independent Living.

Section 504 of the Rehabilitation Act of 1973 prohibits discrimination against people with disabilities. "No otherwise qualified individual with a disability," Section 504 asserts, "shall, solely by reason of his or her disability, be excluded from the participation in, be denied the benefits of, or be subjected to discrimination under any program or activity receiving Federal financial assistance."[17] All programs, projects, and activities that receive financial assistance from the federal government are to operate in accordance with the laws outlined in the Rehabilitation Act of 1973.[18] As declared elsewhere in the act, "Disability is a natural part of the human experience and in no way diminishes the right of individuals to live independently; enjoy self-determination; make choices; contribute to society; pursue meaningful careers; and enjoy full inclusion and integration in the economic, political, social, cultural, and educational mainstream of American society."[19]

Together, IDEA and the Rehabilitation Act of 1973 worked to protect children and adults with disabilities from exclusion and unequal treatment in the workforce, school systems, and public facilities. These acts supported the social model of disability, where focus was put on enhancing the surrounding environment (not on the individual person) in order to be more inclusive and accommodating. Equal access to transportation, employment, and education are foundational aspects of inclusion in society, but only if and when they are implemented. Tragically, these new laws were not initially enforced. Four years after the law had been signed it was still yet to be implemented. This led to letter-writing, lobbying, and finally, in 1977, to widespread protests by disability activists, including one sit-in at a health, education, and welfare office in San Francisco that lasted twenty-five days.[20] Following this and other protests, Section 504 enforcement regulations were put into place, ensuring that programs receiving federal funding could not discriminate based on disability.[21] Section 504 of the Rehabilitation Act of 1973 only applied to federally-funded buildings and organizations, but the antidiscrimination focus set the stage for enactment of the Americans with Disabilities Act of 1990 (ADA).

Figure 1.1.   George H. W. Bush signing the ADA into law, July 26, 1990.
Source: George Bush Presidential Library and Museum/NARA

   The disability rights movement gained additional momentum in the late 1970s in Denver, Colorado, when a group of protesters blocked a major intersection over the absence of wheelchair accessible buses. From there the movement continued to grow, but issues were not immediately addressed because of the stigmatized perceptions of people with disabilities. Activists with disabilities such as Ed Roberts, Judy Heumann, and Fred Fay helped lead the growing movement for change. In March 1990, protesters literally abandoned their wheelchairs and crawled up the steps of the US Capitol in order to bring awareness to disability rights. This public protest, illustrating how people with disabilities had been ignored, made national headlines, and increased pressure on lawmakers to pass the ADA, which had stalled in Congress.[22]

   Less than two decades after the passage of the Rehabilitation Act of 1973, disability rights advocates won another substantial victory: on July 26, 1990, President George H. W. Bush signed the ADA into law. This landmark civil rights law prohibits discrimination against individuals with disabilities "in all areas of public life, including jobs, schools, transportation, and all public and private places that are open to the general public."[23] The ADA added on to the

Architectural Barriers Act of 1968, the Rehabilitation Act of 1973, and the 1975 IDEA. The ADA "built on centuries of activism on the part of people with disabilities, and centuries of public debate over rights, citizenship, and engagement in civic life."[24] The ADA brought public awareness to the environmental concerns confronting people with disabilities.

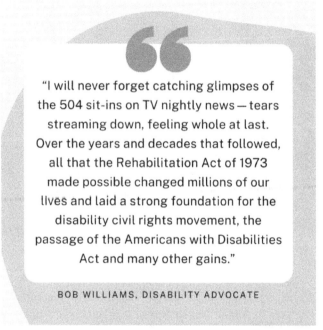

"I will never forget catching glimpses of the 504 sit-ins on TV nightly news — tears streaming down, feeling whole at last. Over the years and decades that followed, all that the Rehabilitation Act of 1973 made possible changed millions of our lives and laid a strong foundation for the disability civil rights movement, the passage of the Americans with Disabilities Act and many other gains."

BOB WILLIAMS, DISABILITY ADVOCATE

Figure 1.2. From "The Rehabilitation Act of 1973: Independence Bound" on the Administration for Community Living blog.

The passage of the ADA was not the end of activism for the disability rights movement. Far from it. There are many more important moments in modern disability history that we do not have space to mention here, but these key junctures and legislative actions did help provide essential protections that promote equal treatment, equal opportunity, and equal access in society for people with disabilities.

MUSEUMS AND DISABILITY LAW

The federal laws outlined above protect and promote the rights of individuals with disabilities and outline the baseline responsibilities museums must comply with to create inclusive spaces. There are a number of reasons and circumstances that confront and prevent people with disabilities from participating in museum programs and events. There are physical barriers, like a multistory building without an elevator, that render spaces inaccessible. There are communication barriers that prevent visitors from accessing information they need on their visit. And there are attitudinal barriers, where museum policies (sometimes unknowingly) act to exclude certain visitors. Oftentimes, museums are unaware of the limitations they are imposing on their visitors because of their spaces and policies. Thankfully, the ADA and the Rehabilitation Act of 1973 together outline a general road map of legal requirements for institutions to follow that address many of these barriers.

The ADA defines a person with a disability as "a person who has a physical or mental impairment that substantially limits one or more major life activity. . . . The ADA also makes it unlawful to discriminate against a person based on that person's association with a person with a disability."[25] The ADA is made up of five parts that relate to different areas of public life: Title I (Employment), Title II (State and Local Governments), Title III (Public Accommodations and Commercial Facilities), Title IV (Telecommunications), and Title V (Miscellaneous). Title I was passed in 1990, with Titles II and III becoming law the following year (Titles IV and V were added later). Titles II and III of the ADA are the sections of the law that most directly impact visitors to museums and cultural institutions. Title II covers programs and services of state and local governments, including museums of any size which are owned or operated by state or local governments. Museums and other places of public accommodation which are privately owned and operated (such as hotels, restaurants, and movie theaters), as well as organizations that function as 501(c)(3) nonprofits, must follow Title III of the ADA.[26] These titles require museums, by law, to take certain steps to avoid discriminating against visitors with disabilities. Here we outline the broad principles and general requirements of Titles II and III of the ADA, and in subsequent chapters we will go into further detail on how to implement them. **Everyone's Welcome: The Americans with Disabilities Act and Museums** by John Salmen provides quick summaries of the Title II and Title III ADA requirements.[27] In a nutshell all museums must,[28]

- provide equal opportunity for visitors with disabilities to participate in programs or services;
- present reasonable modifications to programs and procedures that would otherwise deny equal access to people with disabilities;
- ensure equally effective communication for all visitors, using auxiliary aids when necessary;

- maintain accessible facilities; and
- adhere to the ADA Standards of Accessible Design for any building alterations or new constructions (see below).

State and local government-operated museums must also

- undergo a self-evaluation assessment to identify problems that may prevent or limit access and create a transition plan for any necessary alterations; and
- designate an ADA coordinator to oversee compliance and develop a grievance procedure.

Since being signed into law, the ADA has undergone a number of revisions. The first of these occurred in 2008 when the Americans with Disabilities Amendment Act (the ADAA) was signed into law by President George W. Bush. The most important change to come out of the ADAA was expanding the definition of the term "disability." The Amendment Act broadened the definition of "disability" to make it easier for someone "seeking protection under the ADA to establish that he or she has a disability within the meaning of the ADA" without requiring extensive analysis.[29]

The Justice Department also revised Titles II and III of the ADA in September 2010. The revised regulations adopted enforceable accessibility design standards. The new standards were known as the **2010 ADA Standards for Accessible Design,**[30] which set minimum technical and planning requirements for "newly designed and constructed or altered State and local government facilities, public accommodations, and commercial facilities to be readily accessible to and usable by individuals with disabilities."[31] These standards are helpful for museums to keep in mind when designing spaces within buildings and exhibitions, ensuring that there is adequate room for a wheelchair to maneuver, that counters and tables are the right height, routes are accessible, and so on.

For a more thorough understanding of the current laws, the ADA National Network is a great resource and provides an overview of previous iterations of the law as well. This brief overview of the titles and standards included in the ADA is not meant to be a comprehensive description of what the law is, or a full proclamation of how it impacts your museum. The law will affect each museum differently. The thing to keep in mind, however, is that this law covers the **minimum** of what your museum should be doing to become a more accessible and inclusive space for your community.

DIFFERENT, NOT LESS

Dr. Temple Grandin, autism awareness advocate and pioneer in the field of animal science, once described the mind of someone with autism as being "different . . . not less."[32] In her book **Different . . . Not Less**,[33] she illustrates inspirational stories of achievement from professionals with autism spectrum disorder, highlighting some universal aspects of being human, like experiencing self-esteem challenges and prejudice, as well as perseverance and determination.[34] These powerful personal histories depict the opportunity access can provide for people with disabilities, and reveal the true potential it has to unlock doors to success. On the other hand, however, barriers to access on the account of being seen as different (and perhaps less) can also equally disturb and distress.

MOVING DIFFERENTLY THROUGH THE WORLD

Our friend and artistic director of Phamaly Theatre Company, Regan Linton, shares her experience with the ADA and accessing arts and culture spaces:

I'm 37 years old and I still have vivid memories of visiting museums and art spaces as a kid. I can picture the oversized human organs that I climbed through at the science museum. The indigenous artifacts and artworks available to tactile exploring in the quiet halls of the art museum. The hills outside the children's museum where plastic spindles and mesh mimicked fresh snow, giving kids the opportunity to "ski" as though they were on real fresh powder. I remember the special environments that were miniaturized specifically for kids, including the mini bathrooms at the zoo, and the play supermarket where I would scan plastic food items, and it seemed like the coolest activity ever. I remember the dollhouse-like rooms where optical illusion made me feel like I was shrinking in Alice's Wonderland. These immersive, tactile worlds were full of creativity, and being able to step inside them transported me beyond immediate realities into my imagination. As a kid it felt incredibly special, like everything had been designed specifically with my little child-size body in mind.

Fast forward 25 years. My walking legs had been replaced by wheels after I was paralyzed in a car accident in college. Still imaginative and adventurous, I was in New York City for a performance at a famous immersive theatrical experience in which my friend was performing. I rolled in, excited about what awaited within, and eager to once again be transported to other worlds. But the experience was different. It didn't feel like everything had been designed for me; quite the contrary. I felt like an afterthought. Scenes would begin, and actors would race off up the stairs, with audiences scrambling after them. I would watch them go, with no accessible way to follow. Workers would lift their costume masks and politely try to show me the way to move to the next level in the building. The transition to the elevator extracted me from the fantasy, and once I arrived at the next location, the scene was gone. Whatever creative, immersive story or experience had been designed was completely lost for me, simply because I was on wheels, and no one had given two thoughts to how the experience could be made inclusive. While the other audience members were whisked in and out of whimsical and dramatic other-worlds all evening, I wandered aimlessly through the space trying to find something compelling in the props, noticing flaws in the scenery, and occasionally haphazardly coming across portions of a scene.

I've been in numerous other immersive artistic and cultural experiences on wheels, and been hugely disappointed by the lack of thought around access and inclusion . . . not only for wheelers, but for a variety of humans that somehow don't fit the standard mold due to disability or difference. Spaces, experiences, and performances that leave others feeling awed and inspired too often leave people with disabilities as an afterthought. And it's a shame. Those of us who work in the world of arts and culture are supposed to be the "creative" ones, the folks who can think outside the box and solve problems. But too often I've seen "creative" people and institutions simply get lazy and complacent, and only think to design for a subset of humans that are conventional. Too often museums, theatres, galleries, and the like neglect to consider the humans who move differently through the world, and to plan—even minutely—for the people on wheels, the people whose ears or eyes receive differently, the people whose communication or sensory experience isn't cookie-cutter. And as a result, the spaces that are supposed to elevate humans through arts and culture and be the most open, the most inclusive, and the most transformative end up further marginalizing humans who are already consistently left out.

I think back on those cool immersive environments of my childhood, and realize that most of them would have been exclusionary to me had I used wheels at the time. I think of the kids who have to sit on the side and wait while their counterparts had imaginative fun, simply because the designers and staff didn't think about what diverse types of bodies might be moving through the space, and how to accommodate them. Thankfully, the Americans with Disabilities Act has made it possible for those of us with disabilities to access arts and culture spaces more readily. Which is fabulous. I can sit right next to my fellow humans who stand in a museum or art gallery and partake in many of the works and exhibits that elevate our existence. But just because I can get into the space, that doesn't mean the experience is always as full or complete. It doesn't mean that my low/no vision or Deaf/hard of hearing friends have the same experience of a work of art that isn't described or translated for them. It doesn't mean that immersive experiences are designed to be inclusive of various mobility modalities, or that sensory experiences take into account those who are more easily triggered.

It doesn't take much to make people feel included and significant . . . just a moment of thought and consideration, and a little bit of creativity. The experience of inspiration and transformation that comes through arts and culture shouldn't be relegated to those who have cookie cutter bodies and brains.

—Regan Linton, artistic director of Phamaly Theatre Company[1]

1. Regan Linton, email message to author, March 10, 2019.

We began this chapter with the notion that accessibility cannot be discussed in a vacuum, it needs context. Similarly, context is necessary to understand the reasoning and rationale behind accessibility work. There are a number of reasons why working toward becoming an accessible and inclusive museum is important, and these often fall into four main arguments: it is a legal requirement, it makes good business sense, it is part of your mission, and it is the right thing to do. Let's break these down a little bit:

Legal Requirements

It is illegal to discriminate against individuals with disabilities in public programs, activities, and services (as discussed previously). Avoiding the removal of certain barriers, not taking steps to provide the minimum reasonable modifications, or even ignoring your website's accessibility supports, can all be forms of discrimination that if not cared for, can lead to serious lawsuits.[35] Museums are required by law to maintain accessible public facilities and spaces in which to hold their programs, and furthermore shall not exclude or discriminate against any visitor with a disability.

Good Business Sense

According to the Centers for Disease Control and Prevention, one in four adults in the United States has a disability that impacts their life.[36] If museums and other cultural entities simply refuse to remove barriers from their institutions and engage people with disabilities, they would effectively miss out on potential revenue from approximately sixty-one million visitors, **plus the friends and family members who choose businesses and organizations based on their accessibility**. Furthermore, at some point in their lives, most people will either have a disability themselves or know someone who has one (whether permanent or temporary).[37] Funders give to what they know, so investing in accessible exhibitions, programs, and communications may attract new and different funders to your museum, which can translate into new development opportunities.

Part of the Mission

Mission statements articulate a museum's unique focus, their role and responsibility to the public, and in essence, their reason for existing. The mission sets the strategic direction for the museum, driving policy choices and influencing staff actions and culture. For museums, most mission statements explicitly or implicitly include education as a part of their mission. By excluding a certain portion of the population, museums will never truly be able to fulfill their missions. Even if accessibility and inclusion do not expressly show up in your mission or vision statements, you can connect to the social value or relationship with the community espoused in your mission. People with disabilities are not a small fringe group in your community, but in fact they are an integral part of **every** museum community. Universally designed programs, exhibitions, and communications can be used by any visitor, and more than likely will enhance everyone's overall experience.

Right Thing to Do

Discrimination, segregation, and exclusion are wrong (and illegal). Full inclusion, acceptance, and participation of all people in society is right. Viewing accessibility as a civil rights issue vividly brings into focus the widespread needs, concerns, and rights of people with disabilities. Progressive museums can set examples for their communities. Just as museums have recently begun to address controversial topics and embrace the idea that museums are not neutral, they can also be leaders in their communities by making their spaces accessible and inclusive so that everyone feels welcome. Removing barriers that restrict life choices for people with disabilities is not only good for business and on the right side of the law, but also the right thing to do.

Creating an accessible museum is a process; it takes time to fully ingrain inclusive practices and thinking into the fabric and culture of your organization. We have provided a brief glimpse into the social history of disability in the United States, outlined the groundbreaking legislation that prohibits discrimination against individuals with disabilities, and helped to build the case for why accessibility is essential to each and every museum. Though there is much more to learn about the history and current political issues of

Figure 1.3. "Support Disability Rights" button.
Source: Division of Political and Military History, National Museum of American History, Smithsonian Institution

the disability rights movement, this foundational knowledge is the first step in a museum's accessibility journey. Equipped with this knowledge you can begin to build your case for accessibility and create a plan of action for your museum. You have the background, now it is time to begin.

NOTES

1. Betty Siegel, Keynote Address, Art of Access Symposium, Denver, July 12, 2017. Betty Siegel is the director of VSA and Accessibility, and the force behind the global LEAD® conference (Leadership Exchange in Arts and Disability) from the John F. Kennedy Center for the Performing Arts.

2. For a brief history of disability in the United States, we recommend **A Disability History of the United States** by Kim E. Nielsen (Boston: Beacon Press, 2013).

3. "Social and Medical Models of Disability: Paradigm Change," Art Beyond Sight, accessed March 15, 2019, http://www.artbeyondsight.org/dic/definition-of -disability-paradigm-change-and-ongoing-conversation/.

4. Shirley Wilcher, "The Rehabilitation Act of 1973: 45 Years of Activism and Progress," **Insight Into Diversity**, September 17, 2018, https://www.insightinto diversity.com/the-rehabilitation-act-of-1973-45-years-of-activism-and-progress/.

5. Americans with Disabilities Act of 1990 (ADA), Pub. L. No. 101-336, § 2, 104 Stat. 328 (1991).

6. David Brindle, "Mike Oliver Obituary," March 19, 2019, https://www.the guardian.com/society/2019/mar/19/mike-oliver-obituary.

7. Mike Oliver, "The Social Model in Action: If I Had a Hammer," in **Implementing the Social Model of Disability: Theory and Research,** ed. Colin Barnes and Geof Mercer (Leeds: The Disability Press, 2004), pp. 18–31.

8. "Disabilities," World Health Organization, accessed March 8, 2019, https:// www.who.int/topics/disabilities/en/.

9. This same year (2001), the WHO developed a classification system for disability, recognizing that both the social and medical models oversimplify disability and an individual's outcome in life. Their biopsychosocial definition focuses on function and context. This definition was incorporated into the International Classification of Function, Disability, and the Health (ICF). In-depth information on the ICF can be found on the WHO website at https://www.who.int/classifications/icf/en/.

10. World Health Organization, "Disabilities."

11. World Health Organization, "Disabilities."

12. "A Brief History of the Disability Rights Movement," Anti-Defamation League, https://www.adl.org/education/resources/backgrounders/disability-rights -movement, accessed September 28, 2020.

13. Anti-Defamation League, "A Brief History of the Disability Rights Movement."

14. Nielsen, **A Disability History of the United States**, 162.

15. Nielsen, **A Disability History of the United States**, 165.

16. "Rehabilitation Act of 1973," U.S. Department of Education, accessed January 16, 2020, https://www2.ed.gov/policy/speced/leg/rehab/rehabilitation-act-of -1973-amended-by-wioa.pdf.

17. U.S. Department of Education, "Rehabilitation Act of 1973."

18. Section 504 laws apply to federally-funded museums, whereas the Americans with Disabilities Act applies to all museums whether or not they receive federal funding. If your museum receives federal funds, check with your 504 coordinator if you have any questions about how the law impacts programs and operations at your museum.

19. U.S. Department of Education, "Rehabilitation Act of 1973."

20. Nielsen's **A Disability History of the United States** tells a more complete picture of this event, including how other activist groups, like the Black Panthers, supported the protesters during the sit-in.

21. Nielsen, **A Disability History of the United States**, 168–69.

22. Samantha Michaels, "The Americans with Disabilities Act Is Turning 25. Watch the Dramatic Protest That Made It Happen." **Mother Jones**, July 25, 2015, https://www.motherjones.com/politics/2015/07/americans-disabilities-act-capitol-crawl-anniversary/.

23. "What is the Americans with Disabilities Act (ADA)?" ADA National Network, accessed February 8, 2019, https://adata.org/learn-about-ada.

24. Nielsen, **A Disability History of the United States**, 180.

25. "What is the definition of disability under the ADA?" ADA National Network, accessed February 10, 2019, https://adata.org/faq/what-definition-disability-under-ada.

26. John P. S. Salmen, **Everyone's Welcome: The Americans with Disabilities Act and Museums** (Washington, DC: American Alliance of Museums Press, 1998).

27. Salmen, **Everyone's Welcome**, 20–21.

28. Salmen, **Everyone's Welcome**, 20–21.

29. "The Americans with Disabilities Act Amendments Act of 2008," U.S. Equal Employment Opportunity Commission, accessed February 15, 2019, https://www.eeoc.gov/laws/statutes/adaaa_info.cfm.

30. You can download the **2010 Standards for Accessible Design** from the ADA website. Print copies are also available for purchase from various booksellers.

31. United States Department of Justice, **2010 ADA Standards for Accessible Design** (Washington, DC: Department of Justice, 2010), 1.

32. "About Temple Grandin," Temple Grandin, accessed November 25, 2019, http://www.templegrandin.com/.

33. Temple Grandin, **Different . . . Not Less: Inspiring Stories of Achievement and Successful Employment from Adults with Autism, Asperger's, and ADHD** (Arlington, TX: Future Horizons, Inc., 2012)

34. Dr. Temple Grandin is herself a person with autism.

35. Elizabeth Harris, "Galleries from A to Z Sued Over Websites the Blind Can't Use," **New York Times,** February 18, 2019, https://www.nytimes.com/2019/02/18/arts/design/blind-lawsuits-art-galleries.html.

36. "CDC: 1 in 4 US adults live with a disability," Centers for Disease Control and Prevention, last modified August 16, 2018, https://www.cdc.gov/media/releases/2018/p0816-disability.html.

37. For example, women who have recently given birth are considered to be temporarily disabled by many short-term disability insurance plans.

Chapter Two

Won't You Be Our Neighbor

Partnerships, Part I

Alone, we can do so little; together, we can do so much.

—Helen Keller[1]

Entering into the field of accessibility and inclusion is like moving to a house in a new neighborhood. You can pick up bits of information about the best schools from one neighbor, or the grocery store with the freshest produce from another, but more often than not, no single person possesses all the information you need. With each new person you meet comes a new piece of knowledge. By the time you cover the entire block, you have acquired a more holistic view and deeper understanding of the neighborhood.

Learning from other colleagues and organizations can guide and motivate the work you do. This is particularly true in accessibility and inclusion work. In this dynamic field where terminology, approaches, and best practices are constantly shifting and developing, no single person or organization could possibly possess all the information necessary to effectively practice this work. Knowledge and resources are spread across service organizations, self-advocates, nonprofits, government offices, and various academic disciplines. The need to seek out and share knowledge with others often conflicts with the reality of being the sole person in your organization whose job entails accessibility, let alone being an accessibility or ADA coordinator. You may even be the sole person within your local museum community doing this work. As a result, it can be difficult to know where to turn for information, resources, and fellowship. All too often from colleagues near and far, we have heard comments about the apparent isolation of this work, with reflections of, "I'm the only one" and "Where do I start?" We have found that building comprehensive networks and communities of practice addresses and remedies this isolation.

BUILDING AN INCLUSIVE NETWORK

Networks are essential ways of connecting with people who are working on the same issues. They provide access to expert knowledge, diverse skill sets, and can support participants in growing their craft and developing their individual work. For those of us already embarking on accessibility work in our own practices, we are part of numerous networks. Many of us have built some of these communities from the ground up and have joined others already in existence. Some networks are local and have in-person connections, while others are on a national scale, so peer-to-peer contact occurs virtually via webinars, emails, and online forums. Constructing both local and national networks is good practice, as both have their strengths. National networks tend to have more members to connect with, more resources to utilize (think research and structure), and even potential funding or professional development opportunities to gain from. Local groups, on the other hand, can be more nimble, oftentimes due to their smaller size and more informal structure, and therefore may be more reactive to the particular needs of their communities. Moreover, there are hybrid networks; national organizations who have local chapters where you can often get the best of both worlds with the size and reach of a national network, yet with a local contact more intimately tied to your community. If you are just getting started in the field of accessibility and inclusion, it will be best to first build a foundational understanding of certain audiences that can form the base of the more localized work you want to do at your museum. To get a framework and basic understanding, look to build a network among established organizations that advocate for people with disabilities. Here is a list, by no means exhaustive, that can help get you started:

- ADA National Network
- Alzheimer's Association
- American Alliance of Museums Diversity Committee (DivCom)
- The Arc
- Autism Society of America
- Easter Seals
- National Association of the Deaf
- National Down Syndrome Society
- National Federation of the Blind
- Rape, Abuse & Incest National Network[2]
- VSA Arts[3]

Many of these organizations have an abundance of historical information about the organization and community it represents, as well as training and educational resources, volunteer and advocacy opportunities, links to similar organizations, and individuals to contact for further information. Oftentimes these larger national organizations have local affiliates serving various cities, counties, and states throughout the country. These affiliates support the needs of families and individuals living in their local community or state and therefore have their finger on the pulse of the individualized needs of those they serve.

Looking to city, state, and government agencies can also be a useful resource in helping you to better understand the landscape of accessibility work happening in your community. City libraries are a wealth of knowledge; they can connect you with local agency resources, direct you to available information and research on accessibility and inclusion (some branches may even generate personalized reading lists by request), and are knowledgeable of, and have access to, available adaptive technologies, such as screen readers, braille printers, video magnifiers, and voice recognition software.[4] Many library branches are also diversifying their offerings for communities, including regular Memory Café programs for people with memory loss and their care partners,[5] supplying homebound visitation services for customers who cannot physically visit a branch, and hiring social workers to help connect people experiencing poverty and homelessness with housing, health care, and food resources.[6] City parks and recreation departments often offer adaptive recreation opportunities for their community members as well.

Many city governments have health and human service agencies that advocate in support of human rights issues for their region through various commissions and offices. Denver, for example, has the agency for Human Rights & Community Partnerships which oversees nine offices and ten commissions that work to create a more just and equitable Denver.[7] Among these are the Office of Disability Rights and Office on Aging, which help to develop programs and policies that support and advocate for their respective communities and ensure legal accessibility compliance within the city. At the state level are the Colorado Department of Health Care Policy and Financing and the Department of Labor and Employment. These departments oversee health and human service organizations (who handle case management services) and the Division of Vocational Rehabilitation, which is the leading job placement organization in the state for people with disabilities, assisting people with disabilities to successfully live and work independently.[8] A main provision of these local and state offices, and others like them around the country, is providing their communities with resources like lists of service and support agencies, guidelines for accessibility compliance, insight into effective communication strategies, and oftentimes, free or low-cost professional development training.

An example of a collaboration in action was a partnership that developed between the Denver Art Museum (DAM) and the Colorado Division of Vocational Rehabilitation. These two organizations were able to come to an agreement after a rehabilitation counselor contacted DAM to set up a tour for about thirty adults with vision loss. As they connected and planned out the tour, the representatives involved went over mutual values and outcomes to ensure they were on the same page for this program. From these outcomes they found a way to create a reciprocal experience that could benefit both the clients and the museum as well. The museum happily scheduled a verbal description and touch tour for one of its exhibitions, which provided both education and enrichment for the clients, as well as social interaction with DAM staff and other clients. Participants built up their confidence and competence by navigating their independent travel to downtown Denver and maneuvering around the museum, a place where many of them had not visited since losing their vision. In return, the vocational rehabilitation staff member led a hands-on and experiential training session for the DAM's volunteer docents, which provided invaluable information about the expectations of the group, as well as some potential challenges and opportunities to consider. Years later the volunteer docent group still talks about the positive results of this training.

Local community-based organizations, advocacy groups, and small businesses dedicated to serving children and adults with disabilities are also essential components of a comprehensive network. As with the local affiliates of larger national organizations, these smaller groups can help you to better pinpoint the specific needs of your community and navigate the available resources. These organizations usually fall within a few general categories: respite programs (supporting those who are caring for individuals with any health-care need, such as parents of kids with autism); education and recreation groups (providing support for diagnostics, educational and social experiences, and healthy lifestyle experiences); social and support groups (affords an opportunity for people in similar circumstances to come together to give encouragement, comfort, and advice); social services and employment assistance (aimed to promote welfare); advocacy work (supporting public policy initiatives, and even regional or national legislation); and research and funding organizations (contributing knowledge to the field and connecting people to federal, state, and private funding). The mission of many of these organizations may include community collaborations, meaning they may be eager to share resources, build partnerships, promote your programs to their networks, and maybe even provide free or low-cost training opportunities for you and your staff. Completing a simple online search of any of those general categories should produce quite a few organizations with whom to begin conversations in your area.

Another good rule of thumb in building networks is to look to other cultural organizations, both locally and nationally, who are doing work that you admire or aspire to do. Museums, zoos, theatres, and many more who have committed themselves to inclusive work are often a wealth of knowledge, and usually willing and eager to share advice and resources with those who are inclined to ask. It is helpful to look at the type of accessible resources and programs they offer, whom they are partnering with in the disability community, and how they talk about the work they do. Quite a lot of information can be found with a simple search of their website, but further understanding of their work is best done through connecting directly with staff for a firsthand account. This way you can ask specifics about the genesis of programs and resources, how they build and sustain partnerships, and really get at more nuanced information and perspectives not available on the website. When you are unaware of who exactly to reach out to, there are a few options: look for a contact email or phone number on the staff contact or accessibility page of their website (assuming they have one), search the American Alliance of Museums message boards, ask your friends and colleagues if they know anyone at the institution who can connect you with the accessibility coordinator or someone similar, or send a general query to the museum's general information email or phone number. There is a reciprocal nature of this networking process. We all have questions, and we all have answers. In this field we are consistently learning as we go, building new relationships, and as a result we can all benefit from the triumphs (or even missteps) of others. Everyone has to start from somewhere, so do not be afraid to reach out and ask questions!

DIARY OF AN ACCESSIBILITY COORDINATOR

"In my first few months as the Accessibility Coordinator at the Denver Art Museum, I spent much of my time reaching out to various disability service organizations and advocacy groups in the region through emails and phone calls. Being new to the city and the position, my goal was to familiarize myself with these organizations, make introductions, and forging as many new connections as possible in order to support the work I was undertaking. I felt much like a salesperson making cold calls to these new organizations, but instead of selling goods or services, I was seeking out advice and guidance. While it can feel vulnerable to put yourself out there in such a way, so many great connections with interesting and sometimes surprising partners have come from these spontaneous connections."

—Danielle Schulz, Denver Art Museum

SAMPLE EMAIL COPY

To: Community Partner
From: Your Museum's Accessibility Coordinator

Dear (insert community partner name),

I hope this email finds you well; I would like to make your acquaintance, as I am the new accessibility coordinator at (your museum).

I have been reaching out to different community partners to learn more about their individual work and the communities they represent, as well as to seek their insight into the best ways that my museum can serve as a community resource. I have the pleasure of organizing and overseeing the museum's accessibility programs. At (your museum) we recognize the importance in providing quality programs and services that meaningfully engage members of the disability community.

It is for this reason that I am happy to make your acquaintance—as you are a prominent member of the D/deaf and hard of hearing community. Would you be interested in grabbing a coffee or chatting over the phone about the work you do, the values and interests of your community, and discussing the ways that (your museum) can become a better resource in our community?

Thank you for considering, I hope to chat with you soon!

(Your signature)

Building a diverse and inclusive network of peers—comprised of organizations big and small, local and nationwide—will aid in expanding your knowledge base and guide you to identify the best places and people to tap for resources at whatever point in your practice. As you develop a stronger understanding of the needs of your local communities, you may naturally begin to see both the strengths and weaknesses of your museum and identify areas in which you need more support. You may find, for example, that your website is inaccessible to screen readers, and therefore poses a barrier to a large portion of the population who are blind or have low vision, or you may have a parent support group urging your museum to open early for sensory-friendly hours. If you are eager to learn and do more to actively address the weaknesses found in your museum's accessibility practice, you can connect more closely with contacts in your network, creating what is called a community of practice, in order to build more mutual knowledge in the specific areas where you need more support.

BUILDING A COMMUNITY OF PRACTICE

A community of practice is a group of active practitioners who share a field of study, or a passion for something they do, and by interacting regularly over time, they learn to do their work better.[9] Communities of practice evolve from networks; individuals with an interest in learning more deeply about some aspect of their work can come together, formalize their conversations, and intentionally create new knowledge for their field of practice. Individuals venturing into accessibility and inclusion work can create a community of practice to share resources, support one another, and address problems that are too challenging to solve alone.[10] By joining with others, communities of practice can build collaborative relationships that enable people to learn from each other, and share expertise, knowledge, and best practices. The peer-to-peer quality found in communities of practice can bring together museums, individuals, and organizations of different sizes, perspectives, and missions who can benefit from deeper collaboration by sharing experiences, stories, tools, and ways of addressing recurring issues around accessibility and inclusion.

As with networks, communities of practice can also vary in size, scale, and scope, ranging from simple lunch and learn groups, all the way to larger, city- or region-wide associations of professionals. Metropolitan cities and regions around the United States have begun creating more formalized communities of practice dedicated to promoting accessibility and inclusion in the cultural arts sector. These groups, comprised of people working as cultural administrators, educators, accessibility coordinators, and self-advocates, host professional development workshops centered on best practices, provide a platform to promote city-wide accessible events and programs through web listings and online calendars, and offer a network of mutual support for their local area. If you live within these regions, we highly recommend getting involved with any of these groups: ARTabilityAZ (Arizona); Art of Access Alliance Denver (Colorado); Arts Access for All (North Dakota/Minnesota); Bay Area Arts Access Collective (California); Chicago Cultural Accessibility Consortium (Illinois); Cultural Access Network Project (New Jersey); Cultural Access New England; D.C. Arts & Access Network (Washington, DC); Florida Access Coalition for the Arts; Greater Pittsburgh Arts Council's Accessibility Initiative (Pennsylvania); Inclusion Network of Nashville (Tennessee); Louisville Cultural Accessibility Association (Kentucky); Michigan Alliance for Cultural Accessibility; Minnesota Access Alliance; and the Museum, Arts and Cultural Access Consortium (New York), which was the first access consortium to officially form around 1990.[11] As this is an evolving field, check your local area as one of these groups may have formed since the printing of this book.

   In addition to regional groupings, communities of practice may also organize themselves around a specific topic or audience. In 2009, a group of museums, nature centers, and cultural organizations in Wisconsin came together
to collaborate and connect their thinking on the practical aspects of engaging
visitors with memory loss. Ten years later this group, known as the SPARK!
Alliance, has expanded to twenty-two institutions spread across Wisconsin
and Minnesota, and have developed tried and trusted policies and procedures that support organizations in their region to cultivate and strengthen
engagement programs that are accessible to families living with dementia
and memory loss.[12] Similar communities of practice have evolved around
such topics as sensory-friendly programming, approaches to crafting audio
description for people who are blind or have low vision, and even discussions
around accessibility consultation.[13] Technological and social advances have
also expanded the ways in which communities of practice can exist. Moving
beyond in-person connections or simple online forums, peer-to-peer sharing
can now take place online via video chat platforms such as Google Hangouts

Figure 2.1.   Based on Community of Practice model.
Source: Based on concept proposed by Jean Lave and Etienne Wenger.

or Zoom, through social media such as Facebook Groups or Twitter chats, and even podcasts.[14]

It may seem overwhelming to consider starting your own community of practice from the ground up, but if you lack a company of colleagues to learn from at your own museum, you may need to develop your own community from your network of contacts. Luckily, once you have taken time to build meaningful networks as mentioned above, you are nearly there. A community of practice simply needs a well-defined purpose, a curated group of practitioners who can contribute valuable experiences and knowledge to the group, and a space (either in-person or virtual) to regularly convene. We can share examples of two communities of practice built from the ground up of which we, the authors, are a part: Art of Access Alliance Denver and the Denver Creative Aging Forum. Each group is grounded in a specific purpose: Art of Access Alliance Denver develops and promotes inclusive practices across Denver's cultural organizations through professional development workshops and resource sharing. The Creative Aging Forum brings together colleagues working in the fields of health, wellness, and creative aging to surface questions, find future collaborations, and discover the latest resources.[15] The impetus for convening each of these groups was the simple need to learn more about what was happening in the areas of access, inclusion, and creative aging in our local communities. Members of both groups come from diverse organizations: museums, performing art centers, nonprofits, older adult communities, and more, all with a shared interest in learning about the specific purpose of the group. What sets these groups apart is their size and scale; the Art of Access Alliance is a five-year-old, formalized consortium offering regular professional development opportunities and resources, whereas the Creative Aging Forum is a much smaller and more casual quarterly meet-up of colleagues who share ideas and ask questions. Yet despite their differences both groups have succeeded as their own community of practice (even growing in size over time) because they are driven by the needs and interests of the group, with participants engaging not only for their own needs, but to serve the needs of others. There is an intentional commitment to advancing the field of practice, and to share the discoveries made with a wider audience, especially those doing related work. When colleagues come together to pool valuable experiences and learnings, new knowledge is created, which can then be taken back by participants to their individual museums and organizations to utilize and implement.

A community of practice offers a neighborhood of supportive ideas, all working together toward inclusivity of all members of society. While no one person is likely to have all the resources and knowledge you require, together you can build understanding and opportunity. Not only will you find opportunities to learn, but you will doubtless be able to share from your own background as well, thus benefiting from contributing to as well as learning from your diverse community of practice.

WON'T YOU BE OUR NEIGHBOR?

Knowledge and support can be found in the most diverse and interesting of places, if you are willing to step outside your own front door. It is essential to recognize that you are not alone, and therefore should not act alone in this work. There is a wide world of resources and connections waiting for you to simply speak up and ask, "Won't you be my neighbor?" Only with these networks and communities of practice in place, will you then be able to effectively address the needs and interests of your diverse community. As Fred Rogers so eloquently said, "We live in a world in which we need to share responsibility . . . there are those who see the need and respond. I consider those people my heroes."[16]

NOTES

1. "Helen Keller: 'Alone We Can Do So Little. Together We Can Do So Much,'" American Federation for the Blind, accessed October 21, 2019, https://www.afb.org /blog/entry/happy-birthday-helen.

2. More commonly known as RAINN, they can provide resources for programming help in terms of whether trigger warnings may be necessary for people who've experienced trauma and ensure that artistic expressions of abuse, genocide, war, etc., are conveyed with care.

3. "VSA Affiliates Worldwide," The John F. Kennedy Center for Performing Arts, accessed March 14, 2019, http://education.kennedy-center.org/education/vsa /affiliates/.

4. "Services for Persons with Disabilities," Denver Public Library, accessed February 20, 2019, https://www.denverlibrary.org/content/services-persons-disabilities.

5. "What is a Memory Café?," Memory Café Directory, accessed February 10, 2019, https://www.memorycafedirectory.com/what-is-a-memory-cafe/.

6. Lisa Schencker, "Libraries Hire Social Workers to Help Homeless Patrons," **Los Angeles Times**, October 27, 2018, https://www.latimes.com/nation/la-na-chicago -library-homeless-20181027-story.html.

7. "Human Rights and Community Partnerships," City and County of Denver, accessed February 19, 2019, https://www.denvergov.org/content/denvergov/en/human -rights-and-community-partnerships.html.

8. "About Us," Colorado Department of Labor and Employment, State of Colorado, accessed February 19, 2019, https://www.colorado.gov/dvr/about-dvr.

9. Jean Lave and Etienne Wenger, **Situated Learning: Legitimate Peripheral Participation**. (Cambridge: Cambridge University Press, 1991), 91.

10. "Community of Practice," National Council of Nonprofits, accessed February 10, 2019, https://www.councilofnonprofits.org/tools-resources/community-of-practice.

11. "About," Museum, Arts and Cultural Access Consortium, accessed March 6, 2019, https://macaccess.org/about-new/.

12. "Our History," SPARK!, accessed March 6, 2019, http://www.sparkprograms.org/history/.

13. Communities of practice around specific topics include, the Lone Tree Arts Center Sensory Friendly Summit, the American Council for the Blind's Audio Description Project, and Digital A11y.

14. Philip Dallman's **Access Champions** podcast launched in April 2018 and highlights work being done in the fields of accessibility, diversity, and inclusion.

15. "About," Art of Access Alliance Denver, accessed March 5, 2019, https://artofaccessdenver.com/about-us/.

16. "About Fred," Fred Rogers Center, accessed March 16, 2019, http://www.fredrogerscenter.org/about-us/about-fred/.

Chapter Three

Nothing About Us, Without Us
Partnerships, Part II

Now that you have built networks and communities of practice consisting of colleagues and organizations to help guide the work you do, it is critical to objectively look at who is in those groups, and who is not. Representation of diverse perspectives, backgrounds, and abilities is a key aspect of inclusive networks and partners. Creating programs, events, or resources for any specified group of people without first including those people in the design, production, and implementation is ineffective and generally unsuccessful. This attitude can be summed up in the expression, "Nothing about us, without us," which proclaims that no policy or important decision should be made without direct input from the group that is being affected by that policy. In the case of accessibility, and in situations where policies directly affect people with disabilities, it is understood that the individuals **themselves** know what is best for them, not anyone else.[1] In order to effectively engage diverse communities, and be seen as a place that embraces accessibility and inclusion, museums must work to ensure that people with disabilities have a seat at the table from the very beginning, and are empowered to share their expertise by cocreating programs, events, resources, and policies that directly affect them.

MEANINGFUL INCLUSION

The more an organization is representative OF its community, the more people feel seen and heard. The more programming is created BY the community, the more people feel ownership. The more programming is FOR the community, the more everyone wants to participate.

—OF/BY/FOR ALL project[2]

People with disabilities should be the ones leading the conversation about their own needs and interests. When this is not the case, and outside perspectives and opinions (however well-meaning they may be) overshadow the conversation, this can perpetuate stereotypes and misconceptions that create barriers. This could look like generalizing about disabilities (both positive or negative), patronizing or dismissive behaviors, or simply overlooking aspects of the disability experiences. In order to combat this practice, disabilities must be included in accessibility work from the very beginning. This is achieved by dedicating time, space, dialogue, and action to increasing the representation of diverse perspectives, experiences, and abilities in dominant museum conversations and practices. This is a crucial step toward building a stronger and more accessible organization.

INTRODUCING INCLUSIVE EMOJIS

Even digital communication platforms are increasingly understanding the importance of representing the experiences of those with disabilities. In 2019, Unicode Consortium, the global governing body that develops standards for emoji icons, approved the release of a new set of disability inclusive icons, including a person using a wheelchair, a D/deaf person, a guide dog, and a person using a white cane, among others.[1] This decision diversified the options available to users of digital messaging platforms to better represent themselves and their communities through digital means, and more generally enhanced the overall opportunity for more inclusive communication methods for all.

1. Avery Anapol, "Emoji Representing People with Disabilities Approved for 2019," **The Hill**, February 6, 2019, https://thehill.com/policy/technology/428880-emoji-representing-people-with-disabilities-approved-for-2019.

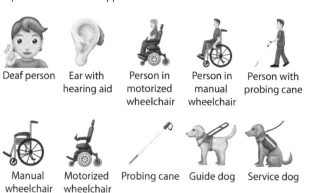

| Deaf person | Ear with hearing aid | Person in motorized wheelchair | Person in manual wheelchair | Person with probing cane |

| Manual wheelchair | Motorized wheelchair | Probing cane | Guide dog | Service dog |

Figure 3.1.   Examples of inclusive emoji icons.
Source: Unicode Consortium, 2019

Inclusion is most meaningful when it is purposeful. When trying to engage diverse audiences, simply putting up a welcome sign is not sufficient. Museums must express and embody a commitment to disability inclusion by intentionally increasing the variety of opportunities by which people with disabilities are represented across the museum. Meaningful inclusion features situations wherein people from the disability community can advise on and design public programs and exhibitions, generate support resources and trainings, act as artists or performers, and of course, work as colleagues through equitable employment opportunities throughout the museum. Organizations that more closely resemble the population they serve, and furnish these inclusive connections, can be more responsive to the needs and interests of their visitors.

COMMUNITY ADVISORY AND ADVOCACY

For years, museums and other cultural institutions have organized advisory committees, focus groups, and community panels in order to gather in-depth information about a community's thoughts and opinions on a topic. The learnings from these feedback opportunities are then used to inform the design and implementation of future programs or exhibitions. Just as you would assemble a group of parents and toddlers to help inform your thinking around the design of a family space or youth exhibition game, similarly you should strive to collect feedback from members of diverse disability communities on the accessibility of your programs, exhibitions, and spaces. Advisory committees advocate for the needs and interests of their communities on different matters, and many museums convene these groups in order to drive their progress toward achieving their mission and expanding their reach and impact in the community. Depending on the aspirations and nature of your museum, an advisory committee will vary in size, formality, and level of involvement. But generally, these are closed, invite-only groups with external community members who have a more sustained engagement with a museum, usually meeting anywhere from quarterly to bi-monthly to provide regular input on decisions. This continual interaction is key, as it builds relationships and rapport among members that cannot only support your museum to better understand the experiences and realities of your local communities, but moreover, it will support long-term strategic guidance.

The ideal accessibility advisory board or committee will consist of people with diverse experiences and abilities, who can bring to the table both a level of community expertise (a finger on the pulse of community needs and activities) as well as an interest in being a change agent with the museum. It is important early on to make clear—to the museum and to the people recruited to join the committee—the goals and purpose for gathering this group. Time is a finite resource and asking someone to dedicate and share this with an organization is a tall order and therefore must be met with respect and purpose. When asking yourself why you are meeting, it is important to zoom out and consider what the museum is hoping to achieve by regularly convening this group. You must dig deep and question the purpose in order to identify a larger issue you want to address. Doing so not only adds meaning to the group but will result in a better outcome for your committee members, your community, and the museum. You may begin by stating that you are gathering an access advisory group because you want to collect their feedback on the museum's exhibitions, spaces, and programs. **But why**? This feedback may help the museum to identify problem areas and access priorities. **But why does the museum need help identifying these problems and priorities**? In order to involve the community to solve problems the museum cannot solve on its own. **And why is that important**? Because access is a process that takes time, energy, and skill, and sharing authority around decision-making with people who are impacted by such decisions is good inclusive practice. Drilling down with these questions until you hit upon a belief or value is important as it connects the work of the advisory group to the museum's larger mission. If people cannot see themselves as part of the museum's work, then they will not see the work it does as essential to their lives. Moreover, consider whether your museum has the capacity to accept, and even invite, criticism. Establishing an advisory group is a process of asking for feedback, but more importantly, it is being able to bravely receive that feedback and put it into action.

Once you have decided why to meet, next is the consideration of how you meet. When recruiting members to be in your group you must make clear what you are asking of them. What is the time and energy commitment? Consider whether what you require is commiserate with the incentives you are providing. Ideally, this group will receive a stipend for their advisory work, but when that is not possible, what other ways can you impart value for their participation? Consider offering free admission or memberships to participants and their families. Give them free tickets to an upcoming event or exhibition preview. At the very least provide a meal during meetings with them.

For this access advisory committee, make sure there is a plan of action for setting expectations and measurable goals with the group. Partners must see that their feedback and energy is being appropriately utilized, and not overlooked or misused. It is important to regularly illustrate how their ideas are being integrated into the museum as a whole. Inviting leadership from across the museum to join in on advisory meetings is a great way to both spread awareness of the group's work across departments and to demonstrate the museum's high level of respect and commitment to the members of the group. Another way to set expectations is by articulating the ways in which your institution will be accountable to act upon the input given by the group. Access is a process, and the process is not a straightforward pathway from point A to point B. It is often your job to mediate the ambition of the advisory group with the reality of the museum. This balance comes by setting goals you can be accountable for and achieve in a realistic time period. Depending on size, staff, and institutional buy-in, museums will have to prioritize different accessibility actions to tackle first. For some organizations, physical access may be an immovable barrier at the moment (e.g., take many historic houses). So while this may be the long-term focus or goal, in the short term you and the advisory group can find more easily attainable solutions to start with (e.g., creating a virtual tour of physically inaccessible spaces). These may be incremental victories, but they can motivate the group, you, and the museum as a whole, and illustrate the progress that is being made.

SHARING EXPERTISE

If you are just starting out in this work, or at an institution with limited staff buy-in, it may seem daunting or nearly impossible to convene an advisory group. But fear not, there are other ways of seeking feedback that may better fit your current point on your journey to accessibility. One opportunity is to recruit people from diverse disability communities to form a focus group to give feedback on a certain exhibition, program, practice, etc. Focus groups can be more compact methods of evaluation, as they are often assembled over anywhere from one to two days to even an hour, and therefore may be more feasible options for your organization to convene starting out. They can also be conducted virtually fairly easy if meeting in person is not possible. The feedback provided by these groups can be immensely helpful when designed appropriately: for example, assessing your website, editing the content and flow of an audio guide, or critiquing the general wayfinding of your museum. Focus groups allow visitors to feel heard and pertinent and avoid having only the "experts in the field" sharing their perspectives.

The same rules apply to focus groups as advisory committees in terms of setting expectations, paying for participation, and outlining achievable goals. Despite the difference in time investment, advisory groups and focus groups should be handled with the same thought, care, and respect for those involved. The design of these groups is dependent upon the goals of the feedback session and what the museum wants to find out. For example, if you want to determine the best approach for designing a tour for members of the D/deaf community, it would follow that your focus group would consist of persons who identify with this group. You can then recruit members by reaching out to your personal connections, if any, and the advocacy groups and service organizations connected to the community you are interested in engaging (as we discussed in chapter 2). It is equally important to consider how focus groups for more general museum matters—like exhibition evaluations, family space reviews, or adult tour planning—could also be inclusive of these members of various disability communities. Focus group recruiters often concentrate on representing members with diverse socioeconomic status, gender, or race, but usually overlook inclusion of diverse abilities. If nearly one in four visitors to your museum has some diagnosable disability, whether visible or not, should it not then follow that one in four members of its focus groups should represent this extensive population? Tapping into diverse communities as content experts can be extremely helpful to building a better museum; oftentimes the ideas unearthed during feedback sessions can lead to important learning opportunities for the entire organization. Moreover, if the museum is willing to accept and even invite their criticism and critique, these groups can be partners in problem-solving and resource-sharing. Consider inviting the community to provide feedback on a specific program, say public tours. You can invite them to attend a tour at your museum, and following the experience, take some time to assess the activity with them. What was successful? What could be done better? Fruitful pieces of information that arise from this conversation can then be turned into future training and educational moments.

This was the case at one museum, when a negative tour experience turned into a teachable moment. A group from an adult day center for persons with developmental and cognitive disabilities visited the museum for an hour-long, volunteer-led collection highlights tour. A few days after the tour, the museum staff asked the activity coordinator from the day center to share some of her thoughts about the tour experience. The leader was candid with her account of the tour, and outlined some issues and practices that needed improvement, particularly around communication techniques and tour leader demeanor. The comments were welcomed and accepted by the museum staff. Beyond just taking note of these recommendations and filing them away, an idea sprouted: Could this be an opportunity to build empathy and understanding among the museum's volunteer docents? The museum staff invited the program coordinator and participants of the adult day center to return and speak as part of a regularly scheduled volunteer docent training, where the participants could share insights about themselves and their experiences at the museum. This casual meet-up afforded the opportunity for the volunteer docents and day center participants to meet on equal footing (as opposed to tour leader and tour followers). The day center participants were able to share their interests and stories, and the volunteer docents gained first-hand insights on ways to welcome and engage the group, which they could carry with them on future tours and interactions.

Barriers like patronizing behaviors, misconceptions, and stereotyping are some of the biggest societal challenges reported by people with disabilities. These negative and misinformed attitudes can often be corrected through exposure to new and different experiences, which can encourage perspective-taking. Museums can be the catalyst for this exposure to new experiences by introducing their staff and volunteers to new communities, new situations, and new ways of being through training initiatives focused on inclusion and accessibility (more on this in chapter 11). When preparing staff and volunteers for welcoming and engaging diverse needs and abilities, you should invite self-advocates, family members, and service providers to share their perspectives and have an open discussion about the needs of their community. Confront the misconception that people with dementia are angry or confused all the time by inviting an educator from the Alzheimer's Association to share stories from real people. Debunk the myth that people with autism cannot express or understand emotions by inviting a self-advocate or parent of a child with autism to come and explain the different communication techniques they employ. The connection and understanding forged through training that encompass first-person narratives can support an affirmative staff culture around accessibility that is grounded in empathy.

H.I. = HAVING INTERDEPENDENCE

Brian Be is an artist, autism self-advocate, and a Diversity Fellow with The Colorado Leadership Education in Neurodevelopmental and Related Disabilities (LEND) program at The University of Colorado Anschutz Medical Campus and JFK Partners.[1] Brian explains that much of his life has been "in the grey area, in and out of special education, living as both able and disabled." This causes regular adjusting for him, where he often asks himself, **So what is my life now?** but he always sees the answer as simple: opportunities. In Brian's own words, "Living with disability and knowing similar people with disabilities who have great community value and skills inspires my artist/advocate work where I can foster individual, team and community capacity in others; refocusing from disability to ThisAbility."[2]

Through Brian's LEND fellowship, he created an interactive arts workshop that utilizes improvisation and theater techniques to encourage people with and without disabilities to connect better with each other. Titled

H.I. = Having InterDependence, these collaborative workshops encourage attendees to focus on social engagement, community building and collaboration, individual empowerment, and reflection (topped off with a communal dance party!)[3] The long-term vision for this workshop is for people with disabilities and their allies to teach compassion and empathy, illustrate lived experiences and outcomes, and demonstrate to leaders and decision makers how to create policy and programs informed by people they affect. One of the attendees of Brian's workshop expressed his delight of the program, saying how "illustrating the concept of interdependence through activities where we had to depend on others was a great reminder that we all have value and something important to contribute."[4]

1. "Leadership Education in Neurodevelopmental and Related Disabilities (LEND)," School of Medicine JFK Partners, University of Colorado, accessed April 28, 2019, http://www.ucdenver.edu/academics/colleges/medicalschool/programs/JFKPartners/projects/Pages/LEND.aspx.
2. Personal communication with authors, July 2019.
3. "H.I. = Having InterDependence," School of Medicine JFK Partners, University of Colorado, accessed April 28, 2019, http://www.ucdenver.edu/academics/colleges/medical school/programs/JFKPartners/educationtraining/fellowships/hi/Pages/default.aspx.
4. Testimonial from H.I. workshop, School of Medicine JFK Partners, "H.I. = Having InterDependence."

Figure 3.2. Workshop participants cheering with hands in a circle.
Source: Brian Bernard, JFK Partners at University of Colorado Anchutz Medical Campus

CONFRONTING TOKENISM

The pitfall that can sometimes trip up organizations when engaging self-advocates or disability service providers in focus groups and training sessions is the assumption that their work is complete after convening one or two of these groups. Guess again. As we have said before, and as we will say again and again, access is a process, and one that is constantly ongoing. Collecting feedback from the community—whether from a group with a disability or not—just once or twice, is not creating real impact at your museum, and this practice runs the risk of derailing accessibility efforts. Inclusion is incorporating ideas and strengths from diverse perspectives into your organization. But if the practice is to pull ideas from these diverse perspectives only a few times, and then tout the inclusiveness of your museum for doing so, this is terribly misguided. Moreover, this could be leaning toward tokenism. Tokenism is making a symbolic effort to do something (e.g., convening an advisory group), only to give the appearance of equality and inclusion.[3] Meaningfully engaging your communities is an ongoing operation, rather than a one-time activity. Pause for self-reflection and consider whether people with disabilities truly have a seat at the table, and a real opportunity to contribute to the larger museum conversation over time, or are they just figureheads for inclusion?

A critical step to avoiding tokenism is ensuring that your museum is not asking a single person to represent their entire community (such as yourself if you are a person with a disability). No one person can speak on behalf of everyone. Therefore, if you engage someone with low vision, do not ask them to speak for the entire low-vision community, much less the larger general population of people with disabilities. In that same vein, do not believe that by knowing one person with low vision, no matter how well, that you now have insight into the needs and interests of an entire segment of that population. People are individuals, and should be recognized as such, and not delineated by their ability. There is an adage that goes, "If you have met one person with autism, you have met **one** person with autism."

There is a great diversity within the lived experience of people with disabilities, even if there is commonality in certain characteristics. It is important to recognize that "each person with a disability has different needs, different opinions, different personalities."[4] One individual cannot and should not be asked to represent and symbolically speak for their entire group. Furthermore, having a disability does not mean that a person can speak on behalf of every other person who identifies as having a disability. It is misguided to assume that someone with autism can address the interests and needs of someone who is D/deaf, or someone who uses a mobility device. These experiences are unique to the individual. Self-advocates, parents of children with disabilities, and staff at service organizations can speak to their **own** individual experiences and may be able to cite some general statistics and statements that can be broadly applied to a group, but they should not be asked to be the singular voice for their entire community, much less for the entire disability population.

Avoiding the pitfall of tokenism in your organization is possible. Museums can commit to engaging with their communities through frequent and ongoing advisory committees or focus group meetings, interspersed with informal feedback sessions that engage diverse community members over multiple occasions. Yet for more sustained commitment to inclusion and to forestall tokenism, ensure that there is more than one person with a disability in the conversations you take part in.

INCLUSIVE EMPLOYMENT

If inclusion is not taking place behind the scenes, then the misconceptions, stereotyping, and patterns of exclusion in the exhibitions, programs, and stories being told in your museum are going to be difficult to change. Fostering a culture of diversity in the workplace is appreciating and valuing individual differences and utilizing these varied perspectives to address institutional challenges and successes. There are many organizations working hard to change attitudes about disability and employment (see appendix A). Through marketing and media campaigns, they are encouraging businesses, and cultural organizations specifically, to recognize the value that individuals with disabilities bring to the workplace, and more generally, the benefits that come with full inclusion. Inclusive employment opportunities will vary by organization, but we have provided a few examples that can be integrated into museums of any size. In 2019, 80 percent of working-age Americans with some form of disability were unemployed. This is why we are focusing our discussion on paid employment opportunities, rather than unpaid volunteer opportunities.[5] The National Organization on Disability explains, "The preeminent challenge before us, as . . . a nation, is to ensure that people with disabilities enjoy full opportunity for employment, enterprise and earnings, and that employers know how to put their talents to work."[6] Museums and other cultural organizations have an important part to play in facing this challenge.

One of the easiest ways to begin is by expressing a commitment to disability inclusion in your museum. This could be achieved by including an equal opportunity statement that specifically mentions disability on your institution's job descriptions and website. This statement illustrates, both internally to current staff and externally to potential new team members, your museum's commitment to including workers of all abilities. Another way to let your community know that your institution is dedicated to this work is by creating an accessibility statement for your museum as a whole. Similar to a vision statement for the museum at large, an accessibility statement publicly states your commitment to being an accessible and welcoming institution (and nods to the fact that accessibility is a continuing process). Creating such a statement is something that can be done at any point in your accessibility journey. Some museums prefer to create this statement after they have begun to make changes and even create it in conjunction with their access advisory group, while others prefer to use an accessibility statement as a way of stating their intentions and keeping them on track and accountable. Figure 3.3 contains sample accessibility statements from museums and cultural institutions around the world.

 At Shedd Aquarium, we believe there should be no boundaries to your experience.

The Queens Museum strives to be accessible to all visitors, including those with varying abilities.   QUEENS MUSEUM

Museum of The MCA welcomes all visitors and is committed
Contemporary to making its programs and services
Art Australia accessible to everyone.

The History Center welcomes all visitors.
We recognize the diverse needs of our audience and
strive to offer accessible programming to enable all
visitors to explore this historic site.   ATLANTA **HISTORY** CENTER

 The Museum is a space for everyone to play and learn.

The Fine Arts Museums of San Francisco are   **de Young**
committed to offering services that make its   museum
collections, exhibitions, and programs accessible to all visitors.

 The Roald Dahl Museum and Story Centre is a small family-friendly Museum that welcomes all visitors... We look forward to welcoming you.

Figure 3.3.   Collection of public accessibility statements from cultural organizations around the world.

The accessibility statements included in figure 3.4 are all different, from diverse types of museums and cultural institutions, and from all over the English-speaking world. One thing you will notice they all have in common: at their core, **accessible museums welcome visitors**.

Figure 3.4. "Accessible museums welcome visitors." These are the words that stand out in a word cloud visualization of accessibility statements.

The next step in this process for inclusive employment is to review your internship program (if you have one). Is there an opportunity to turn this experiential learning program into a more inclusive structure that provides skill-building, leadership, and management growth to a wider pool of potential applicants? The US Department of Labor Office of Disability Employment Policy created a how-to guide for organizations wishing to lay the groundwork necessary for proposing and implementing an inclusive internship program.[7] This guide provides a comprehensive list of recommendations that you can adapt to meet the goals of your specific program, including sample job descriptions, an orientation agenda, and even evaluation plans. Many cultural organizations are doing this work and can be looked to for guidance. For example, the Smithsonian has their Project SEARCH internship program designed specifically for people with disabilities in Washington, DC,[8] while in the New York area the Museum, Arts and Culture Access Consortium has their Supporting Transitions program, which provides increased cultural opportunities for adults with autism.[9]

As outlined earlier in this chapter, it is critical to include people with disabilities in the design of programs and support resources that impact them. Many museums consult with experts for exhibition design, guest curation, and evaluation, so why not for accessibility? Accessibility consultants can be hired for everything from large-scale accessibility audits, to crafting accessibility statements, and even for program feedback (this is how most advisory and focus groups are paid). These individuals should be provided a stipend or honorarium to pay for their time as a program consultant, just as you would do with any other outside expertise. Depending on the size of your institution this practice may start small, with just a gift card perhaps, but it can grow with time. Even from a single focus group, or small-scale assessment, you have tangible feedback in hand that can be used to build a case for why it is important to have (and to pay for) outside advisory voices.

Disability inclusion is representation behind the scenes and in public view. While it is essential that people with disabilities provide guidance on program design and resource development, it is equally important that people with disabilities are actually leading and implementing the programs as well. Hire artists, performers, and instructors with disabilities to be part of your public events, to teach classes, lead tours, and give artist talks or demonstrations. Equally important, people with disabilities should also sit at the boardroom table as members of museum boards of directors and trustees, helping to guide the vision of the museum. On the exhibition side, consider how to integrate artwork, performances, oral histories, and more which are commissioned from artists with disabilities. When interpreting collections of artwork, artifacts, and historical objects, how can you incorporate the diverse stories and firsthand perspectives of past and present persons—artists, scientists, historians—with disabilities into exhibition narratives?

A SEAT AT THE TABLE

We began this chapter by encouraging you to take a critical look at your networks and communities of practice, prompting you to reflect on who is at the table making policy and programmatic decisions, and who is, notably, being left out. A key aspect of building strong and meaningful community partnerships is championing the representation of diverse perspectives, backgrounds, and abilities in larger museum conversations, particularly when those conversations lead to choices that directly affect your visitors. People with disabilities should be the ones leading the dialogue about their own needs and interests, and institutions must work to ensure that they have a seat at the table from the very beginning and are empowered to share their expertise by cocreating programs, events, resources, and policies that directly affect them. Museums can gain a better understanding of the many barriers facing their visitors and how best to meet and support their needs by placing these narratives, and these individuals, front and center.

NOTES

1. James I. Charlton, **Nothing About Us Without Us: Disability Oppression and Empowerment.** (Berkeley: University of California Press, 1998.) **JSTOR,** www.jstor.org/stable/10.1525/j.ctt1pnqn9.

2. "Vision," OF/BY/FOR/ALL, accessed April 3, 2019, https://www.ofbyforall .org/vision.

3. Paraphrased from Merriam Webster dictionary.

4. Burgandi Rakoska, "Disability and Tokenism: Why No One Can Speak On Behalf of Everyone," **Rooted in Rights,** December 21, 2016, https://rootedinrights.org /disability-and-tokenism-why-no-one-can-speak-on-behalf-of-everyone/.

5. "Services," National Organization on Disability, accessed April 29, 2019, https://www.nod.org/services/.

6. "About," National Organization on Disability, accessed April 29, 2019, https:// www.nod.org/about/.

7. **Inclusive Internship Programs: A How-To Guide for Employers**, US Department of Labor. Office of Disability Employment Policy, accessed April 30, 2019, https://www.dol.gov/odep/pdf/InclusiveInternshipPrograms.pdf.

8. "Project SEARCH," Access Smithsonian, Smithsonian, accessed April 30, 2019, https://www.si.edu/Accessibility/Access-opportunities.

9. "Supporting Transitions," Museum, Arts and Cultural Access Consortium, accessed April 30, 2019, https://macaccess.org/rescources/supporting-transitions -cultural-connections-for-adults-with-autism/.

Chapter Four

Environmental Access

The ADA and Inclusive Design

Now that visitors with disabilities have a seat at the proverbial museum table, it is time to ask an important question: Can visitors and staff physically get into the museum, and once inside can they easily interact with the space? It is essential to consider how to remove barriers that may exist within the museum environment in order to provide equal access. By keeping in mind disability legislation and the principles of universal design, you can create inclusive spaces that provide broad environmental access for visitors and staff.[1]

The term "environmental access" may not be immediately clear in regard to museums and cultural institutions. In regard to accessibility and inclusion, environmental access simply means the ability to easily move through and interact with the spaces around you. Environmental access goes beyond just the built environment and looks at whether visitors and staff can effortlessly get up the ramp to the door and easily open that door (whether manually or electronically). It also considers once someone is through that door and inside the museum, whether or not they can efficiently move around and engage with the space in the way it was meant to be used. Environmental access means that environments (or any service, product, or building in the environment) have been designed so that anyone who wishes to use it can do so.

Museums are required by law to maintain public facilities and spaces in which to hold their programs and activities for staff, visitors, and volunteers. Section 504 of the Rehabilitation Act of 1973 states that no person with a disability shall be "excluded from the participation in, be denied the benefits of, or be subjected to discrimination" from any program or activity receiving federal financial support.[2] Similarly, the Americans with Disabilities Act (ADA) prohibits all museums (federally funded or not) from discriminating against people with disabilities by calling for removing barriers in buildings and taking necessary steps to communicate with visitors with vision, hearing, and speech disabilities.[3] One goal of passing these two pieces of legislation was to ensure that visitors with disabilities could navigate any museum with ease and be able to safely interact with spaces and exhibitions as any visitor would. An accessibility audit can support this process by providing a baseline standard from which to approach barrier removal and program accessibility.

ACCESSIBILITY AUDIT

At the beginning of any accessibility journey, a museum should conduct a self-evaluation, or accessibility audit, where it examines the full range of programs, policies, services, and facilities in order to identify existing barriers and determine the extent to which these barriers are preventing people with disabilities from participation. State and locally-funded government organizations are required by law (Title II of the ADA) to conduct an audit and self-evaluate the accessibility of their facilities. Title III facilities—private entities that operate facilities, including museums—are not required by law to conduct a building accessibility survey; but only with an audit can an organization ensure that its programs, services, or facilities are in compliance with the ADA and other federal accessibility laws. A successful self-evaluation closely examines program accessibility, barrier removal, and effective communication.[4]

There are a number of available resources for conducting an accessibility audit within your institution, both fee-based as well as free. If funds allow, hire an ADA compliance consultant who can assist in the oversight and coordination of organizational evaluations. For a more economical approach, there are many resources readily available to conduct an audit yourself. The ADA National Network has a wealth of fact sheets, videos, guides, and handbooks to support your understanding of ADA requirements.[5] The ADA Action Guide, a project of the Institute for Human Centered Design, provides self-evaluation forms that can support you to conduct your own accessibility surveys and to help develop transition plans to implement changes that need to be made.[6] We have listed several "do it yourself" checklists in appendix A that provide clear and helpful instructions on how to conduct an effective survey at your organization.

One particularly helpful resource is the ADA Standard for Accessible Design Checklist, created in partnership by the Institute for Human Centered Design and the New England ADA Center. This checklist reviews the facilities in which programs, services, and activities take place, and can be edited to fit your organization. This checklist follows the four priorities listed in the ADA Title III regulations:[7]

- **Existence of accessible approach and entrance.** All visitors should have an accessible route from their exterior arrival point to an accessible building entrance. The condition of a building's available parking, types of exterior ramps, and entrance accessibility should also be reviewed.
- **Access to goods and services.** The physical arrangement of the space should enable people to acquire goods and services and engage in activities and events without assistance. Review the condition of interior accessible routes and doors, availability and type of interior ramps, elevator scope and design, signage design, seating, and more.
- **Access to public restrooms.** All visitors should have access to restrooms. Accessible routes to and entrance of the restroom, nearby signage, space design inside the restroom, including soap dispensers and hand dryers should all be examined.
- **Access to other facilities.** All visitors should have access to drinking fountains and public telephones. Review the placement and design of water fountains, public telephones, and fire alarm systems.

Very few supplies and resources are needed to complete your accessibility audit: a copy of the ADA Standards for Accessible Design Checklist (or other checklist of your choosing), measuring tape, a level, and something to write with. Before you begin, ask yourself who should be involved in this process. Who are the internal and external partners who can both help identify barriers and brainstorm solutions? If you have an advisory group, call on them for their expertise and help. Involve staff or community partners who identify as disabled and are committed to (and compensated for) helping complete the audit and develop a plan of action. After all, people with disabilities are the only people who can truly speak to what it is like to move through spaces with a disability and can therefore provide more comprehensive and holistic views of both challenges and possible solutions. Begin outside, scrutinizing accessible routes and entrances first, before moving your investigation inside and around the facility. While completing your survey, keep in mind that the ADA, as well as any city or state codes and standards, are the **baseline** of how accessible your building and organization should be. Going beyond this basic level will broaden the potential use of your space and programs for a wider variety of visitors. By identifying issues with the accessibility of your museum, you can begin to provide a roadmap to possible solutions and alterations that can enhance your museum's ability to reach a wider audience.

ADA
Checklist
for Existing
Facilities

Based on the 2010 ADA Standards for Accessible Design

Produced by

Institute for Human Centered Design
www.HumanCenteredDesign.org

www.ADAchecklist.org
Copyright © 2016

ADA National Network
www.ADAta.org

Questions on the ADA 800-949-4232 voice/tty
Questions on checklist 617-695-0085 voice/tty
ADAinfo@NewEnglandADA.org

Priority 1 – Approach & Entrance				Comments	Possible Solutions
1.1	Is there at least one route from site arrival points (parking, passenger loading zones, public sidewalks and public transportation stops) that does not require the use of stairs? [See 2010 ADA Standards for Accessible Design – 206.2.1]	☐Yes ☐No If yes, location of route:		Photo #:	• Add a ramp • Regrade to 1:20 maximum slope • Add a lift if site constraints prevent other solutions

 **Parking** Accessible parking spaces should be identified by size, access aisle and signage.

| 1.2 | If parking is provided for the public, are an adequate number of accessible spaces provided? [208.2] | ☐Yes ☐No

Total #:

Accessible #: | **Total Spaces** / **Accessible Spaces**
1 - 25 → 1
26 - 50 → 2
51 - 75 → 3
76 - 100 → 4
100+ see 2010 Standards 208.2 | Photo #: | • Reconfigure by repainting lines
•
• |
| 1.3 | Of the accessible spaces, is at least one a van accessible space?* [208.2.4] | ☐Yes ☐No | *For every 6 or fraction of 6 parking spaces required by the table above, at least 1 should be a van accessible space.

Photo #: | | * If constructed before 3/15/2012, parking is compliant if at least 1 in every 8 accessible spaces is van accessible

• Reconfigure by repainting lines |

Figures 4.1.1. and 4.1.2. ADA Checklist produced by Institute for Human Centered Design and the New England ADA Center.
Source: Institute for Human Centered Design and the New England ADA Center

PLAN OF ACTION

After completing your audit, the next step is to create a transition plan. Title II organizations are legally required by the ADA to create a transition plan, while Title III private entities are not legally required to, but it is highly recommended.[8] As mentioned above, the only way to know whether your museum facilities and programs are accessible is to undergo an audit and address the barriers that arise. If you have taken the steps to conduct an audit, your work will only be enhanced by creating a transition plan to go along with it.

Transition plans articulate how your organization will address the myriad of access barriers identified during the audit with concrete solutions and realistic timeframes. Some access issues will have straightforward solutions: for example, if there is no sign indicating the location of an accessible entrance, the solution is to install one. Other access barriers may be more complex and thus require creative solutions either because there are multiple solutions with varying cost and complexity or because the principal solution is not easily achievable for some reason. Solutions to access issues can be long term and structural, like installing a ramp for people to enter the building. They can also be nonstructural and more short-term solutions, such as holding a meeting on the first floor of a multistory building that does not have an elevator. It may be that moving a meeting location is a more immediate and cost-effective solution to addressing the barrier for a smaller, underresourced museum. This short-term fix can buy time to fundraise and plan for the longer-term solution of an elevator.

Let's move through a hypothetical transition plan brainstorm using the barrier posed by an office doorknob as an example. For a door to be accessible, it should not require more than five pounds of force to open, and its hardware (handle) must be operable with one hand, limb, or fist and not need tight grasping, pinching, or twisting of the wrist.[9] In this thought exercise, the front door that leads into your museum's staff office space has a round knob that is difficult to grasp and turn, which poses a barrier to entering the office. Examine the identified challenges, in this case accessing the office, and start creating solutions. Be sure to ask yourself if the solutions are convenient, flexible, realistic, and equitable. By asking these questions you are keeping in mind the principles of universal design, which will be discussed in detail below. For each barrier there are most likely multiple possible solutions. In the case of the office doorknob, there are at least four possible solutions to consider. You could: prop the door open, remove the doorknob altogether, replace the round doorknob with a levered handle, or install an electronic door opener. When determining what should go into your transition plan, be sure to consider the practicality of each option. Depending on your museum, propping open your office door may not be realistic in terms of security or safety. Removing the knob entirely disrupts the function of the door, so it is also not a realistic option. Installing an automatic door opener would be most convenient and flexible, yet it is also the most expensive and time-intensive option. Replacing the current knob with a levered handle, which can be grasped without twisting and turning the wrist, is a far less expensive option, and also makes the door more immediately accessible. This choice may be the best short-term, nonstructural compromise for your transition plan as it is cost-effective, has a short target date, and still solves the barrier of accessing the office.

Taking the time to work through all the different possible solutions and their costs allows you to take the barriers you have identified in your accessibility audit and translate the solutions into a plan of action. Completing a cost/benefit analysis of time and available resources for each issue helps determine the time and resources needed for each activity, which then will inform what projects are put into action first. Depending on the scope, some of the projects on your list may have two or more phases. Let's take a look at the doorknob example again. The first phase of the project plan may be to replace the round knob with a lever handle, but later, once you have been able to secure funds, you might want to add an electronic opener. Determine what projects (and steps) can be done immediately and easily—these will be at the top of your action plan. Next will come what can be done in the short term, with a bit more effort or resources, and finally, what can be completed with some long-term planning. There may not be a single solution that immediately works but remember that accessibility is a continuous process involving the development of "ever more responsive solutions to a changing human reality."[10] Developing a realistic plan and timeframe for completing the steps of your transition plan is key. Budget and staff time can be seen as the biggest hurdles when creating and implementing a transition plan; these will often be cited as reasons **against** implementing action items. However, as the **NYC Guidebook to Accessibility and Universal Design** argues, "If buildings were usable by everyone from the start, then fewer renovations would be necessary in the future and those renovations that were required would be less expensive."[11]

HISTORIC SITES

You may wonder what to do in the case of a historic site or house museum: Do the same laws for new constructions apply to historic buildings? Should you conduct an accessibility audit? The ADA applies to **all** places of public accommodation, including museums and other cultural facilities. Therefore, historic sites are not exempt from being accessible locations. That being said, a historic property's spaces, features, and significant materials should not be destroyed in the pursuit of accessibility. Sites should increase accessibility whenever possible. As we discussed in chapter 1, barrier removal in historic buildings is required by the ADA if it is "readily achievable."[12] If the barrier removal threatens or destroys the historic significance of the building or facility, it is not considered "readily achievable."[13] To determine what steps you can and should take, you will want to use a three step process to get started. First, conduct a review of the historical significance of the property and identify any character-defining features of the building and site.[14] Second, conduct an accessibility audit to determine your current level of accessibility. Compare this to the required level of accessibility based on the ADA. Third, create your transition plan for changes, within a preservation context. After you have created your transition plan, begin the work. Just as with nonhistoric sites, you will want to review your plan periodically to ensure that the changes you are planning to implement are still needed and feasible within the budget. You may not be able to do as much to your site as a nonhistoric/ protected site, but remember, the goal is to provide a high level of accessibility by selecting appropriate solutions without compromising significant features or the overall character of the historic property.

Do not be afraid to think outside the box when it comes to modifying your historic structure to be more accessible. This can be a challenge for historians and preservation enthusiasts alike. In the case of many older buildings with historic status and protection, and with limited budgets to boot, drastically changing the structure of the building for accessibility improvements may not be feasible. Making these sorts of complex modifications can be very costly and require specialized trades to complete. However, modifications do not have to be all or nothing. Take for example the Molly Brown House Museum in Denver, Colorado. The museum completed a multiyear restoration and capital project in 2019. As a part of these capital projects, the museum installed an accessible lift so that all visitors could now reach the basement exhibit space, as well as the first floor of the historic home—areas which were previously inaccessible throughout the history of the museum. Installing the lift did require some alterations to the physical structure, but the impact was limited to a small corner of the enclosed back porch. The museum could not install an elevator that reached all floors of the house without dramatically altering the structure and having to completely remove one of the historic bedrooms. Instead of taking this as defeat and leaving the structure inaccessible to anyone with a mobility device, the museum decided to make a small modification to the back porch to open up the house to a whole segment of visitors that, up to that point, had otherwise been excluded from visiting. This example serves as a good reminder that access is a process; do what you can to welcome all visitors without compromising the integrity of the building's history.

Figure 4.2.   Exterior view of accessible lift at the Molly Brown House Museum.
Source: Heather Pressman

If you simply cannot make changes without compromising the building's structure or history, you can create programmatic access, or nonstructural changes, in place of physical access. For historic properties where physical access is impossible, this means providing services, information, and experiences in a different way. This could include things like offering a video or an interactive tour of the space. In the case of the Molly Brown House Museum, for the areas of the house that remained unreachable even with the lift, the museum created a video tour of these spaces that visitors can watch, along with a basket of touchable objects which highlight the furniture, fabrics, and even architectural details that visitors see on the tour. Another option is to provide interpretive panels on the exterior of the museum that vividly illustrate the inaccessible areas of the museum. If you have the space and ability, you could even create a tactile model of the museum that enables visitors to explore areas they could not otherwise. In addition, you could also provide touchable items (replicas, copies, etc.) of clothing, furniture, or other items visitors might see in the spaces. For example, if the walls are covered in fabric, provide a touchable piece of it for guests to engage with. Other multisensory items to make available for visitors include plaster pieces, molding, wallpaper, reproductions of historic photographs laminated or mounted on something sturdy (such as foam core), scent jars, and so on. For gardens, you could provide a selection of potted plants that visitors could see and touch, miniature tactile versions of statuary, or other similar items that help to translate the museum experience. Offering a variety of objects for visitors to engage with will enhance their visit overall. Per the Institute for Human Centered Design, if you design for people on the periphery, it will benefit everyone in the middle as well, thus enhancing everyone's visit to your institution.[15]

OLD MEETS NEW

For more than one hundred years, Vizcaya Museum & Gardens has survived Miami's hurricanes and tropical climate. Now an accredited museum and National Historic Landmark, Vizcaya Museum & Gardens was conceived as a modern and subtropical interpretation of an eighteenth-century Italian villa. It is said to be one of "the finest private house[s] ever built in America."[1] Like many historic houses and gardens, there are some areas of Vizcaya that are inaccessible to the public due to concerns for the preservation of the structures. In 2019, Vizcaya released an interactive tour of two of these spaces: the Barge and Swimming Pool Grotto. To create this look into these two special places they used scanning and 3-D modeling to study and preserve these spaces. The interactive video tour allows all visitors to be able to access these two spaces, which cannot be physically entered by visitors of any kind. Using these new technologies, Vizcaya was able to transport visitors to areas of this National Historic Landmark that are otherwise publically inaccessible.

With its location right on the Biscayne Bay, near Miami, Florida, Vizcaya is vulnerable to tropical storms, rising sea levels, and other impacts of climate change. The Barge and Swimming Pool Grotto are both particularly vulnerable due to their locations within the estate. The Barge, designed playfully to look like a boat, is a breakwater that was built to protect the house and its terraces from waves. James Deering, who had the estate built, commissioned all the sculptures from American artist Alexander Stirling Calder in 1915 (father of Alexander Calder of modern art fame). The Barge is made from local limestone that is soft and porous. The Barge has been impacted by significant erosion from the salt water and storm waves, which threaten the stability of the decorative reliefs and statuary. The lower landing steps of the Barge are no longer visible, submerged under rising sea levels.

Figure 4.3.   Detail of Swimming Pool Grotto ceiling by artist Robert Winthrop Chanler.
Source: Vizcaya Museum and Gardens Archives, Miami, Florida

Vizcaya's original guests experienced a whimsical and fragile grotto created out of limestone, shells, metal, concrete, plaster, and paint as they entered the swimming pool. The grotto features underwater scenes by artist Robert Winthrop Chanler on a plaster ceiling. Due to the nature of the Swimming Pool Grotto, it is subject to salty air, high relative humidity, and periodic storm surges during hurricanes. These conditions compromise the fragile materials that were used to create the grotto.

The Vizcaya virtual video project is an excellent example of creating universal programmatic access to areas of a historic property that would otherwise be inaccessible to visitors. While Vizcaya is a large organization and this was a well-funded project, other organizations can still use this project as inspiration for their own small-scale projects. Creating a simple video of inaccessible spaces for visitors, whether unreachable to all or part of your audience, offers the opportunity for people to explore the space one way or another.

1. "Director's Welcome," Vizcaya Museum & Gardens, accessed April 21, 2019, http://vizcaya.org/about-directors-welcome.asp.

ACCESS THROUGH INCLUSIVE DESIGN

The regulations enforced by the ADA and Rehabilitation Act of 1973 are intended to eliminate some of the physical barriers which limit the usability of environments for people with disabilities.[16] However, accessible design of the built environment is just the starting point. Once through the door and inside the museum, visitors should be able to safely and effectively engage with the space and exhibitions in the way they were meant to be used. Inclusive design, often called universal design or human-centered design, is a design framework intended to create environments, communications, and policies that are usable by as many people as possible without the need for adaptation or retrofitting later on.[17] The goal of inclusive design is to eliminate disabling environments through creative, imaginative, and equitable design approaches.

The idea of design specifically tailored to the needs of people with disabilities gained momentum in the second-half of the twentieth century, with a push toward barrier-free design that removed obstacles in the built environment for people with physical disabilities.[18] Thanks to the disability rights movement of the 1970s, design was being recognized, for the first time, as a condition for achieving civil rights. "Accessible design" was the phrase used to describe this new design movement that argued for equal opportunities to engage with facilities and environments. In 1985, Ronald Mace, an architect and wheelchair user, coined the term "Universal Design" to explain the concept that people, both with disabilities and without, can "benefit from a more accessible built environment."[19] Architects and designers, Mace argued, rarely took into consideration the needs of disabled and older adult users when creating their designs. This consistent oversight led to often costly retrofitting and specialized adaptations after the fact. Mace therefore proposed that all environments be made accessible from the start, which would result in more usable spaces, products, and policies that would benefit all people.[20]

In 1997, Mace collaborated with nine fellow architects, product designers, engineers, and environmental design researchers and the Center for Universal Design at North Carolina State University to establish the Principles of Universal Design, in order to explain the characteristics of this design approach.[21] These seven principles are:[22]

1. **Equitable Use.** The design is useful to people with diverse abilities. Provide the same means of use for all users: identical whenever possible; equivalent when not.
2. **Flexibility in Use.** The design accommodates a wide range of individual preferences and abilities. Provide choice in methods of use.

3. **Simple and Intuitive Use.** Use of the design is easy to understand, regardless of the user's experience, knowledge, language skills, or current concentration level. Accommodate a wide range of literacy and language skills.
4. **Perceptible Information.** The design communicates necessary information effectively to the user, regardless of ambient conditions or the user's sensory abilities. Use different modes (pictorial, verbal, tactile) for redundant presentation of essential information.
5. **Tolerance for Error.** The design minimizes hazards and the adverse consequences of accidental or unintended actions. Provide warnings of hazards and errors.
6. **Low Physical Effort.** The design can be used efficiently and comfortably and with a minimum of fatigue. Allow user to maintain a neutral body position.
7. **Size and Space for Approach and Use.** Appropriate size and space is provided for approach, reach, manipulation, and use regardless of user's body size, posture, or mobility. Make reach to all components comfortable for any seated or standing user.

Along a parallel timeline, the Commission for Architecture and the Built Environment in the United Kingdom (now an arm of the UK Design Council) came up with their own set of inclusive design principles in the 1990s.[23] According to their principles, inclusive design is:

- **Inclusive**. Everyone can use them easily, with dignity, and safely.
- **Responsive**. Considers what people say they need and want.
- **Flexible**. Can be used in different ways by different people.
- **Convenient**. Requires little effort for everyone to use them.
- **Accommodating**. Designed for everyone, regardless of their age, ethnicity, gender, mobility, or circumstances.
- **Welcoming**. Removes barriers that might exclude some people.
- **Realistic**. Balances everyone's needs by offering more than one solution (one size may not fit all).
- **Understandable**. Easy for everyone to understand and use.

Unpacking these two sets of principles we find that universal and inclusive design is the process of embedding the choice and needs of people into the spaces and things we create. Author John Salmen describes universal design as "the art and practice of design to accommodate the widest variety and number of people throughout their lifespans."[24] **Design for Accessibility: A Cultural Administrator's Handbook,** one of the primary accessible design guides for museums, notes that "[i]n the best of all possible worlds, the concept of universal design would guide the creation of all facilities and programs. Universal design benefits people of all ages and abilities because what is an accommodation for one person may be a convenience for many."[25] To others, however, the principles of universal design appear vague and seemingly difficult to put into action in a concrete manner. And still others object to the principles' omission of references to specific users, such as specifically calling out people with disabilities.[26] While there are indeed principles of universal design, as stated above, there is not, however, a universal design checklist that all museums and public accommodations can follow in order to achieve full accessibility. Universal, inclusive user-centered design is a "**process**, a beginning point, rather than a measurable end."[27] As with any design process, universal design is still in formation; one experimental tool used to design a more usable built environment. Salmen explains, "As more is learned about human needs and abilities, and as technologies develop, the practice of universal design improves, evolves, and changes."[28] Emphasis should be on the decision-making process demonstrated by the principles rather than solely on the spaces or products created.

PUT INTO PRACTICE

Inclusive and universal design principles can be a lens through which you determine the solutions involved in your museum's transition plan. They can expand upon the basic requirements set forth in the ADA guidelines. Try to overlay the universal and inclusive design principles onto the four ADA priorities to explore ways architecture and building features, and also policies and programs, can be designed to provide an environment that is supportive of more people.

ADA Priority: **Existence of accessible approach and entrance.** ADA guidelines require that 50 percent of public entrances be accessible.

Inclusive design overlay: Providing automated doors at all primary and accessible entrances. This is flexible (provides choice, people can use the door with or without the automated button) and accommodating (can be used by everyone regardless of circumstance).

ADA Priority: **Access to goods and services.** ADA guidelines require an adequate number of wheelchair accessible spaces to be provided in an auditorium or classroom.

Inclusive design overlay: Ensure that **all** spaces with seating areas (within exhibitions, near the front desk, outdoor seating, etc.) have clearly identified spaces for mobility devices such as motorized scooters or wheelchairs. This is equitable (providing the same means for all users) and welcoming (removes a barrier that excludes people).

ADA Priority: **Access to public restrooms.** ADA guidelines require at least one accessible toilet room.

Inclusive design overlay: Have at least one single-user toilet room, or family toilet, on each floor and identify it as an all-gender toilet room. This is responsive (considering the needs of the LGBTQ+ community) and is simple and intuitive to use (presents a single choice of where to go).

ADA Priority: **Access to other facilities.** ADA guidelines require at least one drinking fountain.

Inclusive design overlay: Cluster other amenities (like a coat rack, garbage receptacles, even museum maps, etc.) together at an easily visible location. This is convenient (little effort to find amenities) and equitable (everyone goes to the same place to find what they individually need).

This brief exercise illustrates the larger concept that employing an inclusive decision-making process can support you to move your museum beyond the basic elements of accessible design into a more universally accessible location. The ADA regulations are the minimum standard for environmental access and should therefore be viewed as representing the **least** an institution should do. Accessibility audits help illuminate what barriers exist and what problems need to be solved when they are readily achievable. Just as your organization will continue to design new exhibitions and programs year after year, while incorporating the newest technology and best practices, so, too, should you approach finding thoughtful and innovative ways to incorporate inclusive design principles that address environmental barriers at your organization. Aimi Hamraie, in the book **Building Access: Universal Design and the Politics of Disability,** perfectly explains this ongoing process as "the aspirational project of access," which is "open-ended, [and] never completed by checking boxes or gaining building permits."[29] Inclusive design principles coupled with the ADA and Rehabilitation Act guidelines support the creation of a more inclusive, functional built environment.

BEYOND ENVIRONMENTAL ACCESS

Environmental access is an essential component of any accessible institution, however, it does not paint the full picture. You should approach finding novel and innovative ways to incorporate universal design standards that address accessibility and inclusion barriers at your organization, just as your organization will continue to design new exhibitions and programs year after year, incorporating the newest technology and exhibition best practices. Endeavor to go beyond the minimum standards for all your visitors because physical access is not the only barrier facing them when they attempt to visit your museum. It does not matter if people can get into and around your building if once there, they do not feel welcome. The next several chapters discuss some of these other barriers (cognitive, sensory, financial, attitudinal) and how to reduce or eliminate them for your visitors.

NOTES

1. Universal design is also known as human centered design, design-for-all, life-span design, or inclusive design.

2. "Section 504, Rehabilitation Act of 1973," Statues, Executive Orders and Federal Regulations and Policies, Office of the Assistant Secretary for Administration & Management, U.S. Department of Labor, accessed August 26, 2020, https://www.dol.gov/agencies/oasam/centers-offices/civil-rights-center/statutes/section-504-rehabilitation-act-of-1973.

3. "What is the Americans with Disabilities Act (ADA)?" What is the ADA, ADA National Network, accessed February 8, 2019. https://adata.org/learn-about-ada.

4. "Self-Evaluation Forms," Resources, ADA Title II Action Guide for State and Local Governments, New England ADA Center, accessed February 26, 2020, https://www.adaactionguide.org/resources#.

5. "ADA Publications and Videos," Resources, ADA National Network, accessed February 18, 2019, https://adata.org/national-product-search?keys=&type=All&tid=All.

6. New England ADA Center, "Self-Evaluation Forms."

7. "ADA Checklist for Existing Facilities," Institute for Human Centered Design, accessed February 18, 2019, https://www.adachecklist.org/checklist.html.

8. "ADA Title II Requirements," ADA Title II Action Guide for State and Local Governments, New England ADA Center, accessed February 26, 2020, https://www.adaactionguide.org/ada-title-ii-requirements.

9. "Opening Doors to Everyone," Fact Sheets, ADA National Network, accessed May 8, 2019, https://adata.org/factsheet/opening-doors-everyone.

10. "History," Institute for Human Centered Design, accessed May 8, 2019, https://www.humancentereddesign.org/inclusive-design/history.

11. Danise Levine, ed., **The NYC Guidebook to Accessibility and Universal Design** (Buffalo: University at Buffalo, The State University of New York, Center for Inclusive Design and Environmental Access, 2003), 10. http://www.nyc.gov/html/ddc/downloads/pdf/udny/udny2.pdf.

12. As a reminder, according to the ADA, "readily achievable" means that it is easy to accomplish and can be done without too much difficulty or expense.

13. If the building or facility is designated as historic under state or local law or eligible for listing in the National Register of Historic Places under the National Historic Preservation Act (16 U.S.C. 470, et seq.).

14. If you need help with this, contact your local State Historic Preservation Office or other local preservation organizations.

15. "Mission," Institute for Human Centered Design, accessed May 8, 2019, https://www.humancentereddesign.org/about-us/mission.

16. Levine, **The NYC Guidebook to Accessibility and Universal Design**, 6.

17. Institute for Human Centered Design, "History."

18. Institute for Human Centered Design, "History."

19. Aimi Hamraie, **Building Access: Universal Design and the Politics of Disability** (Minneapolis: University of Minnesota Press, 2017), 6.

20. Hamraie, **Building Access**, 6.

21. Participants are listed in alphabetical order: Bettye Rose Connell, Mike Jones, Ron Mace, Jim Mueller, Abir Mullick, Elaine Ostroff, Jon Sanford, Ed Steinfeld, Molly Story, and Gregg Vanderheiden.

22. We link to the comprehensive list of all seven principles with all thirty-nine guidelines in Appendix A.

23. "Principles," Institute for Human Centered Design, accessed April 23, 2019, https://www.humancentereddesign.org/inclusive-design/principles.

24. John Salmen, "U.S. Accessibility Codes and Standards: Challenges for Universal Design," in **Universal Design Handbook**, 2nd ed., ed. Wolfang F.E. Preiser and Korydon H. Smith (New York: McGraw-Hill, 2011), 6.1.

25. **Design for Accessibility: A Cultural Administrators Handbook** (Washington, DC: National Assembly of State Arts Agencies, 1994), 55.

26. Aimi Hamraie dives deeply into providing a more critical and historical account of accessibility and universal design in **Building Access: Universal Design and the Politics of Disability.**

27. Hamraie, **Building Access**, 249.

28. Salmen, "Accessibility Codes," 6.1.

29. Hamraie, **Building Access**, 250.

Chapter Five

Not an Afterthought

Cognitive Access

As a destination designed for public use, museums must be mindful of the way in which they present information to visitors. When entering a museum space—be it for the first time or the fiftieth time—guests must use their cognitive functioning to navigate a complex path, steering themselves from entrance to ticket counter to elevator to galleries and more, and then discerning the information provided along the way. Throughout their visit, guests make contact with a series of decision points (where to go and how to get there), as well as rules and expectations (where it is safe to eat or drink, what you can and cannot touch, etc.). Successful museums consider how to both prepare and guide their visitors safely and confidently throughout their space without disorientation or anxiety. By focusing on cognition—how visitors input and store information—museums are better designing information, services, and programs that help their communities to better understand and confidently engage with the museum.

DESIGNING FOR UNDERSTANDING

When you concentrate on serving the needs of a particular group, you learn to design better for everyone. Consider the previous case of ramps: these serve the needs of people using mobility devices, but are equally important for people using strollers, bicycles, pushing delivery carts, and more. Therefore, by definition, design promotes accessibility.[1] Similarly, by designing curb cuts, sidewalks have, in general, become more readily available and usable to a wider portion of the population. We have discussed how some aspects of accessible design can and should be applied to address environmental needs and barriers, and now we want to focus on how this ethos of accessible design can be effectively implemented in ways that promote cognitive access in museum spaces and programs.

Cognitive access is ensuring that information, materials, and communications are readily available, and easily understandable, to people with diverse cognitive abilities. Intellectual or developmental disabilities, learning disabilities, trauma (such as traumatic brain injury), age, and even access to education can affect cognitive ability. These circumstances can affect how people process information and may impact comprehension, literacy or numeracy skills, reasoning and problem solving, memory and recall, attention and perception, and even language capacity. Barriers that could affect those with differing cognitive abilities include complex building maps or text-heavy signage, both of which can leave visitors uncertain of how to find their way around your museum. Or, perhaps, there are long and jargon-filled wall labels that seem to require a PhD to read and understand. These cognitive barriers, among others, could result in confusion, anxiety, or alienation in some visitors. Museums can be inclusive of potential cognitive limitations by fostering access in a more expansive way across the museum. Moving beyond ramps and physical components, museum staff can consider the mental and intellectual side of accessibility, and craft opportunities that enable visitors to interact with content and process information in ways that are more usable to them.

COMMUNICATING EXPECTATIONS

Visiting a museum is a social occasion. Even if initially a person planned to visit a certain museum because of its collection or special exhibitions, their experience is going to include interacting with more than just the objects. From the moment they arrive, visitors are entering into a shared museum space, consisting of various social conventions, cues, etiquette, and interactions with other people, objects, and spaces.[2] As a result, a typical museum visit consists of a series of guidelines, rules, and expectations, and the ways in which people act in a museum is directly informed by the guidelines and rules the museum puts forth. Some of these expectations are overtly stated—such as not touching the art, artifacts, animals, or plants—while others are more implied. Just as you sit silently during a symphony performance, and energetically clap and laugh during a comedy show, museums, too, have their own (often unspoken) appropriate and inappropriate behaviors that vary among museum types. For example, in art museums visitors are expected to whisper rather than talk in galleries; to show appreciation by making the right type of comments; to know how and where to stand (finding an optimal viewpoint to examine the art object, but taking care not to obstruct others); to walk slowly enough to pay attention to exhibits but fast enough to give room to others; and above all, to touch absolutely nothing.[3] In a children's museum, however, visitors are encouraged to touch and climb nearly everything, and are not afraid to make a mess. Dimitra Christidou offers the analogy that museums expect visitors to "know how to act on stage as well as how to read the script provided," meaning visitors are expected to publicly demonstrate their ability and competency to look at art and artifacts.[4] Often, those visitors who more easily recognize these unspoken rules have past experience visiting museums or similar cultural centers, and therefore are far more familiar with these behavioral assumptions and the best ways to act accordingly. The implicit nature of these rules, and the social conventions closely associated with these, create serious barriers to a positive museum experience for someone with affected cognitive ability. Discerning which behaviors are suitable in the museum environment takes skill in perception, reasoning, and comprehension, all of which can be impacted if someone has affected cognitive ability. Take an individual with Alzheimer's disease or a developmental disability for example; the changes in reasoning and judgment caused by these disorders can influence a person's ability to recognize the subtle social cues of a museum visit. Many visitors look to others for guidance on how to act, so may whisper in a gallery or stand a safe distance from an artwork as they see others doing. Whereas an individual with impacted cognitive ability may be unable to pick up on these subtle cues from other visitors, and instead speak loudly in an exhibition or stand too close when examining an artifact (and perhaps even try to touch it), consequently and unknowingly disturbing other visitors. The effects of acting incorrectly in a social space like a museum can be shame, humiliation, and even reprimand (depending on the severity of the action) from staff and even other visitors. All this can result in a negative and unpleasant visit. Faulting people for not recognizing implied expectations of how to act within a museum, without first outlining expectations, is bad practice.

To combat this cognitive barrier, many museums have begun to overtly illustrate to visitors the ways to safely and appropriately act within their museum space. In light of our recent experiences with physical distancing, and mask mandates in public spaces, indicators of how to be safe in a space is more important and present than ever. Guidelines vary from place to place, often depending on the collection, museum vision, and intended audience, but simply type "museum manners" into an internet search and you will find numerous examples of ways that museums are creatively presenting information visitors may need to know before and during their visit. Most often these guidelines are written somewhere on the visit page of the museum's website, or visible on signs inside the museum, and outline any rules and behaviors that keep both the collection, and the visitors, safe. Sometimes museums take more creative routes and share this information in a video, social story (more on this below), or even as a decorative vinyl wrap inside an elevator. The ways in which the information is presented can also be playful and approachable. Take the Dallas Museum of Art (DMA) guidelines, for example. Rather than presenting a long list of restrictions, their approach is to infuse a bit of humor and focus on how to **enjoy** a visit. The mindset being, if a space becomes "a never ending list of restrictions, visitors will never feel relaxed nor engaged."[5] In the DMA's approach, rather than simply stating that umbrellas and backpacks are not allowed in the galleries (which is true), they instead encourage visitors to "lighten up" by checking these materials at the complementary coat check. This subtly shifts the focus on how visitors can have a more positive experience (without the load of added materials) rather than focusing on what they **cannot** have. In another manner, rather than establishing eating and drinking as a negative, they actually encourage this activity but instead direct visitors on where they can safely and appropriately do so. Rules are in place for a reason, but rather than focus on what people **cannot** do, another technique is to point visitors in the direction of what they **can** do; thus transforming a negative "don't" into a more positive "do it this way instead."

Figure 5.1.   Dallas Museum of Art Museum Guidelines.
Source: Dallas Museum of Art

Including information on appropriate museum behavior and rules in a transparent and easily accessible manner, whether via the museum's website or physically inside the museum building, empowers visitors of all cognitive abilities (and their caregivers) to better regulate their encounters at the museum by being able to reference concrete concepts. Furthermore, arming all visitors with clearly stated guidelines and rules supports a more socially cohesive museum experience overall, where visitors more clearly know what to expect, and what is expected of them.

ACCESS TO INFORMATION

As museums and other public areas become increasingly complex and intricate in their layout, it is more important than ever to support people in knowing where they are and where they are going. By scrutinizing the role of communications and information exchange within their buildings, museums can consider how to create coherent and cohesive strategies to get their information across to visitors, and to support them while navigating the complex path and series of decision points involved in a museum visit. People rely on signs and wayfinding support for orientation and guidance when in a space, and not surprisingly, "a well-designed space or sign system will meet the needs of the entire population, not just the needs of a special interest group."[6]

Wayfinding was a term originally associated with travelers seeking passage across uncharted territory.[7] More recently it has come to define how people move through an environment to reach their desired destination, and it considers how signage, graphics, and other recognizable landmarks support navigation. People rely on cues—visual, auditory, and spatial—to orient themselves to a space and create a mental map of the environment. Some visitors may have a more difficult time forming a mental map of the space because of impacts on comprehension or perception, for example.[8] Therefore, they may require additional materials and supports to orient themselves in the space. Signs are some of the most traditional and straightforward ways of conveying messages in the museum. Signs can direct a visitor to a specific gallery or a location of a program; can indicate where to find a gender-neutral bathroom or nursing room; can guide away from closed or staff-only areas; and can educate and inform visitors on the content of an exhibition. All these various types of signs—be they directional or informational—serve a purpose, and as a unit, they create a language that communicates to visitors what is most important to the museum. Because going beyond simply pointing toward a place, a sign can set the tone and give your space an identity. Take an airport for example; the goal of this space is to facilitate travel for thousands of people each day. Airport signage achieves this goal by providing clear directions that guide visitors, in a quick and direct manner, along a set pathway to their desired destination. A children's museum, on the other hand, seeks to stimulate imagination and creativity in children and families, so while they, too, want to usher people through their space, their approach to signage will look different. Directional signage may be as whimsical and playful as it is helpful.

Figure 5.2.   Children's Museum of Pittsburgh directional signage.
Source: Designed by Pentagram design studio

Consider your own museum. If the goal is to support visitors to more easily understand and navigate your space, how can your signage reflect and communicate this attitude of accessibility? Determine what information is important for people to know about navigating your museum. Begin with accessing your space. Is it clear where people enter the museum? If there is a separate accessible entrance, you must clearly communicate its location (and include this on any related maps). Once inside is it clear where and how to purchase tickets? Do not just assume that all visitors will know they need a ticket, or to look for a front desk. Next, consider navigating the space and knowing where to go. Is there a prescribed pathway that visitors should take when touring the museum? Could a sign help indicate where to start (and end)? Is it clear what people can see and do in your museum? A map may be best in this role, but signage illustrating what is in each gallery, or on each level, can also be supportive especially if you have a particularly well-known artwork or artifact.

Next, reflect on what needs people have when visiting a museum. Are there clear signs indicating the location of elevators, stairs, or escalators? What about directing to bathrooms (both individual, family, and/or all-gender) as well as nursing rooms? For those who need to take medication with food or drink, have you indicated areas of the museum where they're allowed? Are there nearby cafes or places to easily purchase food? Finally, revisiting museum rules and guidelines, consider what behavioral cues you want to communicate. Are there clearly marked signs with these rules, particularly "please don't touch?" Similarly, in locations where there **are** touchable or interactive objects or activities in a gallery, is it clearly marked that you can touch?

Figure 5.3.   Interactive gallery element inviting visitors to touch.
Source: Denver Art Museum

After determining the baseline directional information to communicate, take the next step and consider what other information could support a visitor in your museum. A place to start is reviewing the questions that are posed to your frontline staff or on comment cards. Could it be valuable to alert visitors before they enter galleries with high volume? Would a visitor benefit from knowing why exhibitions containing textiles or works on paper are kept dark? (To protect the objects from being damaged by light.) How can signage be used as an educational tool that supports and empowers people to better own and understand their experience?

Well-designed signs enable people to extract the information they need from a quick glance before continuing on their way. There are many design variables that support readability, including contrast, color, typography, size, materials, placement, and viewing distance.[9] In addition to these variables, many museums and other public spaces are looking to use symbols and icons to enhance visitor's access to signage, particularly if language, vision, learning disability, or other impacts on cognition pose a barrier to reading text on a wall.

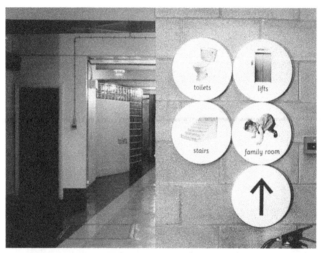

Figure 5.4.   Directional signage for The Basement, Science Museum, London.
Source: Designed by Norman Hathaway

There are easily recognizable accessibility symbols that museums use to indicate programming and support materials, such as for verbal description, closed captioning, and braille. These icons are often posted in areas, such as theaters or auditoriums, where the services they represent are in use. Or the icons are posted on a museum's website to advertise the availability of a program or support to future visitors. Increasingly, however, symbols and icons are being integrated into universal signage and wayfinding supports intended for all visitors. Icons are used to represent spaces (like restrooms, lockers, or a children's gallery), rules and guidelines (no touching or photography without flash), or activities (please touch areas or places to eat and drink). This practice widens the availability of information to a larger segment of visitors, all the way from nonnative English speakers to those with impacted cognition. For a person with a learning disability, seeing an icon of a person using a wheelchair with an arrow may more quickly (and directly) indicate where an accessible entrance/exit or bathroom is located.

One way that museums can support visitors in knowing what to expect even before they come through the door is by providing a social story. Social Stories are visual and written guides which describe various social interactions, situations, behaviors, skills, or concepts. These guides use a combination of text and photographs to deliver information and are designed to help people prepare for situations they may encounter at the museum. These can be reviewed by families, adults, and caregivers with groups before visiting new spaces. Social stories simply take visitors through what a typical visit to the museum might look like, from the front door, to the restrooms, to how to identify someone who works for the museum. Social stories are simple and can be put together by almost anyone (there are a number of samples available in appendix A). Social stories cost no more than the employee's or volunteer's time in producing them. They can be put on your website for easy access by people in your community to review and download before they visit. Printed copies can also be made available on site.

When I get to the Museum, I will wait in LINE. I will wait patiently for my turn.

Then Museum Staff or my parent will put a STAMP on my HAND. I will feel the stamp press on my hand, and it will not hurt.

Figure 5.5.1. Excerpt from "My Visit to Boston Children's Museum."
Source: Developed in collaboration with Boston University Department of Occupational Therapy. With special contribution by Allison Boris, MA. © Boston Children's Museum 2019

If the Museum gets too loud, my family and I can find a **QUIET SPACE** on the third floor bridge to sit and take a break.

In the quiet space I can look out the **WINDOWS** at the **WATER**, and I can take slow, deep breaths until I am ready to explore more.

Figure 5.5.2.   *Source:* © Boston Children's Museum 2019

While social stories were originally designed for children on the autism spectrum, they have found use by a variety of audiences including teachers preparing their classrooms for a field trip, first-time visitors, or even people with dementia. Their universal appeal stems from their goal to prepare people for new environments and situations in a simple and straightforward manner.

To go a step beyond a social story, a museum can also provide a customizable visual schedule for visitors to download and use. A visual schedule tells an individual what to expect during a visit to a museum through images or icons. The goal of the visual schedule is to provide previsit information for visitors in order to personalize their visit. Visual schedules frequently use "first/then" language. For example, "First we will go to the dinosaur exhibit, then we will go see the mummies." Visual schedules can be extremely useful for decreasing anxiety and therefore reducing the chance someone with a cognitive disability will have a meltdown in your museum. For both visual schedules and social stories, you will often see examples written with children in mind, however, the reality is that many older children and even adults use either or both these tools to prepare for new and unknown events.

Hopefully, as museums recognize the varied ways that visitors understand and take in information, they will continue to diversify their communication techniques to support and arm **all** visitors with the knowledge to confidently navigate their spaces.

MODES OF ENGAGEMENT

Universal design aims to create environments that are usable by the broadest spectrum of the public. This includes crafting a range of activities to support visitors with varied learning styles to interact with the content.[10] In terms of

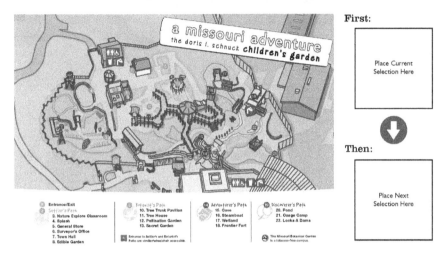

Figure 5.6.   Example of a "First, then" visual schedule.
Source: Missouri Botanical Garden

Figure 5.7.   Images provided by the Missouri Botanical Gardens for visitors to use with a visual schedule.
Source: Missouri Botanical Garden

cognitive access, this is making information available in a wide variety of formats (written, auditory, tactile, etc.) so that every visitor can find a mode that is truly suitable to their specific needs. A multimodal approach considers the complexity of accessibility and encourages museums to become "nimble and flexible in their responsiveness to providing multiple points of access for a changing and diverse audience."[11]

One point of entry to a museum's content is through reading and linguistic means. For example, a primary way for visitors to access information about a work of art or artifact is through a written wall label or audio guide. Museums can enhance the accessibility of their labels by paying attention to reading level. By avoiding technical terms (without defining them), overly complex sentences, and jargon, museums can increase readability for visitors, particularly those with impaired cognition. This places every visitor on the same level in terms of understanding, since no prior knowledge is required to read or understand the label. Furthermore, limiting label length to about seventy-five to one hundred words is ideal, as is sticking to more straightforward "subject-verb-object" sentence structure (e.g., "The Maya created this clay vessel in 635 AD.").[12] This practice avoids nuance and subtlety that could be easily overlooked or misunderstood by some visitors.

Another entry point into an exhibition's content is through visual means. Images and other graphic elements can be used to explain the concepts, ideas, and relationships important to a work of art or exhibition story. For example, a visual timeline can tell the story of a specific region or individual artist's history more simply than an extended label or wall panel. Similarly, a large-scale map can highlight important regions in an artifact or culture's history in a more straightforward manner than something written down. Some visitors, including those with impacted cognitive ability or language differences, may respond more directly when presented with visual representations of concepts in an exhibition. However, the information presented visually should also be available in other formats as well to encompass different learning styles and abilities.

Other visitors will prefer to access information through discussion; both listening to and talking with others about an exhibition's content. Meaning and understanding is derived by talking through concepts and ideas. In an installed setting, for example, this mode of engagement could be designed as a listening corner, where visitors have the option of listening to (or reading a transcript of) recorded stories connected to an object. Or perhaps it is a written response area, where visitors are invited to pose comments or questions about an exhibition to future visitors, as well as answer those responses left behind. This type of engagement could also be designed as a dedicated live program, such as a conversation-based tour. The Museum of Modern Art's

Meet Me at MoMA program, for example, designed specifically for individuals with dementia and their care partners, provides a forum for conversation and exchange through looking at art.[13] Replicated at numerous art, history, and science museums around the country, this interactive format supports visitors with memory loss to express themselves and their life experiences through talking about objects. During this program connections to artists, time periods, and even other participants, are voiced and shared as a group through dialogue and storytelling. Very likely, these connections would not be uncovered without the dialogic format; it is an essential entry point for many visitors with this type of cognitive limitation. It is the social component of being in a group, viewing an object together, and discussing it collectively that creates the connection and meaningful experiences for all involved.

Many visitors learn best through experiential means, by doing and creating. They understand the concept of painting more directly by handling different sized paintbrushes, stretching a canvas, smelling the scent of paint in the tube, and actually putting down a mark. Activities installed in an exhibition that support hands-on learning could be designing your own midcentury modern living room through a computer-generated design program, or stepping into a simulation of the 1960s civil rights movement where you are immersed in a visceral experience of the sights and sounds of a nonviolent sit-in protest.[14] Many museums are recognizing that visitors who respond to hands-on learning opportunities need an immersive experience, as opposed to a wall label, in order to better understand a certain concept or story behind an object or person. The New Children's Museum in San Diego, California, for example, has four different open studios and makerspaces that offer the opportunity for hands-on artmaking, and the Queens Museum's ArtAccess program provides regular opportunities for adults with developmental disabilities to engage with art following a guided tour of the museum. In each of these instances, a creative technique or concept highlighted in the museum's exhibitions, or uncovered during an interactive tour, are further illustrated through creative, hands-on exploration of high quality materials.

By focusing on presenting a variety of access points in which to engage with exhibition content, museums are transforming themselves from a traditional one-size-fits-all approach to a place "populated with a range of experiences that acknowledges museum audiences as individuals with preferred ways of learning."[15] A museum that embraces a multimodal approach to engaging visitors delivers their collection, content, and interpretive experiences through a variety of formats. In doing so, museums are both recognizing and actively supporting the diverse cognitive abilities and learning styles of visitors and providing equal opportunity for all learners to "explore, experiment, and make personal discoveries."[16]

A REWARDING EXPERIENCE FOR ALL

Navigating a museum experience is a complex task. Finding your way around an environment, adhering to the subtle guidelines and rules in place, and then engaging with complicated exhibition content are demanding tasks for any visitor. This complex activity even leads to a specific type of fatigue known as "museum fatigue," which is "both physical fatigue and cognitive saturation."[17] This process is compounded for individuals with impacted cognition who may have difficulties with comprehension, memory, or problem solving. By focusing on supporting visitor's diverse cognitive needs from the start, museums can provide the means for a fulfilling and rewarding experience for all.

NOTES

1. Association of Registered Graphic Designers of Ontario, **AccessAbility: A Practical Handbook on Accessible Graphic Design** (Toronto: RGD Ontario, 2010), 1, https://www.rgd.ca/database/files/library/RGD_AccessAbility_Handbook.pdf.

2. Dimitra Christidou, "Social Interaction in the Art Museum: Performing Etiquette While Connecting to Each Other and the Exhibits," **The International Journal of Social, Political and Community Agendas in the Arts** 11 (2016): 27–38.

3. Helen Rees Leahy, **Museum Bodies: The Politics and Practices of Visiting and Viewing** (Farnham: Ashgate Publishing, 2012), 5.

4. Christidou, "Social Interaction," 28.

5. Karen Hughes, "Museum and Gallery Wayfinding: Tips for Signage, Maps and Apps," **The Guardian**, August 25, 2015, https://www.theguardian.com/culture-professionals-network/2015/aug/25/museum-gallery-wayfinding-tips-signage-maps-apps.

6. Craig Berger, **Wayfinding: Designing and Implementing Graphic Navigational Systems** (Brighton: Rotovision, 2005).

7. **AccessAbility**, 20.

8. For people who have experienced trauma, such as Post-traumatic Stress Disorder, it is important for emotional security to know the way around an environment, especially the location of exits and restrooms. It may also be beneficial to have information available (similar to airplane safety cards) that outlines what to do and where to go should an emergency situation arise. These materials may help visitors feel greater control over unknown situations while within your museum.

9. **AccessAbility**, 20.

10. We are focusing on four learning styles: visual, auditory, reading, and kinesthetic.

11. "Mining the Dimensions of Accessibility," Disability and Inclusion: Resources for Museum Studies Programs, Art Beyond Sight, accessed June 18, 2019, http://

www.artbeyondsight.org/dic/module-5-museum-access-multimodal-engagement /mining-the-dimensions-of-accessibility/#Multimodal.

12. "Smithsonian Guidelines for Accessible Exhibition Design," Smithsonian Accessibility Program, accessed June 18, 2019, https://www.si.edu/Accessibility /SGAED.

13. The MoMA's Alzheimer's Project provides research, resources, and training modules that can be used by museums interested in creating a program for people with memory loss.

14. "American Civil Rights Movement," Exhibits, National Center for Civil and Human Rights, accessed June 19, 2019, https://www.civilandhumanrights.org/exhibit /american-civil-rights/.

15. Art Beyond Sight, "Mining the Dimensions of Accessibility."

16. Art Beyond Sight, "Mining the Dimensions of Accessibility."

17. **AccessAbility**, 1.

Chapter Six

A Spectrum of Experience

Sensory Access

Every day we are surrounded with sensory input: sights, sounds, smells, textures, and tastes. We are bombarded by the sounds of honking car horns during our morning commute, the smell of garlic cooking in the Italian restaurant we go to for lunch, the distant hum of the fluorescent overhead lights in our office. Most people can filter out or ignore the constant stimuli we are surrounded by; however, many people have difficulties processing sensory inputs due to sensory sensitivities or sensory processing disorders which can affect the way they experience a museum. People with sensory processing disorders misinterpret sensory information such as sounds, touch, or movement. Whereas people with sensory sensitivities may feel bombarded by sensory stimuli and are overwhelmed by the vast amount of sensory information their brain is trying to process. For many people they may be overly sensitive to environmental stimuli, such as loud noises or bright lights, while, on the other hand, other people need additional sensory input and will actively seek out sensory stimuli. Visitors have a spectrum of sensory experience that museums must try to support.

SENSORY DIVERSITY

Creating an inclusive environment is striving to support hypersensitive (oversensitive) and hyposensitive (undersensitive) individuals, and everyone in between. Sensory differences are not yet fully understood by doctors and scientists and is an area that needs additional research. What is understood is that some people have sensory processing sensitivities, meaning their senses can become overwhelmed when trying to process sensory stimuli.[1] While others have a sensory processing disorder, a neurological disorder in which sensory input gets mixed up in the brain and results in atypical responses.[2] The nuanced differences between these diagnoses is not as important to museums as is the work museums must do to support the spectrum of sensory experiences that we as humans have. Sensory access is ensuring that information, materials, and communications are readily available and easily understandable in order to support the sensory needs of visitors. Just like universal design approaches, making small accommodations for people with sensory-diverse experiences, based on individual needs, can create a more accessible and comfortable museum for all your visitors. In this chapter, for simplicity, we will refer to all sensory sensitivities and sensory processing disorders as sensory-diverse experiences.[3]

One of the biggest differences between people with sensory-diverse experiences is that some are sensory **seeking,** while others are sensory **avoiding.** Sensory inputs are any number of things that we can sense, including touch, taste, vision, sound, smell, and things we can feel (pain, temperature, and so on). People who are considered sensory seeking, or hyposensitive, will crave more intense sensory experiences and therefore actively seek out stimulation (perhaps through jumping, touching, or tasting). While sensory avoiders, those who are hypersensitive, recoil from sensory stimulation so will actively avoid stimuli such as bright lights, loud noises, or even touch. Sensory seekers and avoiders react differently to diverse external stimuli. Individuals who are sensory seekers use input from sensory stimulation to help them regulate themselves and better understand their worlds. On the other hand, people who are sensory avoiders are easily overwhelmed by the same environmental stimuli, which can lead to extreme behaviors. Examples could be a child screaming when they hear a loud noise or getting upset when putting on dress-up clothes. These behaviors occur because the physical sensations in these scenarios are overwhelming. Understanding these sensory differences will empower museums and their staff to better appreciate how their visitors experience their spaces.

Hypersensitive individuals can have strong reactions to stimuli and become overwhelmed easily.[4] These visitors may

- not be able to tolerate bright lights or loud noises;
- dislike the feel of certain fabrics or textures;
- not tolerate stark contrasts in environments (such as severe contrasts in wall colors, for example, going from a pastel blue in one gallery to a bright neon pink in the next);[5] and
- be easily distracted or distressed by ambient or background noises that most others do not notice (such as whirring of an HVAC fan).

Some hypersensitive visitors may utilize certain tools to modify the environment to make it less overwhelming. For example, in noisy settings such as museums or amusement parks, you may see individuals wearing noise-cancelling headphones. Loud places can make hypersensitive individuals uncomfortable and wearing these headphones can help cancel out the noise,

---

INVISIBLE DISABILITIES

If someone asks you to picture a person with a disability, what pops into your mind? A person with autism or sensory processing disorder? Not likely. Chances are, the first image you formed was of someone using a wheelchair or perhaps someone who is blind and uses a cane or a guide dog.[1] When we picture people with disabilities we tend to first picture someone with a **physical** disability. However, the reality is that the majority of disabilities are not obvious to passersby. They are invisible or hidden disabilities. Disabilities that fall into this category are just what they sound like, that is, not something you can tell just by looking at someone. Rather, the term invisible disability refers to symptoms that a person experiences but may not be seen by others. These symptoms range from mild to severe, and can limit a person's daily activities, however, they may never be obvious to strangers. This includes seizure disorders, chronic pain, sensory disorders, vision or hearing impairments, brain injuries, learning differences, and especially mental health disorders. According to one study, 74 percent of Americans with a severe disability do not use mobility supports, like a wheelchair, crutches, walker, or cane.[2] This means that the vast majority of people with disabilities do not noticeably appear to have a disability. The seeming invisible nature of some illnesses and disabilities can lead to misunderstandings or judgment. Perhaps the fastest growing segment of the invisible disability population are people with sensory disorders, such as autism.

1. "What is an Invisible Disability?," Invisible Disabilities Association, accessed May 29, 2019, https://invisibledisabilities.org/what-is-an-invisible-disability/.
2. Invisible Disabilities Association, "What is an Invisible Disability?"

Some disabilities are visible.   Some are not.

Figure 6.1.   *Source:* René Moffatt

making the environment more bearable for them. Other people may wear sunglasses inside to reduce bright lights, or strobe-like lights, which could cause agitation and discomfort. These are just a few examples of different ways hypersensitive individuals may reduce and regulate stimuli in their environment and are important for museum staff to be aware of.

For every individual who is sensory-avoiding, or hypersensitive, there is one who is sensory-seeking, or hyposensitive. Hyposensitive individuals are **undersensitive,** which leads them to seek out stimuli. They may

- constantly want to touch things (a challenge for many museums!);
- need to fidget and are unable to sit or stand still; and
- love movement, including jumping, spinning, or other similar actions.

Similar to sensory avoiders, some hyposensitive individuals utilize tools to help them regulate their environment. In this case it is to increase environmental stimuli, so they will use things like fidgets (small, highly tactile objects) or weighted vests to provide the stimulus they need. The ways in which hyposensitive, or sensory seeking, people regulate themselves or their environment can often be misunderstood or misconstrued by those not familiar. For example, fidgeting, or moving restlessly, is a way for individuals to control or manage their feelings, so while they may appear agitated or out of control to outsiders, this activity may actually have a calming effect.

Figure 6.2.   Fidget spinners are one popular type of fidgets.

DESIGNING FOR THE SENSES

Museums can support individuals with sensory-diverse experiences through modifying space and exhibition design, including areas of high- and low-sensory input, and by preparing museum goers for their visit ahead of time. There are previsit supports and modifications to lights, sounds, smells, and tactile elements you can make to your museum programs and spaces that will increase accessibility for visitors who have sensory-diverse experiences.

The first step to making sensory modifications to your museum environment is identifying potential triggers in the museum and making necessary adjustments. This is something you can easily add to your accessibility audit (see chapter 4). As you review the museum for potential physical barriers, take stock of the environmental stimuli. When auditing your environment, be on the lookout for:

Visuals
• Bright or flashing lights (including strobes)
• Motion activated videos or images that appear or play suddenly

Sounds
• Loud or startling sounds (such as motion-activated audio)
• Videos with loud music or sound
• Fluorescent lights (which emit a buzzing noise)

Smells
• Scents that are not contained or that linger
• Off-gassing materials (such as a new carpet or exhibit panels)

Unavoidable Tactile Elements[6]
• Any materials that visitors must or most likely will touch during their visit (such as a beaded curtain at an exhibition exit or a stair rail)

Space
• Crowded gallery spaces that are too small to allow for someone to move around easily.

Once you have identified stimuli that could be disturbing to individuals with sensory-diverse experiences, determine what modifications can be made to adjust the amount of stimuli, whether or not these modifications need to be permanent or temporary, and finally incorporate them into your transition plan. As discussed in chapter 4, there may be multiple solutions for each of the modifications you are looking to make.

Visual

For bright flashing lights (especially strobe lights), one quick fix is installing signage near areas that warn visitors of what to expect. Unexpected visuals can trigger an extreme reaction in some visitors, so if possible, make flashing lights and videos/images something that visitors can control themselves, so that they have the option of using them or not.

Sounds

Similar to bright or flashing lights, an easy short-term fix for loud sounds is to post signage warning visitors what to expect. Additionally, for videos or other loud audio components, consider reducing the volume during certain times of the day. On your website post when these "quiet times" are happening so visitors can self-select when to come. If your museum has the budget for it, keep a few pairs of noise-cancelling headphones on hand, either at the front desk or adjacent to exhibits with loud noises or music, for visitors to check out and use during their visit. Finally, and if budget allows, look to replace overhead fluorescent lights with LED bulbs to reduce buzzing or humming.[7]

Smell

While scents can add to exhibition experiences for some people, for others they disturb and detract from the experience. Rather than permanently install-ing scents in specific spaces, add scent jars or some other way to contain the scent so that visitors can opt into this sensory experience. When exhibition spaces are repainted, ensure that the paint being used is low-odor. For smells that you do not have control over, such as off-gassing carpet or exhibition panel plastics, do what you can to get rid of the smell before opening those spaces. Whenever possible, use higher quality materials that tend to emit fewer odors.

Unavoidable Tactile Elements

Some museums include ancillary tactile items that, despite not being tied directly to the story or experience of the exhibition, visitors must interact with when visiting. An example being a beaded curtain at the entrance to your exhibition that everyone must walk through. One question to ask as your space is being audited is whether or not tactile items like these are strictly necessary. While a beaded curtain can be fun and interesting, is it essential to the story you are trying to tell in a particular exhibit? If the answer is no, consider eliminating it. If it is essential determine if there is an option that allows people the choice to touch and interact with it. You could move the curtain to a place other than the entrance or consider tying it back so that visitors can still enter without having to touch it.

Space

If your museum provides group tours, ensure that if needed, there is enough space for someone to move around and away from others while on a tour stop. This might mean reducing the number of people on each tour to allow room for movement. Be on the lookout for areas in exhibitions where you may have bottlenecks, where a lot of people need to move through a small area at the same time. How can your exhibition design mitigate this buildup or provide space for visitors to pull off the tour path to take a break from the crowd?

The goal of creating a sensory accessible environment is to limit excess stimuli by reducing or eliminating certain elements, like the examples just mentioned, and then introducing features that can be calming to visitors.

Quiet areas in museums allow visitors the opportunity to reflect and recharge. As you audit your space, consider what calm and quiet areas you already have and what extra spaces you could incorporate. Is there an out-of-the-way spot with low traffic and little exhibition-related noise? Consider adding seating to this low-sensory area so that visitors can take a break if they need. How each space is designed is going to vary quite a bit from museum to museum. In some cases it could be as simple as an alcove tucked into the corner of an exhibition or a dedicated corner designed with some comfortable chairs and a few books; in others it might be a separate space, such as a room with low-lighting and a variety of seating areas, a pod swing, fluffy pillows, and various sensory calming tools. The design of this space will depend completely on the available space in your museum, your budget, and whenever possible, input from your community who will be using this space. This is another instance of universal design at work. These types of spaces are not just for people with sensory-diverse experiences but can be reinvigorating for all museum visitors (museum fatigue is a real thing!). These spaces, no matter how simple or how complex, offer visitors with typical and sensory-diverse experiences the chance to pause, recharge, and continue their visit.

A dedicated quiet area is not possible for some museums, but there are a variety of items and tools you can make available to support visitors' sensory access during their museum trip. Fidgets are a low-cost support tool that you

Chapter Six

can provide to visitors They are self-regulation tools to help with focus, attention, and calming. There are a variety of inexpensive options available, everything from stress balls to theraputty (therapy putty). Often, individuals will have their own fidgets with them, but it is a welcoming gesture to have some on hand for people who forget them or for visitors who do not normally use them but feel they need to on their visit. Some museums have started carrying sensory backpacks for people to check out, which contain a variety of sensory aides and are designed to meet any "on-the-go" sensory need (for both hyper- and hyposensitive needs). These backpacks contain items like sunglasses, noise-cancelling headphones, wiggle seats, and much more. You can purchase preassembled packs or easily assemble your own.

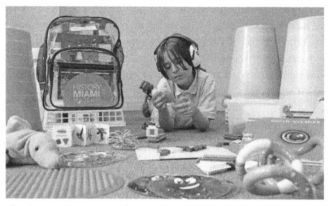

Figure 6.3 Sensory packs can contain a variety of materials to help regulate a person's senses.
Source: Photo by Rodrigo Nuno, Courtesy of History Miami Museum

Another tool museums can offer to support visitors' sensory needs is a sensory map. In addition to typical information such as bathroom locations and exits, sensory maps highlight the areas of your museum that are high-sensory (lots of sensory stimuli) or low-sensory (little sensory stimuli). For example, if there is an exhibition with bright flashing lights or unexpected loud noises, this would be notated on your sensory map as a high-sensory area. Sensory rooms or quiet corners in certain exhibitions would be notated as low-sensory areas on the map. The Museum of Modern Art in New York City encourages visitors to use their sensory map to find "spaces that tend to be quieter and less crowded, spaces that have seating, and spaces with tactile engagement and activities."[8] With this information in hand, a visitor can choose to seek out or avoid particular areas in the museum according to their preferences and comfort level.

If you take stock of the environmental stimuli in your space during your accessibility audit, you can easily create a sensory map from this information. Some important things to take note of include:

- high-sensory areas (areas that tend to be loud and/or crowded);
- low-sensory areas (areas with little ambient noise and which tend to be less crowded);
- areas with natural light and low-light; and
- areas with strong smells (like a cafe);

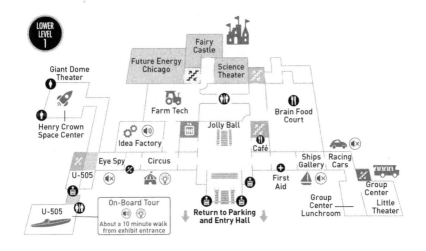

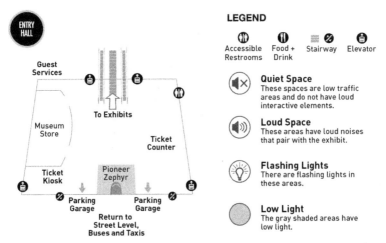

Figure 6.4. Sensory map showing visitors high- and low-sensory areas of the museum.

Source: Museum of Science and Industry, Chicago

- places to safely eat or drink;
- areas with tactile or hands-on activities; and
- locations where visitors can check-out sensory materials (like fidgets, noise-cancelling headphones, sensory backpacks, etc.).

It may also be helpful to note if there are times of the day at your museum that are generally loud (maybe times when there are more school tours) or generally quiet. These louder and quieter times would be good additions to your maps, as well as your website.

When designed well, sensory maps incorporate universal design concepts and are therefore not only useful for people with sensory-diverse experiences, but for all visitors. For example, say there is a family with young children and they need a quiet place with few distractions where a baby can nurse or have a snack. Using the sensory map allows visitors to quickly locate areas that meet their sensory needs, whatever they may be. There are numerous examples of sensory maps out there which can be found through a simple internet search (we ahave included links to a few examples, diverse in style, in Appendix A).

Sensory maps and other supports should be made available on-site as well as online, so as to support visitors before they arrive at a museum. Pairing sensory maps with additional gallery information, such as the average amount of time it takes to go through exhibitions, especially those that have bright/flashing lights or strong or lingering odors, for example, can help visitors with epilepsy or chronic migraines understand how long they could be in a space with significant triggers.

SENSORY-INCLUSIVE PROGRAMMING

Depending on the nature and type of your museum, it may not be possible or realistic for you to always reduce the sights and sounds of an exhibition or public space. As a work-around, many museums have started low-sensory or sensory-friendly programs. Adults and families with sensory-diverse experiences are given access to the museum usually before or after the museum's regular hours and without the general public. This specialized time allows people to visit when there are fewer crowds and enables museum staff to make modifications in terms of lighting and sounds, and even add specialized hands-on activities or performances. These types of dedicated programs offer a time when families and adults alike can come to an event that is targeted for people with similar experiences.

Programming for people with sensory-diverse experiences is not something new. Many museums have been offering specific programs for several years now, targeted in particular for individuals on the autism spectrum and their families. You have probably heard these programs referred to as low-sensory or sensory-friendly programs. Sensory-inclusive is another term that is beginning to be used as well. What is the difference between these three terms? Essentially, they're the same and can be used interchangeably, however, the slight change in wording (from low-sensory to sensory-inclusive) demonstrates a progression to being inclusive of all sensory experiences and not just hypersensitivity. Several icons have been created for museums to use that signals to the public a sensory-friendly program or performance.

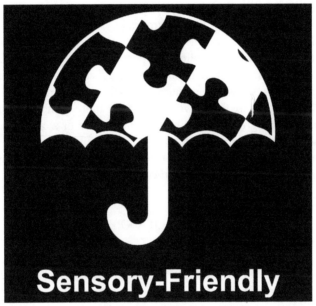

Figure 6.5. One example of a sensory friendly icon museums can use to indicate low-sensory programs or performances.
Source: The Sensory-Friendly access symbol was developed by the Miami-Dade County Department of Cultural Affairs as part of its "All Kids Included Accessible Arts Experiences for Kids" (AKI) initiative. AKI creates inclusive arts and cultural programs in school settings and throughout the community so that kids of all abilities and their families can participate fully in the arts. AKI is made possible with the support of the Miami-Dade County Department of Cultural Affairs and the Cultural Affairs Council, the Miami-Dade County Mayor and Board of County Commissioners, and in part through grant funding provided by The Miami-Dade Children's Trust. The Children's Trust is a dedicated source of revenue established by voter referendum to improve the lives of children and families in Miami-Dade County. For more information visit www.AllKidsIncludedMiami.org

The bit of respite and connection these programs provide, similar to programs for people with dementia and their care partners, is reason enough for many museums to offer these programs. However, it is important to check in with your community to measure interest in attending separate sensory-friendly events. Some cities have found that the sensory-diverse community in their area does not want any sort of special programming, rather they simply want to be included during typical open hours and have sensory supports available (such as sensory backpacks, sensory maps). Other cities, however, have a thriving set of sensory-friendly programs across cultural institutions that are well attended. For these dedicated programs anyone who self-selects to attend should be admitted. No one should be asking for a qualifying diagnosis when visitors check in for the program, rather they should be greeted in a friendly manner, the same as any other guest, and sent on to enjoy what the museum has to offer. In addition to people with sensory-diverse experiences, these events can be beneficial for visitors with developmental or cognitive disabilities, with vision impairments, with compromised autoimmune systems who need to avoid crowds, and many more. When possible, these sensory-friendly programs should be offered for free or at a minimal cost to participants.[9] If providing free or discounted admission to these programs poses a barrier to your museum, know that there are a variety of funding opportunities available to help support them (see chapter 8).

A SPECTRUM OF EXPERIENCE

As we have seen, sensory experiences are complicated, and there is still much to be learned. But what is known is that creating an inclusive museum environment means considering the wide spectrum of sensory needs. There are a variety of elements, many of them low-cost, that can make museums more accessible for people with sensory-diverse experiences, and at the same time more comfortable for all museum visitors. Museums can go a long way to creating a welcoming sensory environment by utilizing previsit preparation materials, employing environmental modifications (both temporary and long term), and offering dedicated programs. Extending this welcome can open up opportunities for visitors to connect deeply with museums.

HELLO, MY NAME IS MAX AND I HAVE AUTISM

My name is Max Miller. I am here to tell my story of how an access day at the Denver Art Museum changed my life. I am 14 years old. I'm an artist, a published author and I have autism.

When I was first diagnosed, as my mother can verify, the experts said that there was no hope for me. I would never learn how to speak or read or take care of myself. They told my mother that I should go to an institution. Well, that wasn't true and my mother knew that. She never gave up on me, and even though I couldn't speak, I could draw. We would communicate through art. Soon, I learned how to speak around age 6. At age 10, I learned how to read.

One thing that my mother did for me was take me places that didn't really want kids like me around. She wanted me to experience life and all of its offerings. We were very poor, so she would look for free things. We got lucky. The Denver Art Museum held an access day for people with disabilities. There are lots of autistic kids and many of our families are poor. The Access Days let our ASD families visit without worry or potential embarrassment as we can be a bit loud. It enables parents to show their kids art without paying a dime. This is important because having autism can be a bit expensive. It was my first trip to the art museum. My mother said that I was very impressed and asked her where all these beautiful things came from—why are they in one place. She explained that artists made them and this was an art museum. I decided that I wanted to become an artist too.

A few years later, in 2013, my mom saw that the art museum was asking for people to participate in a community quilt project. She asked me if I wanted to make an entry. Of course, I said yes. My parents helped me. I did the design and my mother cut the cloth. My dad glued everything with a special glue. I filled out the entry form describing my piece, "My Family." A long time passed and I got the good news. I was going to be exhibited at the Denver Art Museum.

When I found out, I was surprised. I was excited and I was happy. I always thought that getting into the art museum as an artist would be incredible. Many people have autism. People theorized that DaVinci was autistic, but no one really knows. It's speculation. I thought it would be so incredible that someone who has autism, someone like me who is known for having autism,—an adequate artist to be part of such a famous museum in the US. Well, not as famous as our museum back home in Chicago, but good enough that a lot of people know about it when you talk about it.

The Denver Art Museum is known throughout Colorado and I'm known as the autistic kid who wrote a book about having autism so I could contribute to society. You see, I was an outcast. I was kicked out of so many programs and schools, but I was the one who adapted. This opportunity to visit the art museum, the chance to be a part of a community quilt, it changed my life. For the first time, I felt included. I was part of something really special. It didn't matter that I had autism. I was an artist on the wall and for a moment in time, I was normal. Just like everyone else.

It's important for people to realize that I started out with such a horrible path, but the Denver Art Museum changed this for me. It validated me and the museum can spark anyone's destiny. I moved from a bad path, to great path, which led to victory. I became stronger, intelligent and focused on compassion for all humanity. I wanted to contribute to society. I knew I could do so, despite my autism because I, Max Miller, was featured at the Denver Art Museum and that was truly amazingly awesome. I got to participate in such a fantastic activity and show my talents. I wasn't just the kid with a disability, labeled by autism and thrown on the street. Autism did not define me. It was just part of who I am.

There are plenty of kids like me out there, all over the world. There are kids who can't speak, but speak in their own way—they can craft something and tell everyone who they are. And they need access to the arts, because you never know what is going to click for that young person. What happened to me is that I went onto do a Light it up Blue event at my school the next year, featuring my art and essays so I could educate others about autism. That art show was requested to tour, which led to the publication of my book, **Hello, My Name is Max and I Have Autism,** so I could reach more people.

Soon, I started speaking publicly about autism and my book is part of the special education curriculum in several states. I then formed my organization, Blue Ribbon Arts Initiative and I help connect kids with autism to the arts via an art show, art meetups and providing art supplies. We had over 97 pieces of art our first show. I did the show to share with other ASD families what I experienced at the Denver Art Museum. Inclusion, validation and pride in myself.

I changed lives with my art and my words. I'm only 14 years old and it all started with a quilt.

—Max Miller, artist and cofounder of the Blue Ribbon Arts Initiative[1]

1. Max Miller, excerpt from a speech given in April 2016 in support of Denver's Scientific and Cultural Facilities District.

NOTES

1. "FAQ: Is Sensory Processing (or Integration) Disorder (SPD) the same as Sensory Processing Sensitivity (SPS)?," The Highly Sensitive Person, accessed 10/04/2020, http://hsperson.com/faq/spd-vs-sps/.

2. Estimates are that one in twenty people have a sensory processing disorder. "Understanding Sensory Processing Disorder," Star Institute, accessed October 20, 2020, https://www.spdstar.org/basic/understanding-sensory-processing-disorder.

3. There is no term that currently encompasses sensory diversity among people. We chose to use this term and hope that it is both descriptive and inclusive.

4. "Sensory Processing FAQ," Child Mind Institute, accessed June 7, 2019, https://childmind.org/article/sensory-processing-faq/.

5. Having some sort of sensory "palette cleanser" between spaces with sharp sensory contrasts can help visitors from becoming overwhelmed by sensory stimuli. These spaces also give visitors the chance to opt in or out of the space before fully entering it.

6. At the time of this writing, we are still uncertain of the lasting impacts of the COVID-19 pandemic. Based on a pre-COVID world, we have included information on unavoidable tactile and space elements.

7. Most LED light bulbs will not buzz or hum, however, using dimming switches with them can cause them to emit sound.

8. "Sensory Map of the Museum of Modern Art," Museum of Modern Art, accessed October 9, 2020, https://www.moma.org/momaorg/shared/pdfs/docs/visit/MoMA_Sensory_Map.pdf.

9. Many people with sensory processing differences also have autism. The cost of autism is high and offering these programs for free or at a reduced rate can greatly impact whether or not someone can attend your museum (autism costs an estimated $60,000 a year on average during childhood). Over the course of someone's life, the cost is approximately $2.4 million for a person with an intellectual disability, or $1.4 million for a person without. "Autism Facts and Statistics," Autism Society, accessed June 22, 2019, https://www.autism-society.org/what-is/facts-and-statistics/.

Chapter Seven

A Whole New World Wide Web

Digital Access

There is no question that technology is changing the way people interact with the world and perform many of their everyday tasks. Now you can order groceries, purchase a plane ticket, apply for a job, and find love all through a computer, tablet, or smartphone. But imagine, while visiting a museum's website online you are suddenly unable to read the admission ticket price or cannot get a clear description of the exhibition or program you seek to visit. Perhaps you cannot use a mouse to navigate around a website and are unable to complete the admission ticket checkout process. This frustration is the reality for some disabled users who access the internet. When accessibility is overlooked during the digital design process, not only are countless websites, mobile applications, and documents made unavailable, but the online experience in general can become a source of frustration and alienation.

Digital accessibility is the practice of making web and digital interactive content accessible to everyone. In order to be successful, organizations must consider many interrelated components, including how front-end user interaction intersects with back-end web development to create an accessible digital landscape. By reviewing how users interact with content, including the assistive technologies they employ, content creators can author information in a way that supports a user's interaction. Throughout this process museums must continually evaluate and ensure that people with disabilities are involved as coauthors, as they can be the best problem-solvers. There are creative ways of meeting digital accessibility needs, and organizations who take the time to do this work are rewarded.

THE CASE FOR DIGITAL ACCESSIBILITY

As with most initiatives there is a certain level of justification required for organizations to dedicate staff time and resources toward a project. By looking to current news and trends, museums can build compelling cases to support the initial and continued investment in digital accessibility. In addition to legal requirements, the rationale can speak to an organization's business sense, their institutional values, or even their self-preservation.

The ADA and Rehabilitation Act of 1973 prohibits discrimination against people with disabilities and requires reasonable accommodations, which extend to the digital realm. Since 2000, more specific policies around digital information accessibility have been written into law. In 1998, Congress amended the Rehabilitation Act of 1973 in order to require federal agencies to ensure their electronic and information technology is accessible to people with disabilities.[1] In 2010, President Obama signed the Twenty-First Century Communications and Video Accessibility Act into law, which updated federal communications laws to increase access to modern communication services and equipment.[2] Since 2010, a slew of court cases have been raised against art galleries and museums for inaccessible websites.[3] The singer Beyoncé was even swept up in legal issues; her website was sued for allegedly not providing equal access to users with visual impairments.[4] This onset of court cases spooked many museums into auditing and eventually revamping their sites to be more compliant. Adhering to the law around digital accessibility as well as the fear of becoming the next legal lawsuit may be the motivation museums need for change to take place.

There is also a commercial value to focusing on increasing digital access. Consumers who benefit from digital accessibility support represent a largely untapped and high-value market. In the United States the total discretionary income for working-age people with disabilities is about $20 billion.[5] This sizable number does not include family and friends of people with disabilities, who often prioritize going to businesses and organizations that are inclusive of people with disabilities. Chalk it up to business savvy, but museums are beginning to recognize that embedding accessibility into their practices can enhance the visibility of their brand across the museum field and will attract many new visitors.

Finally, embracing accessibility can drive businesses and organizations to do more innovative work. Accessibility is closely related to general usability, as both components focus on providing human-centered and intuitive digital experiences. There is a myth that accessible design means boring design, when in fact constraints often breed ingenuity. Microsoft's Inclusive Design methodology points out that when you solve for one person, you can extend

WORLDWIDE PIVOT

The year 2020 was highly anticipated by many people. It marked the beginning of a new decade. In the United States August 26, 2020, marked the centennial of the passage of the Nineteenth Amendment, which in essence gave many women the right to vote—a commemoration that many museums had been planning for years. July 2020 also marked the thirtieth anniversary of the passage of the Americans with Disabilities Act. It was also the year of a contentious presidential election. It was going to be a busy and exciting year for many museums around the country. Then, in March 2020, the United States came to a halt as the novel coronavirus, COVID-19, raged across the globe leaving a path of chaos in its wake.

Around the world museums shuttered their doors, not knowing when, or if, they would reopen them. During this historic moment, museum staff were quick to pivot and shifted programs, events, and even day-to-day interactions online. Virtual engagement became the new normal in a time when people needed to practice physical distancing in order to keep themselves and others safe. This external circumstance pushed museums and other cultural organizations to be more creative in how they work and how they reach their audiences. Museums large and small created virtual tours, podcasts, online exhibitions, and numerous other digital content to engage audiences who could no longer visit. Museum educators found themselves faced with the challenge of taking engaging, in-person programs and turning them into equally engaging digital content.

The shift to online engagement, in many ways, opened up access to museums for many audiences who, even before a pandemic, could not have visited, whether due to physical restrictions, distance, economic circumstances or otherwise. Online exhibition guides for example, which contain high-resolution images of objects and all the exhibition text, enable people to spend as much time as they need with the content while also avoiding crowded, and possibly inaccessible galleries. Lectures, as another example, broke out of the typical auditorium setting and zoomed onto a computer screen. People could tune in from the comfort and safety of their homes, from anywhere in the world. This new format solved issues with accessible seating and sound—everyone tuning in has the best seat in the house and can control the presenter's volume on their own device. Moreover, in online programs people can move around, eat or take medication as needed, and even talk or make noises without fear of disturbing others. In many ways, increased online content supports visitors to engage with and access a museum's collection and programs according to their own needs and preferences.

Just as with in-person experiences, museums must still ensure effective communication and take steps to support visitors to access online materials. The Web Accessibility Initiative offers guides to help ensure online media and materials are accessible.[1] All content with audio—like narrated tours, behind-the-scenes videos, online classes/webinars, etc.—must have captions or an available transcript. Taking steps to provide real-time captioning, from a live person not a computer, provides access for visitors who are D/deaf, hard of hearing, or need extra support processing auditory information. Access should also extend to live online programs and even video conference meetings (particularly for important meetings attended by all staff, or board/trustee meetings). Provide the option for people to request video remote interpretation, just as you would offer in-person sign language interpretation for a tour or program. For heavily visual content, like virtual tours or lectures that use visual presentations, get into the habit of describing what is on the screen while presenting; providing audio description of the slides and other visual material can support visitors who are blind, have low vision, or are just listening to the presentation. Furthermore, for digital media like online exhibition guides, online collections, or online documents with images, ensure they can be read by a screen reader, and more specifically, that every image important to the context of the document has alternative image text (alt text). Alt text is a brief description that conveys the subject and purpose of an image for someone who cannot see the image and is using a screen reader.[2]

It is hard to know how long the effects of COVID-19 will impact museums and cultural institutions.[3] What we do know is that during the coronavirus pandemic, people engaged virtually with organizations they had not visited recently. One study specifically looking at cultural institutions and the novel coronavirus found people were participating in virtual experiences at fairly high rates, despite the fact that they had not physically visited these museums over the prior year (32 percent at historic attractions, 57 percent natural history museums, with zoos, aquariums, art museums, and botanic gardens all falling somewhere in between).[4] While the study did not break down the percent of respondents with or without disabilities, if on average 20 to 25 percent of respondents are people with disabilities, this is a large number of people engaging that previously had not been. One study respondent said it best: "I'm disabled, so even COVID-19 aside, I appreciate digital access to cultural explorations I might not otherwise have."[5] While it is impossible to tell the future, virtual engagement will likely remain a focused way of connecting visitors to programs and collections for years to come.

1. "How to Make Your Presentations Accessible to All," Web Accessibility Initiative, accessed November 1, 2020, https://www.w3.org/WAI/teach-advocate/accessible-presentations/.
2. "Easy Checks—A First Review of Web Accessibility," Web Accessibility Initiative, accessed November 1, 2020, https://www.w3.org/WAI/test-evaluate/preliminary/.
3. At the time of this writing, the United States was still in the midst of the pandemic.
4. "Culture + Community in a Time of Crisis," Culture Track, accessed November 2, 2020, https://s28475.pcdn.co/wp-content/uploads/2020/09/CCTC-Key-Findings-from-Wave-1_9.29.pdf.
5. Culture Track, "Culture + Community in a Time of Crisis."

to many.[6] Many accessibility features, which are aimed at removing specific barriers for some, actually deliver a more universal user experience for people of all abilities. It is simply universal design in the digital space. Consider the autofill function on a web browser, where content is automatically added into a form or field according to information the user has entered in the past. This application was initially designed for users with disabilities who needed support inputting information, and yet is now widely adopted by a variety of users across browsers and applications. Embedding accessible design practices can lead to innovative thinking and creative problem-solving.

What about the argument that an organization may not need to make changes to their website because they have not received direct complaints? A 2016 study in the United Kingdom found that rather than complaining, 71 percent of users with accessibility needs will actually click away from a website that they find difficult to use.[7] So, if your museum is not receiving complaints from the disability community about your website, it may be because they simply are not using it.

Continued investment in accessibility is the law, and it is also good for business and brand visibility of museums, for both tangible and intangible reasons. Accessibility should be embedded into your museum's services and culture. Organizations must shift their thinking to move beyond the minimum legal compliance and focus instead on the creative challenge, or even commercial opportunity, of building better experiences for all users.

UX: USER EXPERIENCE AND HOW PEOPLE USE DIGITAL MEDIA

Now that we have made the case for digital accessibility, it is important to understand how people interact with digital content. The internet has opened up pathways to a wealth of information for people of all abilities in innovative and exciting ways. Email, for example, quickly grew in popularity among people with hearing loss because it allowed them to express themselves easily and ensure they received messages quickly and accurately.[8] It is argued that no other single invention (since the Gutenberg printing press in the 1400s) has been more revolutionary or more impactful to society than the internet.[9] This is a breath of fresh air for many who have historically faced barriers to accessing information, including people with blindness and low vision, deafness and hearing loss, learning disabilities, cognitive limitations, limited movement, speech disabilities, photosensitivity, or any combinations of these. From ordering groceries to communicating with friends, there is great potential for the web to improve everyday tasks for members of the disability community. Yet despite the fact that individuals with disabilities can most benefit from the expansion of the internet and its associated digital marvels, they are the ones most commonly affected by web inaccessibility. A 2016 Pew Research study found that only 40 percent of American adults with disabilities are comfortable going online, as opposed to 60 percent of American adults without disabilities.[10] When people find going online, or using apps, to be a source of frustration and anxiety, and therefore rarely do so, a digital divide is created. As more and more commerce and information moves to online and digital platforms, this divide widens to become an unequal disparity in experience with far reaching social, economic, and educational implications.[11] Thankfully, there are tools, technologies, and systems being created that are aimed at making the digital experience more accessible and equitable for users with disabilities.

People with disabilities access and navigate the web in a myriad of ways, depending on their preferences, needs, and abilities. Someone may adapt ready-made software and hardware to meet their access requirements, while another may use more specialized tools to complete certain tasks they need. The most common approaches for connecting with the web and other digital content is through using assistive technology and adaptive strategies.

Assistive technology is any piece of equipment, software program, or system that strengthens the learning, working, and daily living for people with disabilities.[12] Adaptive strategies are techniques employed by people with disabilities to improve interaction with the digital content. Social stories and visual schedules are examples of assistive technology used by people with cognitive disabilities. Increasing text size or availability of closed captions are examples of adaptive strategies that offer support when accessing content. Assistive technologies and adaptive strategies can be high-tech or low-tech, and are dependent upon individual needs in certain circumstances. For this reason there is no one technology or single strategy for digital access, rather there are many diverse tools and approaches that support a variety of needs and requirements. Indeed, the ways in which information is accessed depends on a person's individual needs and requirements.

EMPOWERMENT THROUGH TECHNOLOGY

Technology doesn't change your life. . . . What changes your life are the things you do for yourself—and then technology can come in and enhance what you are already doing.

—Carlos Vasquez, drummer and
professional online gamer from Texas who is blind[1]

Accessible design is most powerful when it is customizable and flexible enough to support a person in just the way they need it to. More and more, university programs are interested in exploring the intersection between technology and disability, to explore aspects of human-centered design. Texas A&M University has a Department of Visualization, which focuses on the interplay between art and science, and discerning how to support more natural interactions between people and technology through alternative materials. For example, in order to make technology more approachable for older adults, many of whom experience loss of memory, vision, and hearing with age, the team introduced **Touchology**, a collection of real and artificial plants that, when touched, "produce sounds of running water or bird songs from electronic components in their bases."[2] This tech-based tactile component enabled older adults to experience nature in a new way through technology.

New York University has The Ability Project, an interdisciplinary research space dedicated to the intersection between disability and technology.[3] One of the projects tackled by this group was making creative coding accessible to people who use screen readers. This project promoted software literacy for people with low vision or blindness by redesigning online learning and web development resources.

These program examples illustrate the progress and growing momentum around technological innovations for people with disabilities and illustrate the role of technology in empowering people of all abilities.

1. Katie Dupere, "The Incredible Ways People with Disabilities Customize Their Tech to Thrive," **Mashable**, May 16, 2017, https://mashable.com/2017/05/17/apple-accessibility-videos-disability/.

2. Jinsil Hwaryoung Seo, "Toys, Plants Provide Alternative Digital Interface for Kids, Elderly," **Arch One**, March 10, 2015, https://one.arch.tamu.edu/news/2015/3/10/interactive-toys/.

3. "Home," The NYU Ability Project, accessed July 27, 2019, http://ability.nyu.edu/index.

Perception

People perceive content through different senses: seeing, hearing, and feeling. Perception is dependent on ability and preference. Oftentimes it is necessary for someone to convert content from one sensory format to another in order to help them perceive and understand the information better. For example, a person who is D/deaf may need to convert audio content (like verbal speech) into the visual format of American Sign Language. Likewise, someone who is blind may need to convert visual information into a tactile or audio component. Some assistive technologies that support people to better perceive content are screen readers or braille displays, which convert the visual text of a website, app, or digital document into synthesized audible speech or braille text. Adobe Illustrator supports people to perceive content in a modified way, with a built-in colorblindness inspector. The Color Blind Proof Setup Mode, implemented in 2009, allows graphic designers to preview their work in the same way a red-green colorblind individual would see it, and thus ensure that graphic information is accurately conveyed to people with colorblindness.[13]

Presentation

In order to make content easier to distinguish and understand, some individuals may need to adjust the ways in which information is presented to them. This is primarily because people process information differently. Adjusting how content is presented can be achieved by altering its appearance in a myriad of ways. An example could be changing the font type, color contrast, or spacing of text to make it more legible, or pairing information with a symbol or other graphic representation to support different learning styles (say for visual learners). An assistive technology that supports people to better distinguish content is a screen magnification software, which enlarges text or images to make it easier for people with low vision to identify. An adaptive strategy is including captions, or pieces of audio information put into text form, on every video piece.

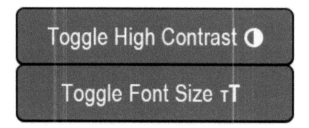

Figure 7.1. Website buttons for increasing high contrast and text size.

Input

People enter information on the web, or activate commands, in different ways. This is important to keep in mind while designing digital interactives. While some people are comfortable using a keyboard/mouse combination, others may require keyboard-only control (due to cognitive or visual disabilities), or entirely hands-free operation (due to physical disabilities). This could be a preference—using spelling tools to help correct text—or a necessity—using voice recognition software when manual keyboard or mouse use is an impossibility. Some assistive technologies that support diverse input techniques are alternative keyboards (with larger sized keys or custom layouts) or voice recognition software that can be used to issue commands to a computer or mobile device.

Interaction

The ways in which people search for content on a digital platform varies greatly and depends heavily on the user's preference, ability, and skill. For instance, someone navigating a website on their mobile device may require more orientation cues or menu navigation than someone searching the same website on their computer (as there is more space to see on a computer). Equally, a first-time visitor to a digital gallery interactive may need clearer guidance to find important information than someone familiar with the activity. How a digital interactive, or website, guides a user to find certain information is known as **usability**. Using descriptive headings is a way to organize content in a clear and consistent manner, and enables users with low vision to easily move through content on a website or app. Another way is to allow sufficient time for a visitor to interact with digital media—be it an image gallery not skipping pictures too quickly or a tablet giving ample time before it times out.

These examples are by no means exhaustive.[14] Yet they help build an understanding of user experience with digital media and can shed light on the barriers to digital content commonly facing people with disabilities. Furthermore, they highlight some of the technologies and strategies available to support the different approaches people employ when interacting with digital content. Understanding the fundamental aspects of how people with disabilities use digital resources helps institutions to better develop and implement accessibility standards that are more effective and efficient to all users.

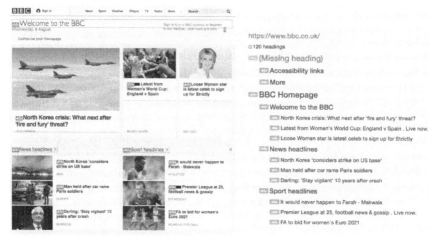

Figure 7.2.   BBC News web page structure.
Source: Darren Wilson, Founder of UXcentric

COMPONENTS OF AN ACCESSIBLE WEB

> The power of the web is in its universality. Access by everyone regardless
> of disability is an essential aspect.

> —Tim Berners-Lee, creator of the World Wide Web[15]

Making information available to everyone is perhaps the single defining goal
of design. Yet all too often accessibility is an afterthought, or sidebar, in the
digital design process. Designers often prioritize creating an aesthetically
pleasing website or app over making it easily understood by a wide audience.
Digital communication is constantly shifting and changing, as is the technology supporting it. Yet even with this fluctuation there can be fundamental
principles defining what accessible web design can and should be. To help
lead the web to its fullest potential, The World Wide Web Consortium (W3C)
was established. Through their Web Accessibility Initiative (WAI), the W3C
has worked with organizations, experts, and interested individuals around the
world to develop recommended standards and guidelines for accessible websites, digital documents, and mobile applications.[16] The guidelines support
the public to better understand and implement accessibility initiatives and are
an excellent foundation upon which to build accessible web content. There
are four general principles that lay the foundation of accessible web design:
perceivable, operable, understandable, and robust.[17] There are many layers of
guidance on how to make content more accessible, and we have included just
a few examples to help better understand and implement these techniques.[18]

Web content is **perceivable** if all components are presented to users in ways they can input and process. When there is a barrier to accessing information in one format, there should be potential to easily convert that information into another format that is more readily perceivable by the user. For people who are blind or have low vision, the key is to provide modifications and alternatives for visual content. Modifications could include adding functions that allow people the ability to magnify text, or alter the color contrast on a web page, in order to better suit user needs. For multimedia content this could be achieved by providing brief audio descriptions, which are narrations that describe the important visual details in an image or video. People who are D/deaf or hard of hearing, require alternatives for audio content. Audible video content can be converted into captions included directly on the video or included on a text transcript nearby. Audio content can also be translated into American Sign Language and made available on a nearby video that accompanies the original.

A website is **operable** if all interactive elements and navigational components can be operated in some way by all users. For people with limited movement, especially that which impairs the use of hands or arms, using a mouse to navigate a website might not be possible, thus they require an alternative method for controlling a computer. An operable website ensures that all controls and functionality available by mouse are also available via keyboard, as well by other inputs including touch activation and voice recognition. For users with limited short-term memory loss, some learning disabilities, or even low vision, websites that include clear headings and labels provide appropriate cues to finding and navigating through desired content.

Web content is **understandable** to users when the information contained on a web page or digital media, as well as the general functionality of the page, is clear. Language should be straightforward and as simple as possible. This supports understanding across a wide variety of cognitive levels and ensures readability (especially for text-to-speech applications). More complex text can be enriched with images and illustrations that support understanding. For users with impacted cognition, intellectual disabilities, or for people who have low vision or who are blind, consistent navigation is key. Successful design provides content components and navigational directions in consistent and predictable locations and formats (e.g., a user always knows where to find a menu). This practice helps users become comfortable with the content and can empower them to be able to predict where they can find things on each page. In 2020, the W3C published a best practices document on how to make digital content more usable for people with cognitive and learning disabilities.[19] The document integrates user stories to illustrate how structure, design, and language choices can make digital content inaccessible.

Robust digital content is compatible with past, present, and future technologies and tools, including assistive technologies. Websites and web browsers are constantly evolving, with new technologies and design techniques altering the user experience. Yet even so a computer (or smartphone) from 2003 should be able to reliably read content as easily as a computer from 2021. Even as progress takes place, baseline web content should still remain accessible. In particular for assistive technologies, robust web content should support these devices to process content reliably and present it in ways the user needs.

All people, regardless of ability, are expected to have a similar experience on all digital platforms and the WAI guidelines help provide a roadmap to achieving this long-term goal. A more universal approach to digital design generates content that improves usability for users in general. Furthermore, adhering to these guidelines also succeeds in supporting older adults whose abilities and needs are changing due to aging. Increasing font size and color contrast on a web page or in-gallery digital media can support users with age-related vision loss or those who have vision loss from birth. However, these four principles alone do not guarantee full accessibility. A more comprehensive understanding of the **why** and **how** behind these standards must be understood in order to do truly effective and accessible work with digital content. We cannot hope to cover all the intricacies extensively in this book, so we recommend diving more deeply into the W3C WAI guidelines and other resources provided in order to more fully understand the many components of digital accessibility standards.

EVALUATING FOR ACCESSIBILITY

Ensuring your museum's website and digital materials align with the web accessibility standards outlined by the W3G is an important step toward legal compliance and creating an accessible digital environment. Ideally, the accessibility of any digital project will be considered early in the project planning, budgeting, and scheduling. Yet when organizations focus solely on conforming to these web accessibility standards, they may miss out on understanding real-world accessibility issues experienced by real users. Involving people with disabilities from the beginning of a project supports museums to better understand accessibility concerns and be more adept at implementing effective accessibility solutions. Accessibility should not be viewed as simply a checklist item; real-life experiences illustrate the human side of accessibility.

One way to user-test web content is by utilizing online resources and trainings, such as the Microsoft Inclusive Design Team's toolkits on inclusive design practice[20] or the WAVE Accessibility Tool.[21] The Microsoft toolkits are designed to help teams learn the benefits of the inclusive design process through interactive activities that bring attention to recognizing exclusion and learning from diversity. Using the WAVE browser extension or online web service, organizations can submit a web page for review and then receive a copy of the review of the page with embedded icons that indicate both the positive accessibility features and potential issues that may or may not be present. This tool does not tell the user whether a web page is accessible, or whether it passes the WAVE test. Rather it is a diagnostic tool that can detect the presence or absence of errors. The WAVE and Microsoft tools are indeed helpful, yet they should not replace the evaluation or direct input of a real user.

Including usability testing and users with disabilities in the development process of a digital project helps organizations more efficiently develop accessible products and approaches that work well for **real** users in **real** situations.[22] First, organizations must learn the fundamentals of how people with disabilities engage with digital content. This can be achieved through focus groups, surveys, interviews, and looking to online resources.[23] Empathy is an important part of the design process. As the Microsoft Inclusive Design team explains, "Learning how people adapt to the world around them means spending time understanding their experience from their perspective."[24] Therefore, the logical next step is identifying a diverse group of individuals, with a range of experiences, who are interested in participating in

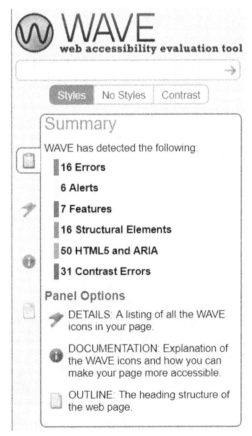

Figure 7.3. Report showing results of WAVE web accessibility evaluation tool.

Source: WebAIM (Web Accessibility In Mind) at Utah State University

your project and providing feedback. The key point, as mentioned in chapter 3, is speaking to **many** different people and sources, rather than assuming that one person with a disability can provide guidance for the full range of accessibility realities. Once this feedback group is formed, learn early and learn often what accessibility concerns are present for them. Utilize your advisory committee to find test users in your community with a wide range of disabilities. Discuss what works well with your current content, and what could be done better. Ask for examples of web pages and applications that work well for them and tease out the key features. Throughout the design and development processes, ask this group to review prototypes at multiple points. And it bears repeating but ensure that you are appropriately compensating this group for their invaluable participation and feedback.

Combining user-centered design with accessibility guidelines from the very beginning not only ensures accessibility is provided to users with a range of disabilities and situations, but it also leads to more innovative solutions to nuanced problems. Take navigation for example; the act of orienting oneself to a web page and successfully maneuvering around the site to find specific content. Under the **operable** principle, a web page should be designed so that users can easily find content and determine where they are. This is easier said than done, and a process that requires repeated human input (through feedback and user testing) to help identify specific issues that may have been overlooked. When done well, accessible design empowers the content creator to see more than just barriers, and instead recognize the universal experiences all people have in common.

COMMITTING TO WEB ACCESSIBILITY

Digital content is quickly becoming a mainstay of daily life for the majority of the population, yet the vast potential of the web and mobile applications to engage people with disabilities is far from being realized. In February 2019, Web Accessibility in Mind (WebAIM), a component of Utah State University's Center for Persons with Disabilities, conducted a widespread accessibility evaluation to determine the current state of web accessibility for people with disabilities.[25] The homepages of the top one million websites were assessed through the WAVE accessibility engine to look for failure to follow web accessibility guidelines. Of the home pages tested, 97.8 percent had detectable accessibility guideline failures. The most common failures were low contrast, missing alternative text for images, empty links, and empty buttons. In May 2019, WebAIM assessed the websites of one hundred nonprofit organizations to gauge their accessibility with the thinking that the nonprofit sector strives to be inclusive and therefore may be more mindful of web accessibility.[26] Failure rates were just as high, with ninety-eight out of one hundred home pages containing detectable guideline errors.

Although museums can contract with web and app developers, or digital engagement strategists, who prioritize digital accessibility and build it into their practice, internally these same museums must realize that inclusion is only sustainable when adopted as a culture, not just a policy. Accessible design and thinking must be integrated more into the culture and design of projects, in order for it to be pervasive. Committing to digital accessibility comes from awareness, leadership, and policy. Most accessibility errors stem from lack of awareness, rather than ill will. If the leadership team at an organization does not express this commitment, both internally and externally, it will not become a priority or embedded in the company culture. Ideally, a museum (of any size) will outline specific standards, methods, and procedures for adhering to and monitoring digital accessibility compliance. This commitment to digital accessibility is essential for museums now more than ever because when approached through an inclusive design lens, web and digital media can be a platform for museums to offer universal access to their collections and programs in innovative and transformative ways.

NOTES

1. "IT Accessibility Laws and Policies," U.S. General Services Administration, accessed October 20, 2020, https://www.section508.gov/manage/laws-and-policies.

2. "21st Century Communications and Video Accessibility Act (CVAA)," Federal Communications Commission, accessed October 20, 2020, https://www.fcc.gov/con sumers/guides/21st-century-communications-and-video-accessibility-act-cvaa.

3. Elizabeth Harris, "Galleries From A to Z Sued Over Websites the Blind Can't Use," **New York Times**, February 18, 2019, https://www.nytimes.com/2019/02/18 /arts/design/blind-lawsuits-art-galleries.html.

4. Laura Snapes, "Beyoncé's Parkwood Entertainment sued over website accessibility," **The Guardian**, January 4, 2019, https://www.theguardian.com/music/2019 /jan/04/beyonce-parkwood-entertainment-sued-over-website-accessibility.

5. Michelle Yin, Dahlia Shaewitz, Cynthia Overton, and Deeza-Mae Smith, "A Hidden Market: The Purchasing Power of Working-Age Adults With Disabilities" (Washington, DC: **American Institutes for Research**, 2018), 3–15, https:// www.air.org/system/files/downloads/report/Hidden-Market-Spending-Power-of -People-with-Disabilities-April-2018.pdf.

6. "Inclusive Design," Microsoft, accessed July 27, 2019, https://www.microsoft .com/design/inclusive/.

7. "Click-Away Pound Survey 2016 Final Report," Click-Away Pound, accessed July 27, 2019, http://www.clickawaypound.com/cap16finalreport.html.

8. Tami Luhby, "Internet Becomes a Lifeline for the Deaf," **New York Times,** February 12, 1998, https://archive.nytimes.com/www.nytimes.com/library/cyber/week/021398deaf.html.

9. "Introduction to Web Accessibility," Web Accessibility in Mind, accessed July 7, 2019, https://webaim.org/intro/.

10. Monica Anderson and Andrew Perrin, "Disabled Americans Are Less Likely to Use Technology," **Pew Research Center**, April 7, 2017, https://www.pewresearch.org/fact-tank/2017/04/07/disabled-americans-are-less-likely-to-use-technology/.

11. Carmen Steele, "The Impacts of Digital Divide," **Digital Divide Council**, September 20, 2018, http://www.digitaldividecouncil.com/the-impacts-of-digital-divide/.

12. "What is AT?," Assistive Technology Industry Association, accessed July 14, 2019, https://www.atia.org/at-resources/what-is-at/.

13. "Accessibility Products," Adobe, accessed July 14, 2019, https://www.adobe.com/accessibility/products/illustrator.html.

14. A more complete list detailing the ways people with disabilities engage with the web is available from the World Wide Web Consortium (W3C) and their Web Accessibility Initiative (WAI). See bibliography.

15. Association of Registered Graphic Designers of Ontario, **AccessAbility: A Practical Handbook on Accessible Graphic Design** (Toronto: RGD Ontario, 2010), 1, https://www.rgd.ca/database/files/library/RGD_AccessAbility_Handbook.pdf.

16. "About W3C WAI," World Wide Web Consortium, accessed July 17, 2019, https://www.w3.org/WAI/about/.

17. "Understanding the Four Principles of Accessibility," World Wide Web Consortium, accessed July 17, 2019, https://www.w3.org/WAI/WCAG21/Understanding/intro#understanding-the-four-principles-of-accessibility.

18. Look to the bibliography for the full list of Web Content Accessibility Guidelines 2.1, published June 2018.

19. "Making Content Usable for People with Cognitive and Learning Disabilities," World Wide Web Consortium, accessed October 20, 2020, https://www.w3.org/TR/coga-usable/#how-to-use-this-document.

20. "Inclusive Design," Microsoft, accessed July 27, 2019, https://www.microsoft.com/design/inclusive/.

21. "Web Accessibility Evaluation Tool," Web Accessibility in Mind, accessed July 27, 2019, http://wave.webaim.org/.

22. "User-Centered Design Basics," U.S. General Services Administration, accessed October 20, 2020, https://www.usability.gov/what-and-why/user-centered-design.html.

23. "Stories of Web Users," World Wide Web Consortium, accessed July 17, 2019, https://www.w3.org/WAI/people-use-web/user-stories/.

24. Microsoft, "Inclusive Design."

25. "The WebAIM Million," Web Accessibility in Mind, accessed July 27, 2019 https://webaim.org/projects/million/.

26. "Top 100 Nonprofits on the Web," Top Nonprofits, accessed July 27, 2019, https://topnonprofits.com/lists/best-nonprofits-on-the-web/.

Chapter Eight

Dollars and Sense

Financial Access

Don't tell me what you value, show me your budget, and I'll tell you what you value.

—Joe Biden[1]

Up to this point, following the resources and guidelines from the previous chapters, a museum may feel like they are finished with their accessibility journey. Let's take a look at a (fictional) example of a museum who has also done these things. The National Waffle Museum has spent the last year working to become a model accessible museum. The museum modified its space to be more physically accessible, created specialized programs for a variety of audiences with disabilities, and made sure their website is accessible. Has the National Waffle Museum done all it needs to do as an institution to become inclusive and accessible? Not quite. Disability is only one barrier that prevents people from accessing museums. Another barrier, which can be just as limiting as physical access, and stands in the way of people with disabilities visiting your museum, is cost.

People with disabilities are overwhelmingly unemployed or underemployed "despite their ability, desire, and willingness to work in the community."[2] Of all the people in the labor force who are of a working age, only about one-third are people with disabilities.[3] This means that there is a nearly 70 percent unemployment rate among people with disabilities, and overwhelmingly, people with disabilities are living on a severely limited income.[4] There are a variety of different and creative ways in which museums can provide free or low-cost programming and admission for people with disabilities without breaking the proverbial museum bank.

OPEN ACCESS

Free or low-cost programs come in all shapes and sizes, anything from free admission to pop-up programming in the community and everything in between. What programs are offered varies by museum size, type, resources, and even location. Based on these conditions, determine what is going to work best for your museum and community. Many of the programs suggested here can be implemented quickly and easily, while others will take more time and require working with both internal and external partners to make it a reality.

Library Passes

A natural partner for many museums is a city or county library. Many metropolitan library systems offer passes to local museums and cultural attractions that patrons can check out for free. Each cultural organization determines how many people can use each pass and the number of passes that are available each day. Oftentimes, these passes are simply donated for community members to use, but some library systems will also pay a small fee to participating museums to be able to provide these passes for their patrons. Depending on how the system is set up, some passes are offered on a first-come, first-served basis, while others are available to reserve online ahead of time for a particular day or time. Check with your local library system to see if this is something they currently offer, and if not, if it is something they would be interested in implementing in the future. Museum/library partnerships occur in communities large and small, so regardless of where your museum is located, you can look into cultivating a partnership such as this.

Museums for All

In 2014, the Museums for All program started as a cooperative initiative between the Institute of Museum and Library Services and the Association of Children's Museums to offer "a signature access program that encourages families of all backgrounds to visit museums regularly and build lifelong museum habits."[5] With the Museums for All program, individuals and families receiving food assistance, also known as Supplemental Nutrition Assistance Program benefits, can gain free or reduced admission to museums by presenting their Electronic Benefit Transfer card when purchasing tickets. Currently, more than five hundred US museums participate in the Museums for All program. As of publication, Museums for All has served more than 2.5 million visitors nationwide across more than forty-eight states, districts, and territories.[6] Museums for All provides an easy-to-implement structure and customizable implementation. It is the only nationally coordinated financial accessibility program in the museum field.[7] Museums set the price (up to three dollars per person) and parameters for admission. So in some cases, museums offer one dollar admission for up to ten people, whereas in other cases they might only admit up to four people, but entirely for free. The flexibility of this program makes it easy and appealing for museums to participate.

Figure 8.1. SCFD campaign image.
Source: The Denver Public Library, Western History Collection, RMN-021-2476.

Free Programming

If offering free or discounted admission through Museums for All is not something that your museum wants to participate in, there are other ways to offer opportunities for people in your community to engage with the museum at no cost.[8] If you have "free zones" in your museum (areas that do not require an admission ticket to enter), you can use these areas to set up activities related to your museum, such as tabletop interactives or other hands-on programming. Or, if you have outreach programs you take out into the community, it may be easy to modify the activities you do in those programs to suit an in-museum, drop-in program. For example, if you are a history-based museum and have a program on pioneer life which includes several interactive activities, you could pull out one of these activities to do as a part of this free programming. Educators can be on hand to help with the activities while also talking about your museum. The individuals leading the program can talk about how the activity relates to the museum, for example, how corn husk dolls were popular toys for pioneer children because they were readily available and easy to make. You can promote and advertise these as free community events with no admission required.

Another option for free programs is to participate in festivals or other community-based events where you can have a pop-up museum—bring your museum to the people rather than the people having to come to you! Pop-up museums are a particularly good way to get out into the community, especially if your museum is fairly inaccessible (due to cost, transportation, physical access, etc.).[9] Again, if you offer outreach programs, these can generally be easily arranged in library spaces and can be another way for members of your community to engage with your museum at no cost to participate. It is also another way to utilize or begin a partnership with your local library system.

Free Days

Perhaps the idea of Museums for All is intriguing but you cannot commit to free admission every day. Consider offering certain admission-free days for your community. Visitors who wish to come to your museum can visit on these specific days throughout the year at zero cost to them. Another option, rather than making these days strictly free admission, could be asking for a suggested donation or pay-what-you-can.

When it comes to funding free admission programs to your museum, there are a variety of options. If a cultural tax district like Denver's Scientific Cultural Facilities District (SCFD) does not exist in your area, look to grant or corporate funding opportunities. Potential financing options could include small, local funders all the way up to large corporate gifts from companies such as Toyota. Funding these programs is in part going to depend on the anticipated number of visitors during these free days and times.

CULTURE FOR ALL

In August 1981, Denver's main city-operated cultural institutions, including the Denver Art Museum, zoo, botanic gardens, and Museum of Natural History (now called the Denver Museum of Nature & Science), received a financial shock. These institutions were informed that in the following budget year, their budget subsidies would be reduced anywhere from 22 to 59 percent. Even by cutting budgets and increasing entrance fees, there was no way to make up that large of a budget reduction. The museums were forced to close off parts of their exhibits and reduce staff to make up their budget shortfalls. These four institutions then came together with several smaller cultural organizations and proposed a tax-collecting district that would specifically support Denver's cultural institutions. The proposed tax was "one penny on a ten dollar purchase to fund arts, culture, and science organizations."[1] Denver voters approved the Scientific Cultural Facilities District (SCFD) in 1988.

At the time that SCFD was proposed, the idea of a special tax district for cultural institutions was fairly new. St. Louis had created a similar tax district in the late 1970s to help fund the city's cultural organizations. Today, the SCFD is the largest tax district in the nation (geographically). The number of cultural tax districts is now numerous, many based on the SCFD model. The SCFD was voted into being, and has been continuously renewed, by residents of the seven Denver-metro counties. As a way of thanking voters, most organizations which are a part of the SCFD each offer a handful of free days throughout the year, adding up hundreds of different free opportunities each year!

1. "Why was SCFD created?" Scientific Cultural Facilities District, accessed July 29, 2019, http://scfd.org/blog-entry/49/2014-05-22-Why-was-SCFD-Created.html.

Figure 8.2. Museums for all tweets.

FUNDING ACCESS

By this point in the book, you may find yourself asking how your museum will pay for all of these accessibility programs and changes. Fortunately, there are a variety of sources you can look to for potential funding.[10] Generally speaking, there are three main types of funding you can seek out: private (individuals and family foundations), corporate (grants or sponsorship), and government (city, state, federal).

Private Foundations

Private funding is available through individual donors or family foundations where funds come from individual assets and are put toward charitable or philanthropic means. Examples of private foundations are the Carnegie Foundation or the Andrew W. Mellon Foundation. Family foundations are often governed by the families themselves who started the foundation, or at least many foundations have family members sitting on the board that make funding decisions. Information on what certain family foundations fund, and the specifics on how to apply it, can be some of the most difficult to find in terms of grants; however, these funding sources can also be some of the most fruitful in terms of developing long-term relationships with a funder. Once you have identified a potential family foundation, it can be beneficial to have a conversation with someone there about the project you are looking to fund, outlining your goals and intended outcomes. While accessibility may not be directly listed as something these foundations fund (assuming they have a website at all), this personal communication can result in an invitation to apply for funding in the future. One of the challenges of small family foundations is that they do not always have a website with information about what they fund, but even if they do, they may not keep the website up-to-date. Also, as a family-run foundation, their priorities may change from year to year (whereas their website may not).

Corporate Funding

Corporations and some larger businesses usually offer two different kinds of funding: sponsorship and grants. Depending on what you are looking for, you may want to apply for one type or the other. For events or one-off programs, seeking sponsorship may be the best route to take since it may be easier and faster to acquire than larger, ongoing funding. If you are looking for more reliable, long-term funding, applying for corporate foundation grants is likely a better option. Many large corporations offer funding to help support free museum admission, such as Target's support for Free First days at places such as the Chicago Children's Museum, the Museum of Modern Art in New York, Denver's Museo de las Americas, and many more.

Government Funding

Government funding opportunities vary from region to region. At the federal level there are four major organizations that offer funding for museums, usually on an annual basis: the Institute for Museum and Library Services, the American Alliance of Museums, the National Endowment for the Humanities, and the National Endowment for the Arts.[11] Grants from these agencies typically range from $25,000 to several hundred thousand dollars, and usually span one to three years. Keep in mind, however, that these are highly competitive grants and have lengthy applications. Before you decide to apply, make sure that your organization has the capacity to allot adequate time for generating (and implementing) one of these proposals. Regional arts councils or other city programs may also offer funding opportunities. For example, Raleigh Arts in North Carolina supports local arts organizations through the City of Raleigh Arts Commission's Grant Program, and in California the City of Oakland Cultural Funding Program funds art and cultural activities in their city.

When looking for funding for accessibility programs, a fourth option is sometimes available through your local regional center or community centered board (the name varies from location to location) and other services organizations that support people with disabilities and their families. Regional centers or community centered boards are organizations that contract with the state to provide services for children and adults with developmental disabilities. These organizations are funded through the Department of Human Services, Disability Services, or similar departments at the state level. These organizations will sometimes help provide funding for accessibility programs so that you can offer them free to participants from that particular service region. Additionally, local chapters of national organizations (such as the Alzheimer's Association) may also provide funding, or at the least may be able to help connect you to potential funding sources.

Not every museum has a development department, let alone paid staff to help find and apply to funders. In cases such as these, and when the impetus for finding and applying to these grants falls on you, connect with your local library. Oftentimes, libraries will have access to grant finding resources, such as the Foundation Directory,[12] or might even have someone on staff who is knowledgeable about how to find resources in your area. One easy source to find potential funders is looking at who is funding other organizations in your area. Peruse the annual reports of similar organizations to see who is funding them and for how much. Taking a look at the foundation's 990 forms can give you a bit more information about the types of programs and organizations that particular funder has decided to support.[13]

In the world of grants, the industry average is that organizations will get approximately one-third of the grants for which they apply. For those grants you apply for but do not receive, it is beneficial, whenever possible, to reach out to the program officer (PO) for that grant or foundation. Conversations with POs can help you get a better idea of why your proposal was not selected, and they may even provide some pointers to make your next application stronger. Ideally, reach out to the PO before you even apply for the grant to see if your museum or program is a good fit for the current focus of the foundation. Generally speaking, funders are more than happy to take the time to talk to a potential grantee since they can eliminate a lot of unnecessary work on the part of both the foundation and the museum if in fact a project is not a good fit.

VISITORS' VOICES

Imagine being a funder. You read proposal after proposal that all say the same thing, something along the lines of, "Our program positively impacts people with disabilities. We have served . . ." Again and again. But imagine coming across this line instead: participating in this program feels "welcoming, energetic, immensely educational and mentally stimulating. It also is uplifting to me as a caregiver because my brain and knowledge base are also very much stimulated by the programs. This is important because caregiving is an ongoing and exhausting experience and so it absolutely energizes my spirits."[1]

Firsthand program feedback like this is critical to collect. The feedback you receive about your programs can be used to strengthen and enhance grant proposals. It is easy to say that your museum has a great program and that a certain number of people attended, but personal quotes and stories like these truly show the impact accessibility programs can have on people. The people participating are going to best be able to express the impact your programs have on their lives. The adage, "Nothing about us, without us" applies to grant proposals as well. Take the time to collect feedback from your participants either during events and programs or just after they end. Use this data to strengthen reports and applications to funders, as well as pass on to museum staff so they too can recognize the importance of the work your museum is doing.

1. Survey response regarding the Denver Art Museum's Art & About program for adults with memory loss and their care partners.

DOLLARS AND SENSE

Financial access is often overlooked, but it is nonetheless important to consider. Using a variety of methods such as free admission, pop-up museum programs, and library partnerships, museums can expand their reach and access. With a little bit of searching you can find a variety of funders to help support your free programs, as well as your other accessibility initiatives. By offering up more opportunities for people with disabilities to visit for free, you open up your museum to a wider, more inclusive audience.

NOTES

1. Rob Berger, "Top 100 Money Quotes of All Time," **Forbes**, April 30, 2014, https://www.forbes.com/sites/robertberger/2014/04/30/top-100-money-quotes-of -all-time.

2. "Employment, Training, and Wages," The Arc, accessed July 5, 2019, https://www.thearc.org/what-we-do/public-policy/policy-issues/employment.

3. The Arc, "Employment, Training, and Wages."

4. "Table A-6. Employment Status of the Civilian Population by Sex, Age, and Disability Status, Not Seasonally Adjusted," Bureau of Labor, Accessed July 5, 2019, https://www.bls.gov/news.release/empsit.t06.htm.

5. "Museums for All," Association of Children's Museums, accessed July 7, 2019, https://childrensmuseums.org/about/acm-initiatives/museums-for-all.

6. "About," Museums for All, accessed October 16, 2020, https://museums4all .org/about/.

7. Museums for All, "About."

8. Many museums offer free programs or tours to Title I schools through the use of grant funding. In this book we are going to focus on nonschool programs.

9. The Santa Cruz Museum of Art and History created a free toolkit available for creating a pop-up museum. You can access the toolkit here: http://popupmuseum.org /wp-content/uploads/2013/09/Pop-Up-Museum-Edited.pdf.

10. While it probably does not need to be said, no funding is ever a guarantee.

11. The National Science Foundation sometimes funds museums as well.

12. Many states also have a more local version of a funding directory. Check with your local library to see what they offer.

13. The 990 form is a publicly accessible IRS tax form filed by nonprofits which provides financial information about a nonprofit organization. The form provides an overview of an organization's activities, detailed financial information, and governance. Guidestar.com is a free online resource you can use to find financial information on nonprofits and foundations, including 990 forms.

Chapter Nine

A Word about Words

Communications

Be careful of your thoughts, for your thoughts become your words. Be careful of your words, for your words become your actions.

—Chinese proverb, author unknown[1]

Language, words, and labels constantly shift over time, sometimes by choice and sometimes by necessity. Take "snowbrowth" for example, a descriptive term from the 1590s meaning freshly melted snow.[2] This word likely faded from our everyday vernacular due to disuse. Whereas a derogatory slur often used to describe people with intellectual disabilities, the "R-word" has drastically fallen in usage due to a concerted effort to eradicate it.[3] This is because words matter. Words can create inclusive communities by opening up doors "to cultivate the understanding and respect that enable people with disabilities to lead fuller, more independent lives."[4] Yet words can also do harm and create "barriers or stereotypes that are not only demeaning to people with disabilities, but also rob them of their individuality."[5]

The language we use in our museums is powerful. What we display publicly through exhibition labels, signage, websites, and more, communicates the values and beliefs of our organization. Moreover, these words then influence the way our staff perceives and interacts with our visitors and each other, even in ways they are unaware of.

OPENING DOORS THROUGH COMMUNICATION

We communicate in order to impart information and knowledge from one person to another. Museums often have entire departments dedicated to communicating information about their exhibitions, collections, and programs to visitors. A museum's website is a key way to share this information, and a place where many prospective visitors first visit. To ensure effective communication have basic information (your physical address, hours of operation, and nearby parking areas) clearly labeled and easy to find, and perhaps in multiple locations on your website or as a footer on each page. Next, consider what other pertinent information people may need in order to visit. What is the price of admission? Are there any discounts or reciprocal programs? Are there certain times that are noisier and more crowded than others? How much time on average does it take for visitors to go through your museum?[6] As for parking and transit information, do you detail the location of the nearest bus or train stop? What about safe drop-off and pick-up locations for ride-share companies? If visitors have a question, who can they contact? Whenever possible, include an email address and phone number of a real person. This could be a general email (like access@yourmuseum.com) which can be read and responded to by multiple staff members, which is especially helpful if there is not a dedicated accessibility staff member.

Equally important to sharing your open hours and ticketing information is communicating your accessibility supports and materials to visitors. Countless museum colleagues have lamented that they have few, and often the same, people attending their American Sign Language (ASL) tours or sensory-friendly programs, for example. The reason? Often, the public is entirely unaware that the museum is committed to accessibility, much less that they offer support materials or dedicated programs. While it is important for museums to promote these accessibility programs to their community, it is just as crucial to publicly affirm their dedication more broadly to access and inclusion. This is most often done through accessibility statements found on museum websites (as referenced in chapter 3). These short statements articulate an organization's commitment to accessibility. There are some online resources to help generate an accessibility statement.[7] These statements should be cocreated, or at the least vetted, by your community advisory group and some internal colleagues.

Accessibility statements should be easy to find on your website. Most often these are located on a museum's accessibility page, which is usually linked to the general visitation webpage. On this page, statements declaring a museum's commitment to accessibility are listed alongside information about the materials, accommodations, and programs your museum has in place for visitors who may require extra support when visiting your space. There are two main categories of information to include when considering your museum's accessibility page. First, highlight materials that are available anytime the museum is open and can be accessed without needing to ask museum staff.

Second, describe services or programs that visitors must ask for (either by requesting ahead of time or upon their arrival). Examples of materials available anytime could be large-print or braille exhibition booklets installed in a gallery, accessible seating in the galleries, accessible restrooms, or exhibition videos with captions. Examples of materials visitors may need to request during their visit could include assistive listening devices, ASL interpretation, sensory or tactile maps, large-print maps, and wheelchair or stroller rentals. While all these materials fall under the umbrella of accessibility supports and services, the distinction between the two categories is a matter of visitor autonomy and independence.

Requesting support materials ahead of a visit, such as renting a wheelchair or an assistive listening device, takes time and planning and thus affects how easily and spontaneously a person can visit. A quick afternoon visit (decided on a whim) instead becomes a planned affair that may take weeks ahead of time to schedule. Additionally, requiring a visitor to ask for materials each time they visit compels them to disclose their personal situation in a public setting to complete strangers. This can add an additional, often unwanted, layer to a visit. Providing accessibility materials or services anytime the museum is open and to any visitor is more in line with a universal design approach, and it supports a more independent visit. Visitors can choose what materials they want to use, or not use, at their convenience. Moreover, highlighting and making these materials available to any visitor (not just those who ask) indicates their universal use and appeal; it says that these materials will support a wide variety of people during their visit. Many museums may not be able to make their materials easily available all the time to visitors, but what is important is clearly explaining what accessibility services are available and how to get them. Many visitors with disabilities will search for a museum's accessibility page for information about the presence and location of accessibility materials before they visit, so they can know what to expect (and potentially what to ask for) when they arrive.

The accessibility page should also include information about any **inaccessible** spaces or paths in your museum. As written about in previous chapters, many historic sites are unable to structurally change their museum space to meet ADA standards (due to historic status), which often results in rendering rooms, floors, or even entire buildings inaccessible to people who use mobility devices. The Durant-Kenrick House in Newton, Massachusetts, for example, a Georgian farmhouse built in 1734, has kept many of its spaces to eighteenth-century standards. The house's accessibility page provides a detailed description of these spaces that, due to historic status, are not ADA compliant, such as doorways and halls narrower than thirty-two inches and rooms that require steps to enter.[8] By delivering this information to visitors, the Durant-Kenrick House is setting visitor expectations by providing information about the reality of the space, rather than trying to hide or ignore those spaces, which some visitors may have trouble accessing. This practice places the decision of whether to visit the museum in the hands of the prospective visitor. If I use a mobility device and I read that the doorways to three of the rooms are narrower than thirty-two inches (meaning my device may not fit) I can decide simply not to visit this house. Or I can decide that I still want to visit, knowing ahead of time which accessible spaces I can expect to see. This information has given me the option to plan for my trip, and make any necessary adjustments ahead of time, as opposed to showing up to the museum only to find out I cannot access certain areas (which could lead to frustration). Knowing all the important information ahead of time can ease some stress and tension and afford visitors the power to independently design their visit. Once people know you are an accessible organization and are aware of the various materials and services you provide, they will be more inclined to visit.

LANGUAGE AS A CULTURAL SIGNIFIER: USE YOUR WORDS

Words are powerful, and the language a museum uses (both internally and externally) can speak volumes about its values. Once the accessibility materials and services a museum wishes to communicate with visitors has been decided, there must be consideration on how to describe these materials and identify the intended audience. An ill-chosen word or phrase can do damage just as easily as a welcome word can open up a door; museums and their staff must be mindful of the language they use and the underlying messages conveyed in those words.

Communication and self-identity are complex matters. It is therefore important to understand two different language concepts: identity-first and people-first language. People using identity-first language view disability as an inherent part of identity and so place the disability-related word first in their self-description (self-identifying as autistic or disabled). People-first language, on the other hand, first emphasizes the person in a description and then communicates the disability second; for example, talking about our friend Sally who uses a wheelchair (Sally as a person is first, and her wheelchair use is secondary). Many people in the disability community embrace disability as an integral part of who they are and therefore describe themselves using identity-first terminology, which rejects the need to separate disability from the person. A self-advocate from the autism community illustrates the difference between people-first and identity-first language through this proclamation: "I'm not a person with autism; I am Autistic."[9] Their identity is closely tied with their autism, it is "an edifying and meaningful component of a person's identity, and it defines the ways in which an individual experiences and understands the world around him or her. It is all-pervasive."[10]

The terms commonly used in identity-first language, such as autistic, disabled, and crip, are examples of reclaimed words. This is a process where self-advocates and allies in the disability community take a derogatory term that was previously used against them as a slur (such as "cripple") and give it a positive meaning that then becomes an expression of solidarity and pride ("crip").[11] Crip in particular is viewed as an inclusive term, meant to represent all disabilities. People who identify as crip can be members of the disability community or community allies, but they all recognize the distinctive disability culture of which they are a part.[12] By reclaiming this word as an integral part of their identity and member culture, some members of the disability community argue that the presence of disability need not be viewed as negative—something to be pitied, feared, hated, or devalued. Instead, disability should be seen as an important aspect of human diversity that brings value to the world.

Within different sectors of the disability community there lies great diversity, and this of course extends to labeling and identification. The deaf and hard of hearing community is no exception. Within this community, for example, people self-identify a myriad of ways. Some may identify themselves by the degree to which they can hear, for example, identifying as "hard of hearing" or "partially deaf." Others will relate to the relative age of onset that hearing loss occurred, saying they are "late-deafened" for example. Even among people who identify as deaf, there is a divergence between deaf and Deaf. The lowercase "d" deaf is used when referring to the audiological condition of not hearing, whereas the uppercase "D" Deaf corresponds to a particular group of people who are deaf and share a culture and a common language—ASL.[13] Like any other culture, Deaf individuals share a complex set of knowledge, beliefs, and practices that are transmitted across their distinctive language, and this practice differentiates them from people who have lost their hearing due to illness, age, or trauma. Furthermore, this culture provides a lens through which to view their connection to the larger society. For example, many people born D/deaf do not view themselves as having a physical disability just because they cannot hear. This distinction between audiologically-deaf and culturally-Deaf is one that takes time and patience to understand, something that a non-Deaf person could not easily recognize without context and insight from someone in that community.

Generally speaking as museum staff, when engaging with or speaking about someone who identifies as having a disability, unless you know their preference for using identity-first or people-first language—whether they have told you directly or it has come up in some other way—it is best to use people-first language, as it is more neutral and objective.[14] This is particularly the case for people who do not have a disability. No one should ever assume to know how someone wishes to be represented, therefore museum staff should always ask their colleagues, visitors, and community partners what language and terms feel most appropriate and respectful. When in doubt, ask!

INCLUSIVE LANGUAGE PRACTICES

When thinking more broadly about communication approaches, when museums are creating content guidelines for their website and other published materials or designing customer service training for frontline staff, there are general inclusive communication techniques to follow. There are numerous online and in-person training materials focused on general disability etiquette that promote respectful ways of communicating with and about people. Here are a few general themes.

Refer to the person first, and the disability second. When it is unknown how the individual or community prefers to identify, descriptions should not place a disability as the primary adjective to identify an individual. Saying a child with autism (rather than an autistic child), or a visitor who is blind (rather than the blind visitor).

Use neutral language. Language can be biased, and very often depictions of disability use negative or passive words that indicate something is missing. Focus instead on impartial language that simply describes the reality of the situation without infusing feeling or opinion. For example, describing a man with dementia rather than a man suffering from dementia.

Emphasize abilities, not limitations. Focus on what people can do (active terminology), rather than what they cannot (passive terminology). For example, describing someone as a wheelchair user (active), rather than being wheelchair-bound (passive). Or explaining that a woman who is D/deaf communicates through ASL (active), as opposed to being "mute" or unable to speak (passive). People are empowered when the focus shifts to what they can do as opposed to what they cannot.

Avoid using euphemisms that are condescending or perpetuate stereotypes. Formerly, it was common practice to say "special populations" or "special needs" when describing people with disabilities.[15] Next came terms like "differently-abled" or "handi-capable," considered perhaps a lighter or more

Table 9.1. People-First Language Basics

Use	Avoid
Child with autism; person on the spectrum	Autistic
Boy who is blind; she has low vision	Visually impaired, visually challenged
Woman who is deaf; boy who is hard of hearing; man with hearing loss	Hearing impaired
People with disabilities; disability community	Handicapped, disabled
Girl with a developmental disability	Mentally retarded
She has an intellectual disability	Retarded, abnormal
He has a physical disability	He's crippled
Congenital disability	Birth defect
Person who has had a stroke	Stroke victim
He has need for a wheelchair	He is wheelchair bound, confined to a wheelchair
A person of short stature or little person	Dwarf, midget
Accessible bathrooms, parking lots	Disabled parking, handicap bathrooms
Woman without disabilities; man who is nondisabled; typically developing child	Normal, regular

polite way of describing people. These descriptors can be condescending and isolating because they still define people as out of the ordinary or somehow set apart. Use terms that promote equity, dignity, and respect.

Refer to disability only when necessary. Is revealing or discussing a person's disability relevant to the story being told, either in a casual conversation or on a blog post on the museum's website? Too often disability-related labels are used even when they are irrelevant to the nature of the story. If a person's disability is not central to your story, then there is no need to mention it.

Following these guidelines should help ensure that what you are communicating—be it in person, on your website, or in other public materials—is inclusive. Next, consider the format in which your communication is being transmitted to your visitors. Is there only one way to receive the information? If so, determine if there are alternative formats that can get your message across. For example, accessible PDFs or Word documents for information that is given orally (such as meeting minutes or training notes), plain text versions of email flyers and newsletters, audio descriptions of training videos with lots of visuals, or providing captioning and signing on videos. Considering how you say something is just as important as what you say.

ABLEIST LANGUAGE

Sometimes with the best intentions, and often unknowingly, people use words or phrases in everyday conversation that are insulting or discriminating to people with disabilities. This is known as ableism: the intentional or unintentional practice of devaluing or discriminating against people with physical, intellectual, or psychiatric disabilities.[16] Very often this practice shows up in the language used to speak about people with disabilities, and the programs or supports they use.[17] Ableist language can come in the form of euphemisms that are intended as polite niceties but in reality are patronizing and divisive. Examples are describing bathrooms or parking spots as "handicapped" rather than accessible; using the term physically or mentally challenged; or calling accommodations and support materials "special" items. Even defining people with disabilities as "special needs groups" or as "access populations" can be condescending. The same goes for the terms "differently-abled" or "handi-capable"; these are often indirect, yet patronizing, ways of saying disability.

Sometimes ableist language will reflect assumptions based on the medical model of disability, where disability is viewed as a problem that needs to be fixed (see chapter 2). An example is describing the people engaging in your program as "patients" rather than attendees or participants. Also using emotional terms that suggest helplessness, such as "afflicted with" or "suffering from." Your museum is not a doctor's office; as such, the people attending your program should not be viewed as suffering, or seeking remedy, from their disability experience. Also, it is problematic to use the term "normal" or "regular" when drawing a comparison between people with and without disabilities. Even if you use people-first language to describe one tour group ("a group of people with disabilities"), if you then describe another tour group as "a normal group," you are effectively implying that the first group is abnormal. This labeling adds to the narrative that people with disabilities are somehow wrong or unusual. It also implies that there is a single norm for people, which there is not. Other options to describe this comparison is nondisabled, typically developing, or group without disabilities.

Ableism can also be seen in more common phrases that have become so integrated into our everyday lives that many people do not think twice about their usage. Adjectives or phrases like "crazy," "insane," "crippled by," "turn a deaf ear to," or "double-blind study" are just a few. These metaphors are problematic because they stem from descriptions of disability or have been historically (and sometimes currently) used to marginalize and oppress people with disabilities. Therefore, when they are used in everyday speech, without thought to how they are tied to the lives of people with disabilities, they exemplify ableist practices by contributing to the narrative that people

REFRAMING AGING

Recently, there has been momentum to reframe how Americans think and talk about aging. Traditionally, aging is associated with decline and deterioration, mirroring the disability medical model perspective. According to the **Journal of the American Geriatric Society**, "widespread negative assumptions about 'getting old' have led the public to take a fatalistic stance that there is not much to be done about aging."[1] This view has manifested in ageist language which, similar to ableism, discriminates against older people due to negative and inaccurate stereotypes. Terms like "the silver tsunami" evoke fatalistic or catastrophic views on aging. Ageism can be seen on television, social media, and in everyday interactions, but perhaps the most serious concern is when ageism is internalized by older adults themselves. Personalizing these negative viewpoints can lead to poor mental and physical health.[2] Older adults who accept that depression, fatigue, and chronic pain are normal parts of aging, do not usually seek medical attention and therefore get less care.[3]

Organizations are taking action toward reframing the narrative on aging, and at the core is a shift in language. And in particular a shift around the word senior. For so long the term "senior" has been the go-to descriptor for people aged sixty-five and older. Yet many people no longer identify with this word, and writers and researchers are recognizing not only the negative connotations it brings, but how it is a label unto itself. The Frameworks Institute is addressing ageism headfirst, by providing a toolkit that provides "empirical guidance on what to say, how to say it, and what to leave unsaid" (see appendix A).[4] With their help, the **Journal of the American Geriatrics Society** is changing its style guide and its language about how to refer to this group, offering the alternative language as a more respectful and neutral way for authors to describe people as they age. There is a shift away from words like "seniors," "elderly," and "aging dependents," to more neutral and inclusive terms like "older adults."[5]

Language matters. Using words and communication can be a way to drive a more informed conversation about aging (and disability) and its implications for our communities. As outreach efforts related to language spread, the hope is for ageist and ableist language and practices to subside.

1. Nancy E. Lundebjerg et al., "When It Comes to Older Adults, Language Matters: Journal of the American Geriatrics Society Adopts Modified American Medical Association Style," **Journal of the American Geriatrics Society** 65, no. 7 (July 2017): 1386–88, https://onlinelibrary.wiley.com/doi/pdf/10.1111/jgs.14941.
2. Paula Span, "Ageism: A 'Prevalent and Insidious' Health Threat," **New York Times**, April 26, 2019, https://www.nytimes.com/2019/04/26/health/ageism-elderly-health.html.

3. "How Ageism in Health Care is Affecting Society," Senior Living, accessed September 25, 2019, https://www.seniorliving.org/health/ageism/.

4. "Gaining Momentum: A FrameWorks Communication Toolkit," Toolkits, FrameWorks Institute, accessed September 25, 2019, https://frameworksinstitute.org/toolkits/aging/.

5. Lundebjerg et al., "Older Adults."

with disabilities are wrong or broken. Again, words are important; they are a way for many people to understand the world around them. Therefore, we must reflect on what our words say:

> If a culture's language is full of pejorative metaphors about a group of people, that culture is not going to see those people as fully entitled to the same housing, employment, medical care, education, access and inclusion as people in a more favored group.[18]

There is nothing wrong with disability and, therefore, we should not use phrases that connect disability with negative and derogatory statements.

Understanding inclusive language and avoiding ableist terminology are key tools in creating an accessible museum. Yet language, words, and labels are constantly shifting and changing over time. Terms deemed acceptable years ago are now revealed to be ableist and disrespectful, while other words (considered slurs) are being reclaimed and used by the community they originally discriminated against. This illustrates the fluidity of language and the importance of consistently checking-in with your communities to determine what is appropriate for the situation at hand.

SPREADING THE WORD

Understanding the nuance of language is a key practice to a museum putting forth an inclusive and accessible communication plan. Yet equally important is recognizing the fluidity of language. As has been shown, terms and phrases used even five years ago may now be seen as out of touch, insensitive, or ignorant. So what are museums expected to do? Play it safe and defer to language approved years ago? No! Show your respect for people by refusing to use outdated or offensive terms on your website, in program descriptions, and as frontline best practice language. People have the right to choose what they wish to be called, either as a group or on an individual basis, and museums have a role in honoring this choice.

Maintaining inclusive communication can be done by keeping up-to-date with research on social justice, language, and communication practices in the disability community. Look to our resources in appendix A for places to start. Next, set up regular intervals to review your website and program descriptions for ableist language, both on your own (perhaps as part of an audit) as well as with community partners (such as your advisory committee). They may flag negative terminology or nuanced phrases that you miss and provide insight about important cultural shifts in language.

Just as you want to build up your own capacity around inclusive communication, it is equally important to do so with your museum staff. People must understand the words they are being asked to use, and perhaps more importantly, what they are being asked **not** to use. For example, explaining why your museum has made the shift to saying older adults rather than seniors, or to accessible restrooms rather than handicapped. This is important for everyone from your volunteers to your director to understand because only if it is understood can it really sink in.

A WORD ABOUT WORDS:
A WORKSHOP ON LANGUAGE, MEANING, AND INTENT

In 2018, the Art of Access Alliance Denver, a group of individuals and organizations who work to advance and connect accessible and inclusive practices across Denver's cultural organizations, came together to outline professional development workshops for the upcoming year.[1] The topic of language and communication—and the fear around using incorrect terminology—was one that continually rose to the top when they reflected upon what they and other colleagues continued to grapple with in their work. They posed the question: How do we challenge the assumptions and fear around how we talk about each other? From this, the workshop, "A Word About Words: Language, Meaning, and Intent" was born. The goal of this discussion-based workshop is to gain greater awareness of the language we use and the assumptions we all have around language. Attendees engage in a focused discussion on the binaries found in language, and through this discussion gain greater awareness of how we can communicate in a more inclusive way.

With a few key ingredients, this workshop can be replicated essentially anywhere and with any group.

- Dedicate enough space to split into small groups, and provide small group facilitators, chart paper, and markers to document the discussion.

- Begin by asking attendees to write down and share what they want to get out of the workshop. This can help the facilitators frame the discussion and key takeaways.
- Next, introduce a set of binary words, often used in community engagement, that will be discussed and analyzed in small groups: access vs. inclusion, ability vs. disability, community vs. communities, and serve vs. engage.
- After breaking into small groups, the facilitators will ask probing questions to support the groups to analyze a different word pair: **What is the difference between these words? When, how, and where are they used? What are the connotations or suggestions these words carry, and for which communities?** Record the thoughts and ideas of the group on the chart paper (to share later).
- After fifteen to twenty minutes of discussion, have the groups rotate to a new word pair. Groups can rotate as many times as there is time for.
- Once groups are done rotating, the facilitators synthesize the notes and share one to two main takeaways and conversation common threads with the larger group.
- Participants are then asked to reflect upon the conversations that took place and write down a personal value statement—something they can prioritize and use to guide their work moving forward.

The beauty of this workshop is that it is dynamic. The discussions, learnings, and takeaways change depending on the group and where their interests and expertise lie. Each time you have this conversation it is different. Even the questions may change, depending on the context of the group. Moreover, despite the fact that facilitators guide the conversation, the power of the workshop is the collective knowledge of the group. Everyone has expertise to provide.

1. "About," Art of Access Alliance Denver, accessed March 5, 2019, https://artof accessdenver.com/about-us/.

So often we overhear comments from museum colleagues who are concerned about saying the wrong thing and insulting someone to the point where they avoid talking about disability entirely. Mistakes will happen, and words will be misspoken, but what is important is to simply try. Try to embrace inclusive wording into your own language. Try to encourage your colleagues (especially in marketing) to adopt inclusive communication practices in their institutional guidelines. Try and then be open to correcting your mistakes. So much of creating an accessible and welcoming environment is being open and receptive to the needs of your communities and being willing to learn from past mistakes. Museums that use inclusive language in their marketing communications, signage, website, and frontline staff, communicate to their communities, "You are welcome here."

Figure 9.1. Banners hung outside the Shedd Aquarium welcoming *all* visitors.
Source: © Shedd Aquarium/Brenna Hernandez

NOTES

1. Robert C. Jameson, "Be Careful of Your Thoughts: They Control Your Destiny," **HuffPost**, April 28, 2014, https://www.huffpost.com/entry/be-careful-of-your-though_b_5214689.

2. Julie Canfield, "Where Have All The Old Words Gone," **Medium**, May 5, 2019, https://medium.com/@juliecanfield_41917/where-have-all-the-old-words-gone-ba665ba9265d.

3. "The 'R'-Word Remains Prevalent Across Social Media," Press Releases, Special Olympics, accessed September 5, 2019, https://www.specialolympics.org/discriminatory-language-about-people-with-intellectual-disabilities-particularly-the-r-word-remains-prevalent-across-social-media.

4. Special Olympics, **Ten Commandments of Communicating about People with Intellectual Disabilities**, 2012, http://www.specialolympicsarkansas.org/uploads/1/6/6/8/16687598/tencommandments_2012.pdf

5. Special Olympics, **Ten Commandments**.

6. Knowing the average time it takes to go through specific exhibitions or the entire museum helps visitors plan their visit. This information is helpful for people

on a tight schedule with other plans, caregivers planning around nap times for young children, or for people needing to take medication at specific times.

7. "Generate an Accessibility Statement," Planning and Policies, World Wide Web Consortium, accessed September 5, 2019, https://www.w3.org/WAI/planning /statements/generator/#create.

8. "Accessibility at the Durant-Kenrick House and Grounds," Durant-Kenrick House and Gardens, accessed September 10, 2019, http://www.newtonma.gov/gov /historic/visit/durant_kenrick_house_and_grounds/accessdk.asp.

9. "Identity-First Language," Autistic Self Advocacy Network, accessed October 1, 2019, https://autisticadvocacy.org/about-asan/identity-first-language/.

10. Autistic Self Advocacy Network, "Identity-First Language."

11. "Crip Theory," Wright State University, accessed October 1, 2019, https:// www.wright.edu/event/sex-disability-conference/crip-theory.

12. Wright State University, "Crip Theory."

13. "Community and Culture - Frequently Asked Questions," National Association of the Deaf, accessed October 7, 2019, https://www.nad.org/resources/american -sign-language/community-and-culture-frequently-asked-questions/.

14. Many advocacy groups argue that people-first language is not neutral and in fact upholds the medical model of disability by portraying disability as something to be ashamed of or changed. Further resources on Identity-first and person-first language usage is in appendix A.

15. In many places the term "special needs" is still very much in use, especially with parent groups that identify with this term. We recommend avoiding the term in the museum but encourage you to determine what works best for your community.

16. "#Ableism," Center for Disability Rights, accessed September 25, 2019, http:// cdrnys.org/blog/uncategorized/ableism/.

17. Center for Disability Rights, "#Ableism."

18. Rachel Cohen-Rottenberg, "Doing Social Justice: 10 Reasons to Give Up Ableist Language," **HuffPost**, August 10, 2014, https://www.huffpost.com/entry /doing-social-justice-thou_b_5476271?guccounter=1.

Chapter Ten

If You Build It, They Will Come

Inclusive Exhibitions and Programming

Because they are a trusted educational source, people visit museums. Museums are often rated more trustworthy than newspapers, the government, or even researchers. Approximately 850 million people visit museums in the United States each year—that is more than all major sporting events and theme parks combined.[1] There are two main ways museums fulfill their missions: through exhibitions and programs. When designing exhibitions, interpretive planners and exhibit designers must consider how to make the included content engaging and memorable for visitors. Another obligation, sometimes overlooked, is considering the accessibility of the content for visitors.

Let us return to our friend Sally. Sally has heard great things about the National Waffle Museum and decides to visit with her friend Harry. Sally has successfully made it into the museum with her mobility device, purchased her tickets from a counter that is low enough for her to easily access, has her printed map (which was also available in several different formats and languages), has met up with Harry and is ready to see the museum's exhibitions. Their first stop takes them to the International Waffle Hall, where, according to the map, they will be able to learn about the history and invention of the world's different waffles. As they walk and roll into the exhibit hall, they are impressed by how new everything looks. Given the museum's recent accessibility upgrades, they are excited to immerse themselves into an interactive **and** accessible exhibit space.

The International Waffle Hall exhibition had won several awards for its innovative design—viewed from above it looks like the grooved surface of a waffle iron. As Harry and Sally explore the exhibition spaces, they are dismayed to find that due to its unique waffle iron design, many of the areas are small and difficult for Sally to maneuver through and turn her wheelchair around in. Many of the text panels, which mimic the dark coating of a waffle iron and the dark golden crisp of a waffle, are challenging to read since the text was layered on images with little contrast between the background image and the actual text. Both Harry and Sally have difficulty manipulating the interactives and are only successful with the help of museum staff. Harry, who is hard of hearing, must ask Sally for a summary of the video showing how to make the perfect Belgian waffle because it lacks captioning, and he cannot hear the audio clearly above the din of other visitors speaking in the exhibition. This was definitely not the experience they were expecting.

ACCESSIBLE EXHIBITION DESIGN

Museum exhibitions should be accessible for **all** people. In the example above the designers at the National Waffle Museum were clearly focused on creating engaging and interactive content but stopped short of taking into consideration the practice of universal design or supporting the needs and interests of people with disabilities, like Harry and Sally. So what do you do to ensure your exhibitions are engaging, interactive, **and** accessible? Start by familiarizing yourself with the basic scope of what makes an accessible exhibition.

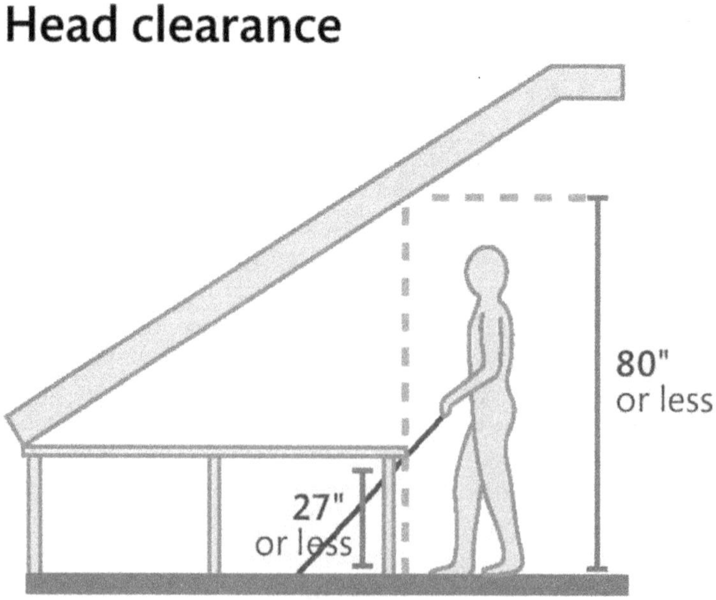

Figure 10.1. Example of head clearance as shown on the Universal Design Quick Reference Poster.
Source: Museum of Science, Boston

When designing a new exhibition, be sure to consider diverse cognitive, physical, and social access. Whenever possible, incorporate planning for these diverse needs early on in the design process, when it is still easy to make changes. After all, it costs a lot more to retrofit something than it does to design it right the first time! When examining a space or exhibition, consider the following questions:[2]

- Can a diverse population of individuals interact with and relate to the space?
- Can people easily and safely move around the space, whether on foot or with the assistance of mobility devices?
- Is the information presented in a variety of ways and formats so that a wide range of individuals can understand it?
- Can people of varying abilities easily manipulate interactives or engage with the space?

There are numerous guides available that can help when designing accessible exhibitions and, more generally, accessible museum spaces. Two of these, **Design for Accessibility: A Cultural Administrators Handbook** (National Assembly of State Arts Agencies, 1994) and **Smithsonian Guidelines for Accessible Exhibition Design** (Smithsonian Accessibility Program), have been around for more than twenty years and are filled with much of what you want and need to know about accessible exhibitions. It should be noted that while **Design for Accessibility** has a wealth of information, some content in this guide is outdated due to changes in the laws. Other guides are more concise, albeit incredibly useful, including the **Universal Design Plan** from the Museum of Science in Boston. In addition to their guide, the Museum of Science, Boston also has a "Universal Design Quick Reference" poster which can be printed to scale so that designers can use it for reference when planning exhibition spaces (it is approximately six feet long when printed out).[2] These tools are helpful for exhibition designers, facilities maintenance departments, and even museum educators and evaluators. If designers of the International Waffle Hall had used the accessibility design guides, Harry and Sally's visit would have been quite different.

Designing for Physical Access

The ability to move around a space is perhaps one of the most important aspects of visiting an exhibition. Using the seven principles of universal design, most environments and products can be produced with physical inclusion in mind.[3] Having exhibit teams who understand and are committed to including these principles in their designs means that the teams "will work to create experiences that are accessible and educational for a broad range of visitors" of all abilities.[4]

Navigation and Pathways

Visitors need to be able to move around with ease within an exhibition space. Pathways need to be clear, "well lit, stable, firm, slip-resistant, unobstructed and at least 36 inches wide."[5] A wider pathway—one that is sixty inches wide or more—is preferable since it allows for another person walking or using a wheelchair to pass by if someone is stopped, or for two people using mobility devices to move through the exhibit alongside one another. Accessible routes should be as direct and short as possible. If every route is not accessible, make sure you have clear signage that indicates the location of the accessible route. If an exhibition space dead-ends into a wall, make sure to leave enough space for a person in a wheelchair to be able to easily turn around to leave (a minimum of sixty inches). Navigation should be clear, especially for people who use a wheelchair or other mobility device. Elevators or ramps should be present, easily connecting all parts of the museum (exceptions of course for historic buildings). For large exhibitions it is important to have more than one exit: "Mid-point exits from exhibitions (particularly large exhibitions) assist those who become tired, confused, or overwhelmed when in an exhibition."[6]

Interactives

One of the most common questions about designing accessible exhibitions is about interactives—areas of visitor engagement like videos, response walls, tactile materials, etc. All cases, pedestals, and interactives should be viewable by people who are shorter, be it seated, or standing. It is important to make sure your interactives, as well as casework, are no higher than forty-eight inches above the floor or else visitors of short stature or who use wheelchairs cannot easily reach the objects or controls.[7] The best height for interactives is a range between thirty-six and forty-eight inches from the floor. This ensures they are accessible to adults as well as children. Additionally, try to minimize the amount of distance a person has to reach to engage with an interactive component. For interactives with some sort of obstruction (a counter, flat surface, etc.), they should be twenty-seven to forty-eight inches off the floor, and the depth of the obstruction should be twenty inches or less. For exhibition components that can be accessed without an obstruction, they should be fifteen to forty-eight inches from the ground if accessible from the front. For side access a component should be thirty-four inches or less from the ground, with less than a ten-inch depth. In addition to thinking about the height and reach of interactive components, you also need to consider the angle of the interactives. For labels and interactives that can easily be read or used by people either sitting or standing, a forty-five degree angle is best for readability. For interactives with buttons, it is recommended to leave a space for people to rest their hands. In this case, a thirty degree angle should be used.[8]

Seating

Every exhibition designer's mantra should be, "There is never enough seating!" In any exhibition space be sure to include comfortable and accessible seating. These seats should have backrests, armrests, and should be between seventeen to nineteen inches off the floor. According to the **Smithsonian Guidelines for Accessible Design,** the additional support offered by back and arm rests "is essential for people who have mobility impairments: arms and backs offer people support points when lowering themselves into as well as when rising out of seats."[9] Back and arm rests are also useful additions for older adult visitors, women who are pregnant, people on crutches, etc. Accessible seating should be located in each gallery or exhibition space. For smaller spaces that may not realistically be able to

Reach

When possible minimize forward reach

Obstructed

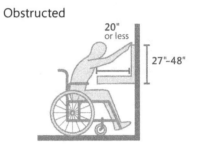

Unobstructed

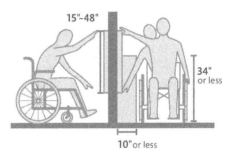

Figure 10.2. Obstructed and unobstructed reach measurements.
Source: Museum of Science, Boston

accommodate seating, place seating in a nearby area. Seating can be fixed in place or moveable (like racks of stools outside exhibition entrances that visitors can take with them if they need). Seating should not be a tripping hazard or barrier for people with mobility disabilities. Many museums will center their seating on an artwork or artifact. Placing seating slightly off-center of the object in focus allows individuals in mobility devices to also view the object from a centralized viewpoint, instead of consistently being stuck on the periphery of good viewing range. It is also helpful to define individual seats, similar to seating on busses and trains. By defining an individual seat, it provides a cue to visitors not to spread themselves or their belongings over the entire seating area. Many people are uncomfortable asking an unknown visitor to move over so they can rest.

Existing Spaces

The suggestions above are particularly useful if you are designing a new exhibition or museum space, but what if you are designing within the confines of an existing space? Start by auditing your space using the checklists referenced in chapter 4 and Boston's quick reference poster. Do you have a wide enough turning radius for people who use wheelchairs? Is there enough circulation space between freestanding objects and pedestals? In the case that you need to remove something to make room for seating, say a bench, you will need to weigh the value of having fewer works of art or artifacts for people to engage with versus visitors possibly skipping entire sections of exhibitions in order to find seating elsewhere in the museum. These are just a few of the things to look for while auditing your existing exhibitions for physical accessibility.

Accessible Cognitive Design

In addition to being physically accessible, exhibition content must be understandable and clear so that "a diversity of individuals can cognitively engage with the materials."[10] Information should be conveyed through a range of media, allowing individuals with different learning styles and abilities to engage with the exhibition materials. The materials used should consider the variety of experiences and knowledge possessed by your wide range of visitors, as well as supporting their range of learning styles and cognitive diversity.

Accessible Exhibition Labels

When writing labels keep in mind who you are writing for. According to the Centers for Disease Control and Prevention, only 12 percent of adults "scored in the highest literacy proficiency levels."[11] Writing clearly does not mean oversimplifying, but it does mean "writing for people who are not experts in the subject."[12] Labels should be suited for as many different readers as possible. Best practice for accessible exhibition labels is writing at a sixth to eighth grade reading level.[13] Keep in mind that you can include higher-level vocabulary words as long as they are used as adjectives, not nouns, and are written in a way that the labels would still make sense without them.[14] For example,

This ornate punchbowl is made out of silver and ruby colored glass.
This ~~ornate~~ punchbowl is made out of silver and ~~ruby colored~~ glass.

Most visitors when given a choice between a short or long label will read the ones that look easier, shorter, and have larger print.

The content of labels is not the only thing you must consider when thinking about accessible labels. Font size, typeface, and text color are also essential features, as well as the placement of text panels within the space. When selecting a typeface to use, designers may want to choose something that is visually interesting (such as a script or handwriting style font), however, sans serif or simple serif fonts are the easiest to read by people with low vision, cognitive disabilities, or early language learners. Decorative fonts should only be used as design elements, provided that the content can also be found elsewhere. At a minimum, the size of the main body text labels should be in twenty-two point font, but twenty-eight to thirty-two point font is preferred. Designers should avoid using all caps or bold lettering (titles excepted), and italics should be used only occasionally. These all help with readability. Text should be left-justified and you should not have any hyphenated words at the end of lines. All these things will make your exhibition labels easier to read and understood by all visitors.

When designing the look of text panels, simple is best. Avoid placing background images, graphics, patterns, etc. behind the text. Panels should be as simple as possible with a high contrast between the text and background color. Some people cannot read text if there is not sufficient contrast between the text and background, for example, light gray text on a light background. Ideally, for fonts smaller than thirty-six point, the contrast should be at least 70 percent between the words and the background. For a basic text panel (those without any sort of interactive element), hang the labels between forty-two to seventy inches off the ground, with the center of the panel at fifty-two to fifty-four inches from the ground.

Up to this point we have been discussing labels written in English. If you have the capacity to create bilingual or multilingual labels, go for it! Many museums are now adding a second or even third language to their labels when they are creating and installing new exhibitions. Determine in which language it would be most helpful to have your labels translated into, based on either your visitorship or community makeup. Many museums automatically assume they should be translating their exhibit text into Spanish. Do not immediately assume this is the second most used language by your visitors. Take for example the Children's Discovery Museum of San

Jose, California. They assumed that Spanish was naturally the language they should be creating bilingual materials in. When they did not see an increase in visitorship from the zip codes closest to the museum after installing Spanish-language labels, they looked at the demographics and discovered that the largest population of people living near the museum actually spoke Vietnamese. They have now added labels and signage in Vietnamese, after which they saw an uptick in local visitation to their museum.[15] Using this example as a lesson, be sure to survey your community or review visitor demographics to determine which language or languages would be the best to include in your museum.

For permanent exhibitions that cannot easily (nor quickly) be changed out, there are several options for including additional languages. Museums with more resources can of course update and redesign current labels to include additional languages. For smaller institutions one option is to create multilingual translations of your labels and make them available for visitors in an inexpensive format to use during their visit. These could be printed in booklet form and made available at the front desk, or even in wall-mounted brochure holders in the exhibit spaces themselves. Simply print, laminate, and attach with a loose-leaf ring. A handy tool to check label contrast and readability is Google's Translate app. Using a smartphone camera, this app can read and translate text into a variety of languages. If your text can be read by an app like this, it is likely that visitors will be able to translate your labels into many more languages than your museum is generally able to provide.

One other type of label to consider including in your exhibitions is an audio label. Audio labels are recorded and read aloud either automatically (by motion sensor) or manually (with the push of a button on an exhibition

Figure 10.3.   Example of a QR code being used to access audio labels.
Source: Flint Hills Design

structure or device). Audio labels can be particularly helpful to a variety of visitors: people who are blind or have low vision, people who have learning disabilities, young children who are learning to read, sighted visitors who want to read along with the audio, or even nonnative English speakers. If you are planning to include audio labels along with your printed labels, be sure to keep the audio label in mind while writing the exhibition text. Write your printed text labels so they can easily be read on a recording. This is not only helpful for the audio labels but also for groups who choose to read the labels

---

GENERAL EXHIBITION DESIGN TIPS

Each of the accessibility design manuals discussed above contains a wealth of information. We wanted to pull together just a few general tips that are helpful to consider (keeping you from having to dig through all of the pages in the manuals):

- Keep entrance labels short! Ideally, these labels should only be forty or so words in length and be conversational in tone. This ensures that almost anyone can read them without needing help.
- When designing labels use a contrast checker to make sure your contrast is high enough between the text and the background. There are a variety of contrast checkers available online.
- Be redundant. Communicate the same information through multiple channels (tactile, visual, auditory, etc.). This provides multiple opportunities for people to be exposed to the information (after all, we know that some people do not read all of the information on labels!).
- Backlit rails fade over time. Use something with more longevity or plan on budgeting to replace these more often.
- Knobs are not the best choice to use on interactives, levers are better. Knobs can be successful provided they pass the pencil test: can you move it with a pencil? If so, then most people with limited mobility will be able to use the knob.
- Sliders are another great alternative to knobs. Use sliders with a cut out instead of a knob so that visitors can catch the slider and move it with whatever they can (hand, elbow, etc.).
- Increase the turning radius clearance in your spaces to account for larger wheelchairs and electric scooters. The current federal requirement is sixty inches, however, a change to sixty-six to seventy-two inch turning radius is likely on the horizon due to an increase of lawsuits by people with larger wheelchairs and electric scooters.
- And of course, seating, seating, seating! Include as much as you can, and ensure they have arms and backs.

aloud. Audio labels can be incorporated directly into the exhibition panels, made available on a website accessible by scannable QR code, or even as part of a mobile app.[16]

Accessible Wayfinding

A wayfinding system is helpful to guide visitors more easily through museum spaces and exhibitions that can be complex to navigate. In addition to a typical handheld paper map, the **Smithsonian Guidelines for Accessible Design** recommends having raised-line or tactile maps available to support people with cognitive disabilities or visual impairments easily travel throughout your exhibitions. A raised line map in a museum setting contains basic information of the location of walls, stairs, doors, and large obstructions (such as a fountain or even the front desk). A tactile map contains even more information and uses a key with different forms of textures representing different types of objects or areas. For permanent spaces and exhibitions (that will not change), a museum could create a fixed position map or kiosk with tactile representation of the space, while for spaces that regularly change a portable map, that can also be changed, is best. All portable museum maps should be available in the same location so that visitors can make the choice on what type of map they would like to use on their visit.

Another consideration for accessible wayfinding is signage. **Design for Accessibility** explains that "signage is a much overlooked accessibility asset."[17] Signs help visitors understand where they are and to make decisions on where they want to go. Signage can support visitors with disabilities when it directs to fundamental facilities like accessible routes and entrances, restrooms, and emergency exits. Often icons or symbols are used because the majority of people can recognize and understand pictographs and international symbols, including non-English speakers, regardless if they understand the primary language in use. Consistency is key with accessible signage, all elements should have a consistent look, placement, and function.

Auditory Access

Currently, the World Health Organization estimates that 5 percent of the world's population has disabling hearing loss. By 2050, that is expected to double to one in ten people (more than nine hundred million in total).[18] In the United States, approximately 20 percent of the population has hearing loss, and this number is steadily increasing with the aging population. Captioning in-gallery video components enables members of the D/deaf and hard of hearing community to still fully participate in museum exhibitions. There are

THE INTERNATIONAL SYMBOL OF ACCESS

Figure 10.4. Original International Symbol of Access, designed in 1968.
Source: Accessible Icon Project

In 1968, Danish student Susanne Koefoed submitted an entry into a design competition held by Rehabilitation International. Her design, with a few modifications, was selected to become the International Symbol of Access (ISA). ISA was adopted by the International Organization for Standardization, and has been the global icon for accessibility for more than fifty years.[1] The symbol is used to indicate, and provide direction to, accessible spaces and elements, including the locations of accessible entrances and paths, parking spaces, accessible vehicles, bathrooms, and even check-out aisles.

There is a movement underway to replace the current ISA static image of a person sitting in a wheelchair with a more dynamic image. The proposed new image features a person in a wheelchair leaning forward, actively appearing to move their body through space. The active nature of this updated design indicates that the person with the disability is the "decision maker about his or her mobility."[2] The movement to change the icon "speaks to the general primacy of personhood, and to the notion that the person first decides how and why s/he will navigate the world, in the broadest literal and metaphorical terms."[3]

Figure 10.5. New symbol of access designed by the Accessible Icon Project.
Source: Accessible Icon Project

Several states and cities have adopted the new symbol, however, not everyone is on board with its use. Some disability rights activists are concerned that the new symbol could imply prejudice toward "people with more serious disabilities."[4] The US government also weighed in on the new symbol. In March 2017, the United States Access Board issued guidance on the use of the ISA symbol and other similar symbols. According to Marsha Mazz, director of the Access Board's Office of Technical and Information Services, "Consistency in the use of universal symbols is important, especially for persons with limited vision or cognitive disabilities."[5] ISA is a worldwide symbol identifying accessible elements and spaces. Many federal codes require the use of ISA. Under the ADA Standards there are no specific substitutes for ISA, however, alternative symbols may be used as long as they "provide substantially equivalent or greater accessibility and usability."[6] So the question remains, should the current ISA be updated to include a more active figure? Or should the symbol remain the same since uniform iconography promotes legibility amongst people with disabilities?

1. ISO is an independent organization that represents more than 160 national entities and develops international, consensus-based, voluntary standards.

2. "International Symbol of Accessibility," Rehabilitation International, accessed October 13, 2019, http://www.riglobal.org/about/intl-symbol-of-access/.

3. "Notes on Design Activism," The Accessible Icon Project, accessed October 13, 2019, http://accessibleicon.org/.

4. Rehabilitation International, "International Symbol of Accessibility."

5. "Access Board Issues Guidance on the International Symbol of Accessibility," News, United States Access Board, accessed October 13, 2019, https://www.access-board.gov/news/1899-access-board-issues-guidance-on-the-international-symbol-of-accessibility.

6. United States Access Board, "Access Board Issues Guidance on Use of the International Symbol of Accessibility."

two types of captions for use on in-gallery and website videos: open captioning and closed captioning. Open captions are always on and are essentially embedded into the video. Closed captioning, on the other hand, can be turned on or off as the user desires. Closed captioning has been around since the 1970s. The American Broadcasting Corporation first tested these out on February 15, 1972, when they embedded closed captions within a broadcast of the television show **Mod Squad**.[19] Closed captioning has gone from being an experimental service intended exclusively for people who are D/deaf to a "truly global communications service that touches the lives of millions of people every day in vital ways."[20] Regardless of which type of captioning you choose, **all** of your museum's videos should be captioned, whether onsite or online (just make sure there is an easy and obvious way for visitors to turn captions on and off if you choose to close caption). Only as a last resort should you have a printed transcript of the video's audio content available for your in-gallery or website videos.

If you are having a video professionally produced, the production company will most likely include an option for captioning (make sure to ask about this if the company does not automatically bring it up). For videos created in-house, there are several options to consider when adding captions. Some video hosting sites, such as YouTube and Vimeo, have the ability to automatically caption videos for free. Automated captions are not completely accurate, so a staff member will need to go in and edit. We detail further captioning resources in appendix A.

Captions on videos can be useful for nonnative English speakers, people with cognitive disabilities, visual learners, and for people who are D/deaf and hard of hearing. Some D/deaf visitors communicate primarily in sign language, a complete language that is grammatically separate from English. American Sign Language (ASL) is often taught to children born D/deaf or who lose their hearing at an early age. So for many D/deaf people, written English is actually their second language. As a result, for some individuals who communicate primarily through ASL it can be challenging to read and understand captions at the rate they are presented in videos. Therefore, to be more inclusive of the D/deaf community, a museum can include ASL video options in their videos (where there is a synchronized video of a sign language interpreter in the corner or beside the video content).[21]

Figure 10.6. Photograph from the Musee d'Orsay showing a split screen with French sign language.
Source: Danielle Schulz

Accessible Social Design

We all have fascinating things we want to share with our audiences—artifacts, artwork, animals—but these are not the only things visitors are coming to experience. They are also visiting as a way to spend time with their friends, family, or social groups. It is our duty as museum professionals to support visitors who wish to experience our artifacts and artworks in a group by designing exhibitions that are accessible to a wide range of people. Ask yourself if your exhibitions are inclusive so that everyone can participate. Does the environment feel safe and welcoming for people of all abilities? Can diverse groups of people easily engage with the exhibitions and each other, or with museum staff? One way to ensure that all your visitors can engage with your exhibition content is by providing multimodal options; that is, using multiple methods (or modes) to share concepts and communicate information (via visual, auditory, spatial, and/or linguistic means). For example, if you have an exhibition on tigers, you can show a picture of a tiger (or the real live animal), play a sound of what a tiger sounds like, and maybe even offer a raised line drawing or a tactile component that would be similar to what a tiger feels like. These multimodal options enable visitors with a variety of abilities and learning styles to access different information and learn something about tigers.

Multimodal components should enhance visitors' understanding of the exhibition. Therefore, whatever elements are available should be both easy to find and use. Avoid tucking away content into some corner that no one can find or making the activity so complicated to use that people are not successful when they try it out. As you are designing these interactive areas, consider how far apart your multimodal engagement options are located from the source object. If they are too far apart, how can you move them closer together? Multimodal options should be proximal to the main component that they relate to. So in the case of the tiger exhibit, having audio description of a tiger around the corner from where you actually see the animal limits the effectiveness of the audio option. Instead, place it closer to the physical location of the animal, specimen, or illustration of the animal.

INCLUSIVE PROGRAMMING

Accessible exhibitions can be a jumping off point for in-gallery educational activities that can create further inclusive connections between visitors and the museum's collection. Museum educators can also use universal design principles to guide program development and create learning environments that are accessible and effective for all. As explained by the Museum of Science in Boston, "Using a universal design approach in museum education ensures that experiences are designed with inclusion in mind . . . so that people with a wide range of abilities and disabilities can interact without relying on specialized devices or other members of their group."[22] Below are a few examples of accessible educational activities meant to spark further ideas for what is possible.

Touch Tours

For people who are blind or have low vision, touch can be the primary way to acquire information. Tactile experiences can support individuals to complete their mental picture of an artifact or work of art. There are a variety of ways to offer touch tours in your museum. You can use original artworks or artifacts from your collection (which can be handled), or you can use replicas, models, or props that are close to the original but safe for visitors to touch. Three-dimensional interpretations or re-creations of objects can replicate basic object form and color as well as translate stylistic properties, such as texture and brushwork, into a touchable experience. Some museums offer visitors the opportunity to touch original artworks with the assistance of a trained educator or volunteer docent (these are typically sculptures, or other 3-D artifacts). Still, other museums allow visitors who are blind or have low vision to have self-guided exploration of certain objects on their own (touchable objects are labeled or identified in some way and staff are given additional training to direct people to these items).

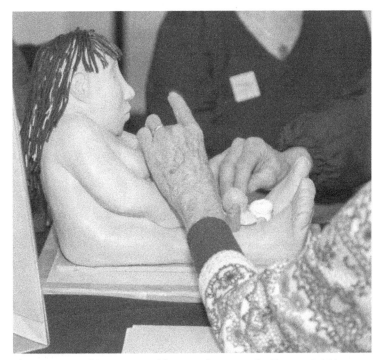

Figure 10.7. Visitors engaged in a touch tour at the Denver Art Museum.
Source: Denver Art Museum

TEN TOUCH TOUR TIPS

1. Tactile experiences are good for all learners, not just your visitors with low vision or blindness. Encourage docents and program leaders to include tactile opportunities in all their tours and programs.
2. When planning a touch tour, work with whomever is in charge of your collection (in most cases the curator or conservator) to determine what objects would be appropriate for a touch tour (you want to avoid fragile objects or items that could easily be damaged). They might have suggestions about how you could create a replica of an object with similar materials.
3. If possible, provide verbal descriptions and background information of the objects you are going to tour on your website or send it to participants ahead of time to help them prepare for what they are going to see.
4. Make sure that the objects included on your tour are physically accessible to participants (remember, people may have multiple disabilities or are different sizes). Make sure that visitors can reach all parts of the object you are discussing. If it is a particularly large piece, provide tactile diagrams to support.
5. Limit guided touch tours to three to five objects and keep your groups small (three to six people) so that people have time to discuss and respond to what they are exploring.
6. When giving a guided touch tour, include a verbal description of the space you are in to help orient people. Also, as you move from one space to another in the museum, give brief verbal descriptions of the galleries and spaces you are passing through (a few words are fine, just enough to give participants information on the size and scope of the museum or exhibit).
7. For any sort of touch tour program, make sure to include additional time for processing the tactile experiences of the tour.
8. Whenever possible, find a way to be involved with early exhibition planning. This will make it easier for you to work with curators to suggest types of art or artifacts that would be useful to have on a touch tour. Of course, by participating in the exhibition planning you can also help bring awareness to accessibility and inclusion in your museum.
9. Think outside the box! There are a variety of different places you can look for tactile objects for your tours, if objects in your collection are not available. Depending on what you are looking for (and of course your resources), you could commission local artists to create tactile paintings, replicas of statues, and so on. Several online retailers offer replica or reproductions sources, particularly for ethnographic or

historic objects. You can even use everyday objects to enhance tours and encourage discussion. Look at partnering with a local design or art school to have students re-create artifacts or works of art as part of a class project.

10. Never underestimate your museum store! Many museum stores carry replicas or models of objects from the collection that you could purchase for use in your tours and programs.

Verbal Description

Verbal description (also known as audio description) is another resource for increasing access to exhibition content, especially for those visitors who are blind or have low vision. Verbal description uses "non-visual language to convey the visual world. It can navigate a visitor through a museum, orient a listener to a work of art, or provide access to the visual aspects of a performance."[23] Recall the beginning of this book when we described the Duke of Urbino. Did the image in your head change when you were given additional details, such as the shape of his hat? That was a brief verbal description in written form. Verbal description, on its own or in conjunction with multisensory experiences, can bring art and artifacts to life for people with vision impairments. Art Beyond Sight, an organization working to make museums and cultural institutions accessible to people who are blind or have low vision, has numerous training materials on its website to use with museum staff to create verbal description scripts for objects that can be used on live tours or recorded for online or in-gallery use. You can download examples of verbal description by searching for Art Beyond Sight on iTunes. Additionally, the verbal description training page of their website has a variety of examples for describing historical objects, paintings, interiors, small decorative items, and more.

Descriptive audio tours are different from verbal description tours. Descriptive audio tours provide step-by-step directions for visitors who are blind or have low vision. For an exhibition on the senses, the Cooper Hewitt museum created a descriptive audio tour to accompany the exhibit. Here is a brief excerpt from that tour:

> Attached to the tabletop are a small push button and two round, black pods, about the diameter of a soda can. A headset hangs on the front of the table to the left of the pods. I put on the headset and then press the button to play some music. Now, I gently rest my hands on the pods, and I can feel the music as a vibration. I'm hearing the music in the headset, and feeling that same sound vibrate through my palms.[24]

Compare this to the verbal description in figure 10.6. Descriptive audio tours contain less specific information about each object, and instead provide more information about the gallery space including what to do and expect in the exhibition. Both types of tours are beneficial to visitors and provide distinct information that can lead to a holistic understanding of an exhibition.

Figure 10.8.   This gilt brass sculpture from the Rubin Museum of Arts collection stands seven inches high by five inches wide and is about 2.5 inches deep. The sculpture is of a comparable size to that of an outspread adult human hand. Created in the eighteenth century during the Shang Dynasty, it depicts a wrathful deity Damchen Garwai Nagpo sitting sidesaddle on a goat frozen in a dynamic pose.
Source: Annotated image of Damchen Garwai Nagpo; China; eighteenth century; Gilt brass; Rubin Museum of Art; C2005.16.65 (HAR 65488). From a demonstration of the Rubin Museum of Art's Verbal Description Tours.

Multilingual Tours

Earlier in this chapter we discussed multilingual labels. Just like labels based on the demographics of your community, determine which languages are most used in your surrounding community and then offer museum tours in those languages, preferably led by native speakers of those languages. While it would be ideal to have multiple multilingual tours each day, the reality is that most museums do not have the resources to provide this variety of tours each day. Whenever possible try to include tours in ASL to be welcoming for visitors who are D/deaf. As a distinct language—with its own rules for word order, pronunciation, and word formation—ASL is a "complete, natural language that has the same linguistic properties as spoken languages, with grammar that differs from English."[25] Since it is a distinct language from English, it therefore follows that there is also a difference between a tour led in ASL and one that is ASL-interpreted. ASL tours are led by a person who is a native speaker or fluent in sign language who delivers the tour content in ASL, without voice interpretation. An interpreted tour is given by a hearing person and then translated into ASL after the fact by an interpreter. A D/deaf person attending an ASL-interpreted tour is similar to an English-speaking hearing person joining a foreign language tour and receiving an English translation. For people whose native language is not English, it can be frustrating to try to understand tours that are only offered in English. As the adage goes, there are things that get lost in translation. People in your community want to visit your museum, but they want to feel welcome doing so. Tours given by native speakers or people fluent in a language is a welcoming and inclusive gesture.

In addition to live tours in other languages, there are also opportunities to use audio guides or self-led audio components to meet diverse language needs. Tours can be recorded in multiple languages, including a sign language video. These audio and video files can be saved on your website and then accessed in gallery using a QR code that a visitor can access with their smartphone. This option may not be perfect, but it illustrates to your visitors that you are trying to do something to meet their language needs. Creating accessible programs is a great opportunity to engage your advisory group (discussed in chapters 2 and 3) and open up to ask for feedback. Your communities can guide you on designing and even leading multilingual tours.

Providing Options

People should have the choice of opting into using additional resources and tools to support their museum visit. For example, someone does not need to be D/deaf or hard of hearing to choose to read the captions on a video. Similarly, someone who is blind or has low vision can choose to participate in a touch tour if they want to, however, if they want to simply visit the exhibition with their friends on their own time, that should be an available option as well. While dedicated programs may be available for a variety of audiences with disabilities, individuals of all abilities should be able to opt in or out of these specialized programs. People with disabilities should not be limited to only attending these programs, which would exclude them from experiences open to everyone.

START AT THE BEGINNING

Anytime you can start a project and make it accessible from the very beginning, the better the project will be. Ask any designer; if you have to retrofit something to make it accessible, it is going to be more expensive than if you designed with accessibility in mind from the beginning. Bring accessibility into discussions early on to get inclusive language in the goal and design principle documents as part of the early design phase. This will make it easier for everyone to understand and stick to the plan. If you wait too late into the design process to suggest or request changes, it is going to feel like a burden and discourage others from embracing accessibility as a part of their work.

In many organizations there is one person charged with overseeing accessibility (if you are lucky). In most cases, it is just one part of a person's job, rather than their full-time role (as is the case with the authors of this book). In reality, access touches upon all parts of an organization. If you are the person whose job it is (whether in full or in part) to lead accessibility initiatives in your museum, whenever you can, get involved in the exhibition design process. But it is important to know your role and remember to be diplomatic. Scale your asks for where you are. Depending on your organization and the people you work with, you may only be able to really push for one thing at a time at the beginning; however, even increasing the size of the font on exhibit labels can make a huge difference for many. Again, thinking about your role, you might pick one accessibility issue on each project to push or one thing to retrofit. But do keep bringing it up. Accessibility should come up in conversation at almost every planning meeting. The goal should be to get to the point where those who always bring up accessibility (namely you!) do not have to bring it up as regularly because someone else does! Once you get to this point, your museum has truly begun to embrace accessibility and inclusion as a part of the organization's identity.

ROLL THE WALK AND SIGN THE TALK

Exhibitions and programs are two of the ways that museums convey information to their visitors. Ensuring that spaces and experiences are accessible to all broadens the reach museums have, making them a trusted anchor in any community. Greater access to exhibitions and educational programs enhances everyone's visit to the museum and ensures people with disabilities can engage on the same level as other visitors.

WORKING DOG OR PET?

There is a lot of confusion about allowing service dogs in museum exhibits. For the sake of museum collections, most museums do not allow pets into their buildings. Service dogs (and miniature horses), however, are legal exceptions to this rule. There are three types of roles a dog can serve to help a person with a disability: service dogs, therapy dogs, and emotional support animals. How are these similar and how are they different?

Service dogs are trained to help a person with disabilities live a more independent life. According to the ADA, a service animal is a dog "that is individually trained to do work or perform tasks for a person with a disability."[1] **Therapy dogs** receive training but have different jobs from service dogs. They provide psychological or physiological therapy to individuals at many different places such as hospitals, schools, nursing homes, etc. **Emotional support animals,** on the other hand, are not specifically trained to do a job. Instead, they provide emotional support and can help ease anxiety, depression, and other related disorders.[2]

According to the ADA, a service dog is just like any other medical device and corresponding legal status, and therefore must be allowed the same access to spaces as its handler.[3] If you are uncertain about whether an animal is a service animal, you are legally allowed to ask the following two questions:

- Is the dog needed to help with a disability?
- What tasks is it trained to perform?

If the answer to the first question is yes, proceed onto the second question. Just be aware that this question can sometimes be hard for people to answer because they may disclose more detail about their medical history than they feel comfortable giving to a stranger in a museum. Legally, you **cannot** ask about a person's disability—on top of being illegal, it is also intrusive to guests of your museum.

Service animals can be trained to do a variety of tasks. These tasks can include:

- Assistance with mobility (such as guiding, bracing, pulling, stabilizing)
- Retrieving items for their handler, picking up and returning dropped items, or even going to get help if their handler needs it
- Alerting their handler to the presence of someone or to sounds
- Alerting their handler to oncoming seizures, or other medical alerts

Staff are not allowed to ask for a demonstration of the tasks the dog is trained to perform, regardless of whether or not they think the dog in question may or may not be a service animal. If someone tries to present an ID card, certification, or vest as proof that their dog is a service animal, understand that there is no federal authority that regulates service animals in the United States. This means there are no **official** ways to ID a service animal. Chances are the person presenting these documents may be simply trying to pass their dog off as a service dog. Vests are not required to be worn by service animals, however many handlers use them with their animals because it sends a visual signal to others that this is a working dog and should not be petted.

If a service animal is being disruptive, it is up to the handler to stop the behavior. The dog should be in a heel position unless it is doing something for its handler. If a service animal is making noise, running around without attending to a task, begging for attention or food from other visitors, or is not potty trained, you can ask the handler to remove the dog. Staff are sometimes concerned that this will come off as kicking out the person with a disability, however, handlers know that their dogs need to behave and that you are asking the dog to leave, not them. Dogs have off days just like people do.

1. "Service Animals," United States Department of Justice, accessed September 5, 2019, https://www.ada.gov/service_animals_2010.htm.

2. Kristi Moore, "Welcoming Service Dogs to Your Museum," **American Alliance of Museums**, August 26, 2019, https://www.aam-us.org/2019/08/26/welcoming-service-dogs-to-your-museum/._

3. "Frequently Asked Questions about Service Animals and the ADA," United States Department of Justice, accessed September 2, 2019, https://www.ada.gov/regs2010/service_animal_qa.html#def.

NOTES

1. "Museum Facts & Data," American Alliance of Museums, accessed September 7, 2019, https://www.aam-us.org/programs/about-museums/museum-facts-data/#_edn23.

2. "Universal Design for Museum Learning Experiences," Museum of Science, Boston, accessed September 9, 2019, https://www.mos.org/UniversalDesign.

3. The seven principles of universal design are described in detail in chapter 4 of this book.

4. Museum of Science, Boston, **Universal Design Plan.**

5. **Design for Accessibility: A Cultural Administrators Handbook** (Washington, DC: National Assembly of State Arts Agencies, 1994), 68.

6. "Smithsonian Guidelines for Accessible Exhibition Design," Smithsonian Accessibility Program, accessed June 18, 2019, https://www.si.edu/Accessibility/SGAED.

7. **Design for Accessibility**, 73.

8. Museum of Science, Boston, **Universal Design Plan**.

9. **Smithsonian Guidelines for Accessible Design**.

10. Museum of Science, Boston, **Universal Design Plan**.

11. Adults were scored as a part of the Program for the International Assessment of Adult Competencies, a comparative study done across twenty-three countries. "Understanding Literacy & Numeracy," Centers for Disease Control and Prevention, accessed September 27, 2019, https://www.cdc.gov/healthliteracy/learn/Understand ingLiteracy.html.

12. Beverly Serrell, **Exhibit Labels: An Interpretive Approach** (Lanham, MD: Rowman Altamira, 1996), 95.

13. Serrell, **Exhibit Labels**, 97.

14. In her book **Exhibit Labels: An Interpretive Approach,** Beverly Serrell gives several other examples of how to do this in her chapter on selecting the right reading level.

15. Jenni Martin and Marilee Jennings, "Tomorrow's Museum: Multilingual Audiences and the Learning Institution," **Museums & Social Issues** 10, no. 1 (2015): 83–94, http://dx.doi.org/10.1179/1559689314Z.00000000034.

16. We recommend consulting Boston's Museum of Science **Universal Design Guide** as to the placement, shape, etc. of audio label buttons.

17. **Design for Accessibility**, 75.

18. "Deafness and Hearing Loss," World Health Organization, accessed September 29, 2019, https://www.who.int/news-room/fact-sheets/detail/deafness-and-hearing -loss.

19. "History of Closed Captioning," National Captioning Institute, accessed September 29, 2019, https://www.ncicap.org/about-us/history-of-closed-captioning/.

20. National Captioning Institute, "History of Closed Captioning."

21. The World Wide Web Consortium has some techniques for how to best do this, available here: https://www.w3.org/TR/WCAG20-TECHS/G54.html.

22. Museum of Science, Boston, "Universal Design for Museum Learning Experiences."

23. "Verbal Description Training," Art Beyond Sight, accessed October 1, 2019, http://www.artbeyondsight.org/mei/verbal-description-training/.

24. "The Senses: Descriptive Audio Tour," Cooper Hewitt, Smithsonian Design Museum, accessed October 2, 2019, https://www.cooperhewitt.org/2018/05/24/the -senses-descriptive-audio-tour/.

25. "American Sign Language," National Institute on Deafness and Other Communication Disorders (NIDCD), National Institutes of Health, accessed October 3, 2019, https://www.nidcd.nih.gov/health/american-sign-language.

Chapter Eleven

All Aboard

Professional Development and Staff Training

Perhaps your museum has successfully created an accessible website, supports visitors to navigate your building through universal signage, and engages them through inclusive exhibitions—but what about their interactions with museum staff? Employee and volunteer training is an essential building block of an accessible museum, and yet it is an element that is often neglected. If paid staff and volunteers effuse bias, use negative and disabling language, or simply do not know enough to speak about the museum's accessible accommodations, all the work you have done to create a welcoming and inclusive environment is effectively canceled out.

To address this disconnect between an accessible environment and unprepared staff, first make accessibility a dedicated part of someone's job. Next, provide focused professional development opportunities to support that person to spearhead this work. Finally, give this person the resources they need to expand their knowledge base and build a framework to understand accessibility more broadly. Once they have this foundation, they can then begin to outline an accessibility plan, which includes staff training, based on the museum's unique needs and circumstances.

NOT MY JOB

Accessibility is everyone's responsibility. But, before it can be a part of **everyone's** job, it must be **someone's** job. That means writing accessibility coordination specifically into a job description, and even a job title if possible. This position can live in a variety of different museum departments. Typically it is found in education, exhibitions, facilities, or community engagement. Ideally, accessibility oversight should be this employee's primary focus;

however, we recognize that in reality coordinating accessibility initiatives may be one of the many duties a person performs. Regardless, it is important to delegate a person to oversee this important work, as this is a way to hold your museum accountable (both internally and externally) to promoting accessibility and inclusion.

If you work at a museum where accessibility has not yet been written into a job, this is your opportunity to start the conversation. Ask your supervisor about the accessibility plan for your institution, and if there is not one in place, ask how this can be prioritized and how you can take part (we're assuming that if you are reading this book, you want to!). As many museums, businesses, and city agencies are committing more time and resources to diversity, equity, and inclusion work, this can also be a way to connect to accessibility initiatives. Refer back to the very beginning of this book where we discuss DEAI work and its importance. Where there is work on inclusion, there should also be work on accessibility.

To get an idea of what duties and responsibilities this person should have, it can be beneficial to connect with other institutions, ideally in your area, which have a dedicated accessibility coordinator. Ask if they are willing to share the job description for that position. This will allow you to see how the work and associated duties are described. Using this information can be a great way to build your case for creating such a position or having the role to be added to your role and title. Oftentimes, you are already doing this work—fielding accessibility questions and requests, interfacing with groups to schedule American Sign Language (ASL) tours, etc. You may just need a bit of help to define and attribute what you do as "accessibility coordination," and getting your supervisor and museum administration to recognize the work as such. Changing position descriptions and work allocation can take time but having this conversation early and often with your supervisor and administration is a way to truly make progress by illustrating your commitment to this work. It seems contrary, but often you must illustrate how integral accessibility work already is to your institution (and your position) before you can make the case for it to be recognized and named as a staple part of your job.

KNOW WHAT YOU DON'T KNOW

Whether you are new to overseeing accessibility at your institution, or have done it for years, professional development should be a key component of your work. In accessibility there are a lot of unknowns as well as best practices that can shift and change quite quickly. In order to have the most up-to-date information, keep current on best practices and new endeavors from self-advocates, colleagues, and research in the field. It can be intimidating to know exactly where to go and what to look for. We recommend starting at the local level. Regional ADA Centers can be a great first stop for general resources and assistance when getting started. There are ten regional ADA Centers in the United States: New England, Northeast, Mid-Atlantic, Southeast, Great Lakes, Southwest, Great Plains, Rocky Mountain, Pacific, and Northwest.[1] These centers provide information, guidance, and training on the ADA, and often tailor these resources to meet the needs of organizations and businesses at a variety of levels in their regions. Through these centers you can take online or in-person trainings, browse relevant publications, collect data and statistics for your individual state and region, and find specific resources to help you in your daily work (such as links to CART or brailling services).[2] Many of these resources are free or offered at a very low cost, making your regional ADA Center a great first stop when discovering what you need to know on your professional development journey.

Sometimes you need to dive more deeply into a content area or learn more about a specific audience. This can be achieved by looking for local chapters or state affiliates of national organizations in your city or region, such as the Alzheimer's Association, Autism Society, Down Syndrome Society, National Federation of the Blind, Special Olympics, and more. These organizations generally offer helpful resources like local contacts and support networks, data and research, advocacy opportunities, and perhaps even introductory trainings or workshops for the local community. Attending these free or low-cost trainings, in-person or online, is a great way to familiarize yourself with specific audiences in the disability community you may not be familiar with. Additionally, look to your city or state government as a resource, as they may offer research and training workshops through various commissions, health and human services departments, or even the department of labor. Receiving regular newsletters, attending meetings or webinars, or even volunteering can be a great way to get involved with these local partners and can support you to learn more about what they do.

Next on your path to collecting useful sources of information, connect with colleagues in your local community. Who else is working on accessibility initiatives within your city or state? Expand your search to include museums, botanic gardens, libraries, zoos, art centers, performing arts organizations, or other nonprofits of all shapes and sizes. Reach out to staff to learn more about the way they and their museum work. You can ask to observe a specific program, or review support materials, to see how they are designed and implemented. Doing this across a variety of cultural institutions is a great way to see the different approaches taken to address similar situations. For instance, does every museum have wheelchairs on site for visitors to check out free of charge? What does the checkout process look like? How are frontline staff trained to field questions about requesting ASL interpreters? Where do they turn for questions they cannot answer? Do some institutions have large print maps and guides, while others have braille guides? What is the rationale for this decision? Compile a list of the materials and programs that various organizations in your area do and do not offer; this will help you to reflect upon the spectrum of available accessibility materials and better determine what your museum should be offering.

There are also state and regional museum associations that can be valuable assets, especially if you are unsure of what resources are available to you. Nearly every state has its own museum association, and sometimes even smaller cities or counties have established hyper-local museum networks for sharing expertise and resources. More broadly, there are six major regional museum associations that span the country: Association of Midwest Museums, Mid-Atlantic Association of Museum, Mountain-Plains Museum Association, New England Museum Association, Southeastern Museums Conference, and the Western Museums Association. These associations offer advice on best practices, post job listings, assist in the development of professional standards, offer skill-building and training workshops, host webinars and conferences, and generally serve as a forum for collaboration between institutions.[3] Attending their annual conferences, or local meet-ups, is a great way to start connecting with local colleagues who may share your passion for accessibility.

Armed with a good foundation of local options, you can widen your search to learn from colleagues and organizations across the country who are leading the way in accessibility. This can be done digitally—through a focused internet search of museums with strong accessibility programs (when looking up a museum, search for their accessibility page for contact information). It can also be achieved by site visits, where you spend a few hours or days visiting the museum in-person, setting up program observations, meetings with key staff members, and soaking up as much time exploring the museum and its materials as possible.

Another way to connect on a more national level is by attending national conferences and meetings. These convenings are great ways to make connections, learn new techniques and approaches, and achieve a deep dive into best practices. Additionally, you are often able to connect with a large number of colleagues in the field over a short period of time. There are numerous relevant conferences held on an annual basis to choose from, so you have to prioritize depending on your budget. The conference, which is the most focused on accessibility in the arts and cultural sphere, is the Leadership Exchange in Arts and Disability (LEAD), put on annually by the Kennedy Center. Each year new and experienced professionals come together to "explore practical methods for implementing accessibility in cultural environments."[4] Information ranges from foundational building blocks to advanced track discussions that address accessibility in action. Both brand new and seasoned accessibility advocates from around the country (and globe) attend this one-of-a-kind conference that expressly focuses on accessibility in cultural venues. The National ADA Symposium provides the latest information on ADA regulations and guidelines and offers strategies for implementation and best practices in the field.[5] The American Alliance of Museums' annual meeting is another staple conference for many museum professionals, where each year professionals from museums of all shapes and sizes come together to connect, collaborate, and share best practices in the field. These annual conferences are held in a new city each year (and sometimes virtually), offering participants a deep dive into the many museums and cultural offerings of the region.

There are also subject-focused conferences that can enhance your development in a specific content area. To name a few, there is the National Art Education Association with a focus on visual arts engagement; MuseumNext, which brings together museum leaders, makers, and innovators to spark positive change in the museum sector; and the Museum Computer Network (MCN), which seeks to advance digital transformation in museums. Accessibility is not the main focus of these conferences per say, but it is a subject that is garnering more and more attention and increasingly becoming the focus of a growing number of conference presentations. For example, the MCN has stated that accessibility (along with diversity, equity, and inclusion) is one of its five strategic priorities to be embedded in their work. To this end they have started rolling out accommodations at the conference, including improved accessibility guidelines and a new Code of Conduct.[6] It can also be beneficial to look at conferences that specialize in distinct audiences. For example, the American Society on Aging offers their annual Aging in America conference, which focuses on the exploration of issues impacting older adults,[7] while the National Federation of the Blind's National Convention provides training, support, and information for the blind community.[8] Oftentimes these conferences offer scholarships to help people pay for the cost of attending, which can get quite pricey, especially if you are planning to attend more than one. All together these conferences combine to create a well-rounded approach to understanding accessibility in the cultural sphere, with each distinct conference contributing one aspect to a holistic understanding.

A culminating professional development experience for any accessibility coordinator would be achieving an ADA coordinator certification. While not required, a professional certificate in ADA coordination ensures that the individual with this title has demonstrated a mastery of content related to the ADA. The Great Plains ADA Center, as part of the ADA National Network, has established a training curriculum, with forty credit hours, that covers the knowledge essential to performing the role of ADA coordinator.[9] After completing the training, both online and in-person, and passing an exam, you receive the professional certification of ADA coordinator and can use the designated initials ADAC as a way to publicly illustrate that you have met the requirements.

One area of staff training that is often overlooked is crisis training. Keeping people safe should be every museum's priority. Institutions should train staff, especially frontline staff, on what to do when they encounter someone in crisis. Crises can take on many forms, from physically hurting or threatening themselves or others to someone becoming emotionally overwhelmed. By teaching staff how to assist visitors who may be experiencing the fight or flight reaction, museums can help avoid someone getting hurt. The Alliance for Response trains cultural institutions on crisis response by bringing them together with emergency management professionals to protect cultural and historic resources. Trainings range from disaster recovery to active shooter situations.[10]

Professional development, of any scope and scale, is a necessary component in equipping anyone to be successful in this field. It builds up a knowledge base, creates connections with colleagues, expands access to resources, and can support the development of an accessibility roadmap and training plan for a museum to follow.

DEVELOPING A TRAINING PLAN

The goal of any accessible museum should be to establish a paid staff and volunteer base who embody inclusivity in their everyday work and interaction with visitors. This is more than just being aware of the accessibility accommodations and supports on-site (though this is important), it is also about a certain disposition and ability to welcome people of all abilities into an institution. This comes from creating a training structure that shifts behavior, builds a solid knowledge base around services and accommodations, and spreads accountability across the museum.

Accessibility is everyone's responsibility but making that known and accepted by your staff can take time, and more importantly, can take a strategic approach. Effective staff training cannot be covered in a single two-hour session. But neither does it have to be an expensive, time-intensive endeavor. It is important to set clear goals so that you and the staff know what to expect each step of the way and to scaffold the information and learning where concepts build upon one another. Many museum staff are unfamiliar with accessibility initiatives and as a result will not naturally see it as part of their responsibilities. To combat this misconception craft a training plan that provides a holistic view of disability as a human rights concern. Begin by sharing the history of the ADA, and even the models of disability, in order to create a foundational understanding of disability and provide context about the people your museum is engaging. Then build by sharing statistics and first-person narratives from those experiencing discrimination due to their disability (when possible, invite community members to share these insights directly with your staff or share your own experiences if you have a disability and are comfortable doing so). Then review disability etiquette and identity-first language and person-first language usage, making sure to touch upon the importance of words and communication when interacting with visitors. The goal of this introductory training plan is to arm all staff and volunteers with these basics—the ADA and models of disability, community perspectives, and the importance of language—so that staff can act from a place of respect and understanding when interacting with all visitors. Furthermore, when a staff member understands the everyday barriers and discrimination facing people with disabilities, they are more easily able to recognize the need for your museum's accessibility services and can even begin advocating for them on their own.

Build upon this basic framework by designing training and information around your museum's specific elements and amenities. The goal is to equip anyone, regardless of their role in the museum—director, educator, conservator, volunteer, etc.—to have a basic understanding of the accessibility supports at your museum. If staff are unsure of this information, support them, at the very least to know where to go to find the answer. When reviewing what to train on, begin with the basics. First, how do people find you? What are the web addresses of your website and accessibility pages and the physical location of where people enter? Once inside the museum, where are the locations of accessible restrooms? Do you have mobility devices that can be checked-out (such as wheelchairs, walkers, or strollers), and what is the protocol for checking them out? Are there specific locations inside the museum where people can and cannot eat or drink? This is important for people who need to take medication at certain times. If a visitor wants to lodge a complaint, or share an accolade, how do they do so? There will be other questions, fundamental to your specific institution, which should be added to this basic list. Take stock of the questions most frequently asked by visitors for more specific ideas of what to include.

For staff who interact on a more regular basis with the public—people working in front-facing departments like guest services, education, or the museum gift shop, for example—there are more in-depth pieces of knowledge (discussed below) that they should have in order to support visitors who may require services.

Physical Access

What are the locations of the nearest public transportation stops, or the safest drop-off locations? Can staff easily direct visitors from these stops to the front door of your museum, and when necessary can they use directions and landmarks that do not rely on vision (for directing someone who is blind or has low vision)? What type of mobility aids are available? Are service animals allowed inside the museum? Are there areas that are inaccessible to mobility devices or strollers inside the galleries, grounds, or exhibitions? What forms of accessible seating are available inside the museum spaces? Do you have dedicated low-sensory times in the museum?

Communications

Do staff know how to use telecommunications relay services?[11] This is particularly important for staff who answer calls from visitors, as this is a telephone service that enables people with hearing or speech disabilities to place and receive telephone calls. Is there a process for responding to requests for communication assistance, such as providing ASL interpreters, Braille, or recorded materials? Do staff know the only two questions they can ask an individual about an animal that may be a service animal (see chapter 10)? Do all videos have captions or at least written transcripts nearby?

Amenities

Does the museum offer exhibition materials in alternate formats, such as Braille, large print, audio, or in languages other than English? Is large print, sensory, or braille/tactile museum maps available? What about transcripts for audio guides? Where do visitors access all these materials? How can people request assisted listening devices for public tours and lectures? Are your audio guide and assistive listening device headphones compatible with hearing aids or cochlear implants? What dedicated accessibility programs or events do you offer, including sensory-friendly times, touch or verbal description tours, ASL tours, etc.

There are ways to approach the design of these training components to be engaging and thoughtful. Rather than just listing the location of accessible restrooms in your building, invite staff to go on a scavenger hunt through the museum to find them, or employ improvisation exercises to help build inclusive communication skills and creative problem solving.[12] Consider creating unique formats for delivering information that staff will check again and again, such as a quick reference guide for people-first language basics, for example.

Mission Accessible Quick Reference Card	
Instead of... 👎	**Say...**
The disabled, handicapped	People with disabilities
Normal	People without a disability
Blind, Sightless	Person who is blind or has low vision
Hearing impaired	Person who is deaf or has hearing loss
Wheelchair-bound	Wheelchair user
Autistic person	Person on the Autism Spectrum
Mute, Dumb	Non-verbal
Crazy, Insane	Person with a mental illness
Handicapped Parking, Restroom, Entrance	Accessible parking, restroom, entrance
Crippled, Deformed, Lame	Person with a physical disability
Downs	Person with Down Syndrome
Slow	Person with an intellectual disability
Midget	Person of short stature, Little Person

It's ok if someone corrects you!

museum of science+industry chicago   9/25/2017

Figure 11.1. Person-First Language quick reference card for staff.
Source: Museum of Science and Industry, Chicago

When you do have a training in which staff must absorb and remember a lot of information, such as the full list of accessible tours and programs you offer, can you test knowledge through an interactive format like a quiz or Jeopardy-style game? Furthermore, are there ways to incentivize and reward staff to practice sharing the knowledge they have collected throughout training? Consider creating small gestures that mark positive behavior (e.g., congratulating the employee during a staff meeting or taking him or her out for coffee when they go above and beyond); this recognition can go a long way in building investment in your training program and promoting positive staff culture around accessibility initiatives. Collecting and sharing visitor feedback, both positive and negative, achieves this as well as it is a way to connect what staff are learning to real-life situations. People feel more invested in learning new content when they see how it shows up in their everyday interactions.

It is also important to engage community partners, area organizations, and your access advisory group to help design and lead these training sessions. They provide invaluable first-person perspectives and authenticity to your trainings, and as previously mentioned, some service organizations will provide free or low-cost training as part of their mission. The Autism Society and Alzheimer's Association are two organizations that often offer free introductory trainings. Two other cost-effective resources are your state ADA Center, which generally offers free online classes in basic ADA topics, and the Job Accommodation Network, a free service of the US Department of Labor's Office of Disability employment, which provides free training and publications through their multimedia training microsite.[13] Furthermore, your community partners and access advisory group can provide more specialized and audience-specific training that will build upon the foundational knowledge you have already introduced to your staff. This could be sighted guide training, an introduction to the autism spectrum, or etiquette tips for interacting with service animals, depending on the expertise of your group.[14] Plus, these partners can help inform the scope of training you should be leading with your staff, as they are familiar with the barriers facing their particular disability communities. Ensure, however, when engaging community partners to help design and lead staff trainings that you are paying them appropriately for their time, energy, and expertise. Even if you have a small budget, it is important to begin carving out resources for accessibility training in order to illustrate the importance of this work to your staff and your museum.

SHARING THE RESPONSIBILITY

Achieving the goal of building an inclusive staff is difficult, and nearly impossible, if you are not able to dedicate financial and staff resources across the board. As we have outlined many times, the responsibility of implementing accessibility traditionally falls (albeit incorrectly) upon a single staff person, and this same mentality often extends to budget implications as well. Many museums are lucky if there is a single line item dedicated to accessibility initiatives. If and when this budget does exist, the number is usually far too low to truly address the complex process of implementing comprehensive accessible programs and inclusive supports while also training a knowledgeable staff. As a result it is essential to make the case for allocating financial support of accessibility initiatives across a variety of departmental budgets. Committing to being an accessible institution is achieved by incorporating "the costs of compliance into the cost of doing business [and] including line items in your budget for facilities, communication and services."[15] Consider where it makes the most sense to distribute funds. In terms of accessible materials, for example, the cost for creating large print or raised line museum maps could be included in the marketing budget; sensory support items (e.g., fidgets and headphones used on school tours) could be in the education line while the bill for ASL interpreters could be under the guest services purview. Staff training costs can be allocated across many departments as well. Marketing dollars could cover identity-first/person-first language training, as these learnings should be incorporated into a museum's brand and voice. The technology department could contribute to training on digital accessibility since this relates to website and digital in-gallery design. The visitor services team could cover an introductory training on autism spectrum disorder since they are often the first point of contact for visitors. With this approach each museum department sets aside a couple hundred dollars within their budget to put toward accessibility initiatives. This relieves a single department from needing to cover every single support and training item, which necessitates a much larger budget (which no accessibility program has!). It also weaves accessibility initiatives into the fabric of the entire museum.

Overseeing the budget, especially of multiple departments, likely falls outside your purview, however, that does not mean that you should refrain from making informed recommendations for utilizing funds to increase accessibility awareness. Staff training costs must be included in annual and long-term budgets because creating an inclusive museum culture and shifting behavior takes time. One cannot expect a single training on accessibility to cover the breadth of information available. While you may not immediately gain ground with your budget allocation proposals, with time, effort, and making your case, people will start paying attention. You can start small. Decide the best use of your limited funds. Rather than creating an entirely new training schedule, consider if there are ways to infuse a discussion about identity-first/people-first language usage into an already designed customer service workshop. Or perhaps, after completing your state's online ADA modules, you feel confident leading a training on service animals for frontline staff. For example, lead this on your own to cut costs and, instead, put your money toward printing large print museum maps. Or focus on bringing in one paid community partner a year for training while filling the rest of your sessions with free resources. This is also a great opportunity to partner with other museums and organizations in your city to share speakers. Propose that a few staff from each institution be given the opportunity to attend the staff training at the other site. This increases the amount of information each staff is exposed to while helping the museums stay within their respective budgets. Plus, it builds camaraderie and a culture of sharing among organizations.

Finally, spreading training resources across museum departments supports the ability to be dynamic and responsive to visitor needs as they arise. Trainings can be designed around the unique feedback received by different departments and can be implemented in a timely manner that is responsive to specific situations. In chapter 7 we mentioned the recent slew of court cases raised against art galleries and museums for inaccessible websites. This is an example of a timely situation that training funds, when appropriately distributed, can respond to. If training resides only within the visitor services or education department, then perhaps digital accessibility was not accounted for in this year's training budget and your museum's digital footprint is showing its age (and potentially in danger of being targeted). However, if the technology team also has funds set aside for accessibility initiatives, then they can bring in an expert to complete an audit of your website and train key staff on digital best practices. Shared responsibility for staff training creates a more comprehensive approach to accessibility and empowers museum staff and volunteers to be responsive to and learn from situations as they arise.

ALL ABOARD

Adopting a museum-wide approach to accessibility is the only way to truly create an accessible and inclusive museum environment. A successful training strategy provides just enough foundational knowledge, layered with specific content, so that each and every person within the museum should understand the role they play in promoting accessibility. The accessibility coordinator can steer the way, but she needs her staff and museum resources to truly power the boat.

NOTES

1. "Contact Your Region/ADA Center," ADA National Network, accessed October 27, 2019, https://adata.org/find-your-region.

2. Communication Access Realtime Translation services, also known as real-time captioning, translates the spoken word into English text using a stenotype machine and computer.

3. "State & Regional Museum Associations," Sustaining Places, accessed November 13, 2019, https://sustainingplaces.com/about/museum-associations/.

4. "Leadership Exchange in Arts and Disability (LEAD)," The Kennedy Center, accessed October 30, 2019, https://education.kennedy-center.org/education/acces sibility/lead/conference.html.

5. "National ADA Symposium," National ADA Symposium, accessed November 7, 2019, http://www.adasymposium.org/.

6. "Code of Conduct," Museum Computer Network, accessed November 17, 2019, https://mcn.edu/conferences/code-of-conduct/.

7. "Aging in America Conference," American Society on Aging, accessed November 6, 2019, https://www.asaging.org/aging-in-america.

8. "National Convention," National Federation of the Blind, accessed November 6, 2019, https://www.nfb.org/get-involved/national-convention.

9. "About," ADA Coordinator Training Certification Program, accessed November 6, 2019, https://www.adacoordinator.org/page/About.

10. You can learn more about the Alliance on their website: https://www.cultural heritage.org/resources/emergencies/alliance-for-response

11. "Telecommunications Relay Service–TRS," Federal Communications Commission, accessed November 12, 2019, https://www.fcc.gov/consumers/guides /telecommunications-relay-service-trs.

12. Linda Flanagan, "How Improv Can Open Up the Mind to Learning in the Classroom and Beyond." **KQED**, January 30, 2015, https://www.kqed.org/mind shift/39108/how-improv-can-open-up-the-mind-to-learning-in-the-classroom-and -beyond.

13. "Multimedia Training Microsite," Job Accommodation Network, accessed November 12, 2019, https://askjan.org/events/Multimedia-Training-Microsite.cfm.

14. "Autism 101 Online Course," Autism Society, accessed November 17, 2019, https://www.autism-society.org/autism-101-online-course/.

15. Job Accommodation Network, "Multimedia Training Microsite."

Chapter Twelve

You Are on the Road to "Welcome"

I wish for a world that views disability, mental or physical, not as a hindrance but as unique attributes that can be seen as powerful assets if given the right opportunities.

—Oliver Sacks[1]

Congratulations! You have made it to the end of this book and to the beginning of your accessibility and inclusion journey. You are now officially on the road to welcoming visitors of all abilities; after all, taking care to better understand the barriers facing visitors with disabilities is the first step in this process. We all can do more to improve access to our institutions, and we hope that within these pages you found a few initiatives you can begin to work on immediately. Our goal is to help museums get to "that day when the concern for accessibility is second nature, an automatic calculation in everything we do."[2] So thank you for taking that initial step with us.

Throughout this book we outlined a number of ideas and principles aimed to help you build more inclusive practices at your organization. We covered both theory as well as concrete tools. We recognize, however, that we are just one voice supporting you as you make your museum more inclusive and accessible. The information included here is by no means exhaustive. We see this as one part of an ongoing conversation. Just like the rest of the museum field, museum accessibility is constantly changing and growing over time, especially as more institutions recognize the importance of this work. With our remaining pages we want to outline some ways you can continue the conversation.

CONTINUING EDUCATION

As mentioned in the last chapter, professional development is key to this work, since vocabulary, practices, and even theories change. As a result we recommend subscribing to newsletters, blogs, and generally staying up-to-date on the latest research in the field of museum accessibility. To help your continued education in this subject, we have provided some additional resources in the appendices of this book. In appendix A we have compiled a list of relevant books, articles, videos, websites, and more on a variety of topics that we have used in our own work, and that we believe you will find useful on your journey. In appendix B you will find a list of questions to ask yourself in order to get started on creating a plan for your museum. Finally, appendix C provides definitions for some of the terms we have used in this book that may be less familiar. In partnership with the bibliography, we believe these appendices will provide a broad base of useful resources and information.

At this point in the book, we hope you have some concrete ideas of modifications or improvements you might introduce at your museum to make it more welcoming and accessible to visitors. Implementing some of what you have learned is a great way to increase your knowledge and comfort with this work. Do not be afraid to experiment with new programs and tools; try new things as you develop your accessibility plan, even if you are unsure how they will work at the outset. Evaluating what works (and what may not) in your specific space is key. Accessibility is not a one-size-fits-all all situation; you must take the best practices covered in this book, and from other resources, and make it fit your organization. This is where having an accessibility advisory committee can be especially useful. Invite members from this group to come in and help develop and test out new ideas, whether that is attending pilot programs, trying out new tools, or helping to craft accessibility goals and outcomes. Afterward, ask participants to provide feedback based on their experience as users. This sort of evaluation can help you adjust programs, tools, and spaces as you go along, rather than after the fact. Your local access consortium is another possible group you can ask for feedback and input. If you do not have an access advisory group, members of the access consortium can most likely connect you with individuals to help you test your ideas. If you live in an area without an access consortium or community of practice, consider starting one yourself. This may seem daunting but start small. Gather a few people for a brown bag lunch or a cup of coffee. Thanks to modern technology like video chats and conference call services, distance is less of an obstacle than it used to be.

BUILDING AN ACCESS CONSORTIUM

Starting an access consortium can be easy enough, however, these groups take time and effort to grow and forge connections in order to make things happen. There are a number of access consortiums in various cities and states around the country. Each group is unique, but as you will see, they all share similarities. We have included a few examples to give you an idea of the size, structure, and origins of each of these groups.

Art of Access Alliance Denver

The Art of Access Alliance (AAA) is a group of Denver-area individuals, disability advocates, and organizations working to develop and promote accessible and inclusive practices across Denver's cultural organizations.

In the fall of 2016, conversations began in earnest among a few colleagues working in the cultural sector around organizing a group dedicated to improving the accessibility and inclusion of Denver's arts and culture venues. The seed was planted during an accessibility symposium held in the summer of 2015, and soon after this small group of colleagues came together to plan another more comprehensive symposium for 2017. Additionally, they explored the beginnings of what a Denver consortium could look like. The second symposium drew nearly one hundred people, further demonstrating the hunger and interest for this sort of organization in Denver. After that, AAA was officially born.

The founding members come from a wide variety of backgrounds, abilities, and types of organizations, and all share a passion for supporting access across cultural institutions in the region. AAA has a website, active Facebook page, monthly newsletter, and calendar where organizations can post accessible programs and events. The alliance hosts multiple professional development workshops each year, covering audience-specific topics like "Art and Aging," holistic approaches like "Staff Training and Cultural Change," and nuts and bolts introductions like "Audio Description 101." The vision for these trainings is to educate and support all who work in arts and culture organizations—especially arts leaders and board staff—to recognize how they can readily increase access in their programming. In 2020, AAA began a partnership with the City of Denver Arts & Venues office to provide workshops and trainings that reach a larger audience while still expanding access and inclusion of people with disabilities at arts centers, cultural venues, and nonprofits around the city.

Bay Area Arts Access Collective

Founded in 2010, the Bay Area Arts Access Collective (BAAAC) started as a volunteer-run network made up of arts and cultural workers, disability community advocates, artists with disabilities, educators, and allies coming together to think collectively about building an accessible and equitable art and cultural sector.

Founders of BAAAC felt it was critical to have people and organizations from multiple communities involved in shaping the vision/goals, programs, and structure of the organization. Steering committee and core members ranged from community leaders with disabilities from disability-led arts organizations, disabled artists, educators, arts professionals, older adults, and transition-age youth. The aim was to build a platform for collaboration across multiple sectors of communities, creating a more nuanced and complex conversation around the barriers and gaps that various communities face around access to the arts. BAAAC also intentionally chose to become a "collective," which allowed for a more fluid and nonhierarchical structure that allowed members of the group to determine and guide the organization forward.

BAAAC organizes free community workshops related to accessibility in museums and cultural institutions, foregrounding the expertise that people with disabilities bring to this wide range of topics. Workshops have included "Making Museums Accessible for Blind and Low-Vision Audiences and Artists," "Employment Equity in the Arts," "Accessible Exhibition Design: A Case Study with the Patient No More! Exhibit," "Beyond Compliance: Advocating for Access to the Arts," to name a few. All of BAAAC's workshops are developed in partnership with local disability community members, all of whom have participated on a volunteer basis. Community workshops provided opportunities to network, exchange resources, and build community capacity in the efforts to create a more accessible Bay Area. BAAAC maintains a Facebook page where it regularly shares events and resources.

BAAAC has strengthened its partnerships with city-wide municipal agencies such as the Mayor's Office on Disability, the Department of Disability and Aging Services, the Longmore Institute on Disability at San Francisco State, and other local disability community organizers, artists, and nonprofits to help shape innovative cultural policies that will provide San Franciscans with greater access to arts and cultural opportunities.[3]

Chicago Cultural Accessibility Consortium

The Chicago Cultural Accessibility Consortium (CCAC) was started by Christena Gunther, Evan Hatfield, and Lynn Walsh in 2013. Gunther was a member of the Museum Access Consortium (MAC) in New York and had relocated to Chicago. She was hoping to find something similar to MAC in Chicago, but at that time nothing existed there. Having heard that Hatfield and Walsh had been doing access and inclusion work for several years (he at Steppenwolf Theatre Company and she at Chicago Children's Museum) Gunther reached out to the two of them and asked about starting CCAC. Together, the three created a plan, developed a mission and organizational values, and began interviewing potential steering committee members. The goal was to find people with and without disabilities who had the same passion as the founders—to make Chicago's cultural organizations as accessible and inclusive as possible.

On February 3, 2014, CCAC presented their first community workshop (ADA 101: The ADA & Cultural Spaces) and have continued presenting workshops since then. In addition to providing free professional development opportunities, CCAC, in partnership with Steppenwolf Theatre Company, also offers short-term accessible equipment loans to Chicago-area cultural organizations. CCAC also has an Access Calendar that was developed with funding from The Chicago Community Trust. The calendar provides the opportunity for Chicagoland cultural organizations to submit their accessible programs and services. Anyone is able to view the Access Calendar through the CCAC website. The sheer number of listings on the calendar speaks to the growth of accessible and inclusive programming that is now taking place in Chicago.

CCAC is now a 501c3 nonprofit that continues to be run solely by volunteers. Steering committee members past and present continue to work hard to provide the resources to make Chicago's cultural organizations as accessible and inclusive as possible.[4]

Michigan Alliance for Cultural Accessibility

Founded in 2016, the Michigan Alliance for Cultural Accessibility (MACA) provides a forum for ideas, resources, and sharing best practices focused around making Michigan's cultural institutions more welcoming and inclusive. MACA hosts three to four professional development workshops per year, produces a quarterly newsletter, hosts a website and Facebook page, and hosts quarterly resource sharing meetings.

MACA got its start when several organizations came together to provide collaborative, sensory-friendly programming at five institutions in Metro Detroit. During the initial planning of meetings for this collaborative programming, the idea was brought up to continue to meet quarterly as a consortium. The organizers spent about two years developing a mission statement and bylaws, deciding on MACA as a name, and planning for the future. While developing these things, board members reached out to other similar organizations across the country to determine how they were structured, what sorts of programming they offered, and their process for developing a mission statement. Since 2016, MACA has grown to include about fifty-five institutions across the state.[5]

EVERYONE IS WELCOME

The responsibility to ensure everyone who comes into your museum feels welcome is not your responsibility alone, it rests with every single person on staff at your museum, both paid and volunteer, because creating a welcoming environment is a shared responsibility. We encourage you to share what you have learned from this book and these resources as a way to talk with your colleagues about accessibility and inclusion at your museum. As you are working to create a more inclusive and accessible museum, keep in mind that accessibility and inclusion affects us all. Accessibility is a legal requirement, makes good business sense, is a part of your mission, and above all, is **the right thing to do.**

NOTES

1. Courtney Seiter, "14 Quotes that Celebrate a More Accessible World," **Chicago Tribune**, May 26, 2016, https://www.chicagotribune.com/business/blue-sky/ct-buffer-14-quotes-that-celebrate-accessible-world-bsi-hub-20160526-story.html.

2. Association of Registered Graphic Designers of Ontario. **AccessAbility: A Practical Handbook on Accessible Graphic Design**. Toronto: RGD Ontario, 2010. https://www.rgd.ca/database/files/library/RGD_AccessAbility_Handbook.pdf.

3. Cecile Puretz, email message to author, November 14, 2019.

4. Lynn Walsh, email message to author, November 12, 2019.

5. Caroline Braden, email message to author, November 12, 2019.

Appendix A

Resources to Continue Your Journey

We hope that the information provided in this book will be useful on your journey toward becoming a more accessible and inclusive museum. Included in this appendix are some of the practical resources we have used in our own journeys, or have been recommended by others on a similar path. In partnership with the bibliography, they should provide a broad base of accessibility and inclusion resources.

ACCESSIBILITY AUDIT

Checklists, guides, and self-evaluation forms for understanding and adhering to ADA requirements.

- **ADA Readily Achievable Barrier Removal Checklist for Existing Facilities**, U.S. Department of Justice, https://www.ada.gov/racheck.pdf
- **Checklist for Existing Facilities**, Institute of Human Centered Design, https://www.adachecklist.org/doc/fullchecklist/ada-checklist.pdf
- **Renewing the Commitment: An ADA Compliance Guide for Nonprofits** by Irene Bowen, https://cct.org/wp-content/uploads/2015/08/2015ADA ComplianceGuide.pdf

EFFECTIVE COMMUNICATION

Captioning, sign language, and other means to communicate with visitors.

- "Transcription Services," 3PlayMedia, http://www.3playmedia.com/services-features/services/captioning-transcription/
- "Assisted Listening Systems and Devices," National Association of the Deaf, https://www.nad.org/resources/technology/assistive-listening/assistive-listening-systems-and-devices/
- The Audio Description Project, http://www.acb.org/adp/index.html
- **Audio Description and Captioning Guide**, New York City Major's Office for People with Disabilities, https://www1.nyc.gov/assets/mopd/downloads/pdf/MOPD-Audio-Description-and-Caption-Guide.pdf
- Dotsub. **Captions and translations for web video into multiple languages,** http://dotsub.com/
- "How to Learn Sign Language: 9 Apps and Resources to Teach Yourself ASL" by Yohana Desta, https://mashable.com/article/how-to-sign/
- Linguabee. **American Sign Language interpretation and video remote interpreting services,** www.Linguabee.com
- Rev.com. **Transcription, captioning, and foreign language subtitles,** www.rev.com
- Telecommunications Relay Service (TRS). **Telephone service that allows persons with hearing or speech disabilities to place and receive telephone calls,** https://www.fcc.gov/consumers/guides/telecommunications-relay-service-trs

DIGITAL ACCESSIBILITY

Guidelines for designing accessible digital interactives.

- **Communicating Effectively with Adults with Intellectual or Developmental Disabilities**, Vanderbilt Kennedy Center for Excellence in Developmental Disabilities, https://www.communitycarenc.org/media/files/communicating-adults-idd.pdf
- "Create Accessible Content," University of Minnesota, https://accessibility.umn.edu/what-you-can-do/create-accessible-content
- Gaining Momentum: FrameWorks Institute Aging Toolkit, **Resources designed to help reframe aging in America,** https://frameworksinstitute.org/toolkits/aging/

- "Guidelines for Accessible Presentations," Museum, Arts and Culture Access Consortium, https://macaccess.org/rescources/guidelines-for-accessible-presentations/
- "Guidelines for Image Description," Cooper Hewitt, https://www.cooper hewitt.org/cooper-hewitt-guidelines-for-image-description/
- "How to Make Your Presentations Accessible to All," Web Accessibility Initiative, https://www.w3.org/WAI/teach-advocate/accessible-presentations/
- **Inclusive Digital Interactives: Best Practices + Research**, a collaboration of Access Smithsonian, Institute for Human Centered Design and MuseWeb, https://access.si.edu/sites/default/files/inclusive-digital-interact ives-best-practices-research.pdf
- Telestream. **Provides closed captioning software for Mac and PC to create and edit video captions for mobile and web,** http://www .telestream.net/captioning/overview.htm
- Vimeo Captions and Subtitles, https://vimeo.com/help/faq/managing-your-videos/captions-and-subtitles
- **Web Accessibility Initiative**, World Wide Web Consortium, https://www.w3.org/WAI/
- YouTube DIY captioning, https://support.google.com/youtube/answer/2734796?hl=en

EQUITABLE EMPLOYMENT

Resources for building an inclusive workplace.

- Employer Assistance and Resource Network on Disability and Inclusion (EARN), http://www.askearn.org
- **Inclusive Internships Programs: A How-To Guide**, U.S. Department of Labor, Office of Disability Employment Policy, https://www.dol.gov/odep/pdf/InclusiveInternshipPrograms.pdf
- Job Accommodation Network (JAN), https://askjan.org/index.cfm
- National Organization on Disability, https://www.nod.org/
- "Diversity and Inclusion," U.S. Department of Labor, Office of Disability Employment Policy, https://www.dol.gov/odep/topics/diversityandinclu sion.htm

FUNDING OPPORTUNITIES

In addition to these national funding opportunities, check with your local Community Centered Board, Regional Center, or equivalent; hospital(s) or health system(s); and local/regional museum association(s) for additional opportunities.

- American Alliance of Museums Grants. **AAM member-only content**, https://www.aam-us.org/programs/resource-library/financial-stability-resources/grants/
- Foundation Directory Online. **Search for potential funders from all over the country. This is a subscription service, but many libraries have access for free with your library card,** https://fconline.foundationcenter.org/
- Institute of Museum and Library Services, https://www.imls.gov/grants/apply-grant/available-grants
- National Endowment for the Arts, https://www.arts.gov/grants/apply-grant/grants-organizations
- National Endowment for the Humanities, https://www.neh.gov/grants

INCLUSIVE DESIGN

Guides and resources for designing accessible facilities.

- **AccessAbility: A Practical Handbook on Accessible Graphic Design** by Association of Registered Graphic Designers of Ontario, https://www.rgd.ca/database/files/library/RGD_AccessAbility_Handbook.pdf
- **ADA Standards for Accessible Design**, 2010, https://www.ada.gov/regs2010/2010ADAStandards/2010ADAstandards.htm#titleIII
- **Design for Accessibility: A Cultural Administrator's Handbook,** produced by the National Assembly of State Arts Agencies, https://www.arts.gov/sites/default/files/Design-for-Accessibility.pdf
- **Inclusive Design: Implementation and Evaluation** by Jordana L. Maisel et al.
- **The Multisensory Museum: Cross-Disciplinary Perspectives on Touch, Sound, Smell, Memory, and Space** by Nina Levent
- "Resources," Institute for Human Centered Design, https://www.humancentereddesign.org/inclusive-design/resources
- **Smithsonian Guidelines for Accessible Exhibition Design** by Smithsonian Accessibility Program, https://www.sifacilities.si.edu/sites/default/files/Files/Accessibility/accessible-exhibition-design1.pdf

- "Why Accessible Design Isn't a Niche Market," AIGA Eye on Design, https://eyeondesign.aiga.org/why-accessible-design-isnt-a-niche-market/

Sensory/Cognitive Experience Supports

- **101 Games and Activities for Children with Autism, Asperger's and Sensory Processing Disorders** by Tara Delaney
- **Feeling the Stars** Blog
  Follows the program development and prototyping of materials to make a planetarium show accessible to its viewers who have low- or no-vision. Start at the beginning of the blog (August 2012). Accessibleastronomy.blogspot.com
- "How to Write a Social Story," Vanderbilt Kennedy Center, https://vkc .vumc.org/assets/files/tipsheets/socialstoriestips.pdf
- **The New Social Story Book** by Carol Gray
- Sensory Processing and Autism Resource Kit (S.P.A.R.K) Explorer Pack, Autism Community Store, https://www.autismcommunitystore.com/spark -pack
- **Visual Supports for People with Autism: A Guide for Parents and Professionals (Topics in Autism)** by Marlene J. Cohen

Specific Museum Resources

- The Metropolitan Museum of Art Resources for Visitors on the Autism Spectrum, https://www.metmuseum.org/events/programs/access/visitors -with-developmental-and-learning-disabilities/for-visitors-with-autism -spectrum-disorders
- Experience Grand Rapids Sensory Friendly Experiences, https://www .experiencegr.com/blog/post/sensory-friendly-experiences/
- Atlanta Children's Museum Social Story, https://childrensmuseumatlanta .org/wp-content/uploads/2018/08/CMA-Social-Story.compressed.pdf
- Missouri Botanical Gardens:
  - Children's Garden Pre-Visit Guide, http://www.missouribotanicalgar den.org/Portals/0/Education/interpretation/Childrens-Pre-Visit-Guide .pdf
  - Parent/Caregiver Narrative, http://www.missouribotanicalgarden.org /Portals/0/Education/interpretation/Parent-Narrative.pdf
  - Children's Garden Visual Schedule, http://www.missouribotanicalgar den.org/Portals/0/Education/interpretation/Visual-Schedule.pdf
- Museum of Science and Industry, Chicago

- ◦ Communication Book, https://www.msichicago.org/fileadmin/assets /plan/Communication_Book.pdf
- ◦ Field Trip Social Narrative, https://www.msichicago.org/fileadmin /assets/plan/Social_Narrative.pdf
- ◦ Sensory Map, https://www.msichicago.org/fileadmin/assets/plan/MSI _sensory_map.pdf
- Museum of Modern Art Sensory Map, https://www.moma.org/momaorg /shared/pdfs/docs/visit/MoMA_Sensory_Map.pdf
- Field Museum **Jurassic World: The Exhibition** Sensory Guide, https:// www.fieldmuseum.org/sites/default/files/sensory_guide_to_jurassic _world_at_the_field_museum.pdf

Universal Design

- **Universal Design Plan: Exhibit Design & Development** by Museum of Science, Boston, https://www.mos.org/sites/dev-elvis.mos.org/files/docs /misc/MOS_UD_Plan.pdf
- "Universal Design for Museum Learning Experiences," Museum of Science, Boston, https://www.mos.org/UniversalDesign
- "Universal Design Guidelines for Computer Interactives," Open Exhibits, http://openexhibits.org/accessibility/UDguidelines/
- **Universal Design Guidelines for NISE Network Exhibits** by the NISE Network, https://www.nisenet.org/sites/default/files/catalog/uploads/2971 /ud_guide_exhibits_10_23_print.pdf
- **Universal Design New York**, City of New York Department of Design and Construction in partnership with The Mayor's Office for People with Disabilities, http://www.nyc.gov/html/ddc/downloads/pdf/udny/udny2.pdf

JOURNALS AND PUBLICATIONS

Research from colleagues in the field.

- **Accessible America: A History of Disability and Design** by Bess Williamson (2020), https://nyupress.org/9781479802494/accessible-america/
- **American Alliance of Museums**, https://www.aam-us.org/category /diversity-equity-inclusion-accessibility/
- **Art Beyond Sight Museum Accessibility Research,** http://www.artbeyond sight.org/mei/advisory-board-for-the-multi-site-museum-accessibility -study/

- **Association of Science and Technology Centers (ASTC),** https://www.astc.org/category/diversity-equity-accessibility-and-inclusion/
- **Building Access: Universal Design and the Politics of Disability** by Aimi Hamraie (2017), https://www.upress.umn.edu/book-division/books/building-access
- **Curator: The Museum Journal,** https://curatorjournal.org/
  - ◦ July 2013 Special issue on Museums and People with Disabilities, http://onlinelibrary.wiley.com/doi/10.1111/cura.2013.56.issue-3/issuetoc
- **Disability Studies Quarterly,** https://dsq-sds.org/
- **Diversity, Equity, Accessibility, and Inclusion in Museums** edited by Johnnetta Betch Cole and Laura Lott
- **Everyone's Welcome: The Americans with Disabilities Act and Museums** by John Salmen (1998)
- **Programming for People with Special Needs: A Guide for Museums and Historic Sites** by Katie Stringer (2014)

NATIONAL DISABILITY ORGANIZATIONS WITH LOCAL AFFILIATES

- ADA National Network, https://adata.org/find-your-region
- Alzheimer's Association Local Chapters https://www.alz.org/local_resources/find_your_local_chapter
- Autism Society Affiliate Network, https://www.autism-society.org/about-the-autism-society/affiliate-network/
- The Arc Chapters
- https://thearc.org/find-a-chapter/
- Easterseals Affiliates
- https://www.easterseals.com/connect-locally/
- National Association of the Deaf Affiliates
- https://www.nad.org/members/organizational-affiliates/
- National Down Syndrome Society Local Organizations
- https://www.ndss.org/resources/local-support/
- National Federation of the Blind State Affiliates, https://www.nfb.org/about-us/state-affiliates
- VSA Programs, https://www.kennedy-center.org/education/vsa/

PROFESSIONAL DEVELOPMENT AND STAFF TRAINING

Videos, webinars, training materials to strengthen the knowledge and skills of staff, volunteers, and board members.

General Disability Information

- 10 Facts on Disability from the World Health Organization, https://www.who.int/features/factfiles/disability/en/
- "The Americans with Disability Act," Chapel Hill Training Outreach Project, https://vimeo.com/6248976
- Disability FAQ, https://www.respectability.org/hollywood-inclusion/disability-faq/
- "DisABILITY Series – Guide to Access Symbols," https://www.disability-benefits-help.org/blog/disability-series-guide-access-symbols
- Global Disability Action Plan 2014-2021, World Health Organization, https://www.who.int/disabilities/actionplan/en/
- Multimedia Training Microsite, Job Accommodation Network, https://askjan.org/events/Multimedia-Training-Microsite.cfm.
- World Report on Disability (2011), World Health Organization, https://www.who.int/disabilities/world_report/2011/en/
- Visitor's Bill of Rights, https://airandspace.si.edu/rfp/exhibitions/files/j1-exhibition-guidelines/3/Visitors%20Bill%20of%20Rights.pdf

Language

- Identity-First Language
  - The Significance of Semantics by Lydia X. Z. Brown, https://www.autistichoya.com/2011/08/significance-of-semantics-person-first.html
  - Identity and Hypocrisy: A Second Argument Against Person-First Language by Lydia X. Z. Brown, https://www.autistichoya.com/2011/11/identity-and-hypocrisy-second-argument.html
- People-First Language, https://adata.org/factsheet/ADANN-writing

Personal Narratives

- "6 Things Deaf activist Nyle DiMarco wants you to know about sign language," https://mashable.com/article/nyle-dimarco-deaf-sign-language/?utm_cid=a-seealso
- "10 Awesome Books for Adults about Disabilities, Accessibility and Inclusion," Easter Seals (**All written by disabled authors**), https://easterseals

.ca/english/10-awesome-books-for-adults-about-disabilities-and
-accessibility/
- Access Champions Podcast, http://www.philipdallmann.com/access
championspodcast-853761
- **Being Heumann: An Unrepentant Memoir of a Disability Rights Activist** by Judith Heumann and Kristen Joiner
- Clip from "Talk" by the UK Disability Rights Commission, https://www
.youtube.com/watch?v=k3AeIFup1qY&playnext=1&list=PL961CE6A2D
1A552BE
- **Crip Camp: A Disability Revolution** (2020) written and directed by James Lebrecht and Nicole Newnham
- #DeafAtWork, National Association of the Deaf, https://www.nad.org
/resources/deafatwork/
- "How Alzheimer's patients rediscovered their identity through graffiti," TEDxMileHigh by Damon McLeese, https://www.youtube.com/watch
?v=PyXZvuxDkC4
- "I got 99 problems . . . palsy is just one," TEDWomen 2013 Talk by Maysoon Zayid, https://www.ted.com/talks/maysoon_zayid_i_got_99
_problems_palsy_is_just_one
- "The opportunity of adversity," TEDMed 2009 Talk by Aimee Mullins, https://www.ted.com/talks/aimee_mullins_the_opportunity_of_adversity
- **Ten Things Every Child with Autism Wishes You Knew: Updated and Expanded Edition** by Ellen Notbohm

Staff Trainings

- **ADA Building Blocks Course**, ADA National Network, http://www.ada basics.org/
- "Arts and Special Education Webinars," The Kennedy Center, https://
www.kennedy-center.org/education/resources-for-educators/professional
-development/arts-and-special-education-webinars
- **Autism 101 Online Course**, Autism Society, https://www.autism-society
.org/autism-101-online-course/
- "Disability Awareness, Sensitivity and Practical Inclusion Training," Easter Seals, https://youtu.be/b_GO4beTspA
- **The MoMA Alzheimer's Project: Making Art Accessible to People with Dementia**, Museum of Modern Art, https://www.moma.org/visit/access ibility/meetme/
- **Museum Education Institute**, Art Beyond Sight, http://www.artbeyond sight.org/mei/

- "Resources," Museum Access Consortium, https://macaccess.org /resources-2/
- **The Visual Made Verbal: A Comprehensive Training Manual and Guide to the History and Applications of Audio Description** by Joel Snyder

US LAWS AND REGULATIONS

Current legal requirements.

- "ADA Resources for Museums, Arts and Cultural Institutions," ADA National Network, https://www.adainfo.org/sites/default/files/Arts-Muse ums-Cultural-Inst-ADA-Resources-4-12-12.pdf
- "A Guide to Disability Rights Laws," U.S. Department of Justice, https:// www.ada.gov/cguide.htm
- Publications and videos, ADA National Network, https://adata.org /national-product-search?keys=&type=All&tid=All
- "ADA Requirements for Historic Properties," **STRUCTURE Magazine,** https://www.structuremag.org/?p=7540
- "ADA Requirements: Wheelchairs, Mobility Aids, and Other Power-Driven Mobility Devices," U.S. Department of Justice, https://www.ada .gov/opdmd.htm
- "Factsheet Highlights of the Final Rule to Amend the Department of Justice's Regulation Implementing Title III of the ADA," U.S. Department of Justice, https://www.ada.gov/regs2010/factsheets/title3_factsheet.html
- "About IDEA Individuals with Disabilities Education Act," U.S. Department of Education, https://sites.ed.gov/idea/about-idea/
- "Information and Technical Assistance on the Americans with Disabilities Act," U.S. Department of Justice, https://www.ada.gov/2010_regs.htm
- "Making Historic Properties Accessible," National Park Service, https:// www.nps.gov/tps/how-to-preserve/briefs/32-accessibility.htm
- "What Historic Sites Have Learned After 25 Years with ADA," Engaging Places LLC, https://engagingplaces.net/2015/07/28/what-historic-sites -have-learned-after-25-years-with-ada/

Appendix B

Questions to Get Started with Museum Accessibility

Answering these questions will help you begin to create a concrete plan for your museum to become more welcoming and inclusive:

- What accessibility materials does my museum currently offer? What are we leaving out?
- Who are we serving right now? Who aren't we serving?
- What is the need from my community (check feedback forms, etc.)?
- How much time can my museum invest?
- How much money can my museum invest?
- Who is the best person in my museum to advance this initiative? How can I partner with them?
- Who else in my museum is interested in this work? How can I connect with them?
- Do I have institutional buy-in? If not, how can I get it?
- What other cultural institutions in my area and region are doing good work? How can I connect with them?

Appendix C
Glossary

Ableism: Stereotyping, discrimination, or prejudice against individuals with disabilities.

Accessibility: Giving equitable access to everyone along the continuum of human ability and experience. Accessibility encompasses the broader meanings of compliance and refers to how organizations make space for the characteristics that each person brings. It is not just about the physical environment: it is about access to and representation in content for all.

Accessibility Audit: A survey of your physical spaces used to identify accessibility problems and solutions and tell you which areas of your museum may need physical changes to be more broadly accessible.

Ageism: Stereotyping, discrimination, or prejudice against people on the basis of their age.

Americans with Disabilities Act (ADA): This landmark civil rights law prohibits discrimination against individuals with disabilities. The original ADA law was made up of five parts that relate to different areas of public life (employment, state and local government, public accommodations and commercial facilities, telecommunications, and miscellaneous). The law made it so that organizations and businesses must make reasonable modifications to serve people with disabilities, as well as take the necessary steps to communicate with people with vision or hearing loss and/or speech disabilities. If creating reasonable accommodations creates undue hardship on the organization, they can be exempted from making changes.

Assistive Technology: Any device, equipment, or software that helps people who have disabilities increase their functional capabilities. Assistive technology can be high- or low-tech and aids people who have difficulties writing, speaking, typing, pointing, walking, and more. Other examples of assistive technology include autocorrect or word prediction and text-to-speech software.

Autism Spectrum Disorder: A lifelong developmental disorder characterized by challenges with social skills, repetitive behaviors, speech, and nonverbal communication.

Cognitive Accessibility: Ensuring that information, materials, and communications are readily available and easily understandable to people with limitations in cognitive abilities which could be impacted by intellectual or developmental disabilities, learning disabilities, trauma (such as traumatic brain injury), age, and even access to education.

Community Centered Board (CCB): Nonprofit organization that is responsible for case management services, eligibility determination, service plan development, coordinating and authorizing services, monitoring service delivery, and many other functions for individuals and children with intellectual and developmental disabilities. Also known as Regional Centers.

Community of Practice: A group of active practitioners who share a field of study, or a passion for something they do, and by interacting regularly over time, they learn to do their work better.

D/deaf: The uppercase D (Deaf) corresponds to people who identify as culturally Deaf and are actively engaged with the Deaf community. The lowercase d (deaf) refers to the medical audiological condition of having hearing loss.

Digital Accessibility: The practice of making web and digital interactive content accessible to everyone.

Disability: Developmental, physical, cognitive, or mental condition that interferes with, impairs, or limits a person's ability to engage in daily living activities, interactions, actions, or certain tasks.

Diversity: All the ways that people are different and the same at the individual and group levels. Even when people appear the same, they are different. Organizational diversity requires examining and questioning the makeup of a group to ensure that multiple perspectives are represented.

Environmental Access: The ability to efficiently move around and engage with the environment, service, or product in the way it was meant to be used.

Equity: The fair and just treatment of all members of a community. Equity requires commitment to strategic priorities, resources, respect, and civility, as well as ongoing action and assessment of progress toward achieving specific goals.

Identity-First Language: Way of speaking that places disability first in the phrase, where it is closely tied to the identity of the person. An example is someone saying, "I am autistic" or "I am disabled."

Inclusion: The intentional, ongoing effort to ensure that diverse individuals fully participate in all aspects of organizational work, including decision-making processes. It also refers to the ways that diverse participants are valued as respected members of an organization and community.

Invisible Disability: Refers to symptoms that a person experiences, but that may not be visibly seen by others. These symptoms range from mild to severe, and can limit a person's daily activities, including seizure disorders, chronic pain, sensory disorders, vision or hearing impairments, brain injuries, learning differences, and especially mental health disorders.

Medical Model of Disability: This model of disability focuses on curing or managing illness or disability and emphasizes that the problem exists within the person. This model supposes that a person's disability may reduce their quality of life and ability to complete everyday activities without medical intervention. This model of disability led to a widespread practice of defining people by a condition or their perceived limitations.

Multimodal: Sharing concepts using multiple methods of expressing and communicating information. Can be through visual, auditory, spatial, and linguistic means.

Paternalism: An infringement on the personal freedom and autonomy of a person (or groups of persons) with a protective intent.

People-First Language: Terminology that focuses on the person first and the disability second when communicating about people with disabilities. For example, "a boy with autism" or "a woman with a disability."

Sensory Avoiding: See Sensory Diversity.

Sensory Diversity: Individuals who are hypersensitive or hyposensitive to environmental stimuli. This can manifest as sensory seeking behaviors (craving more intense sensory experiences) or sensory avoiding behaviors (recoiling from sensory stimulation).

Sensory Map: Maps that indicate the sensory areas of a specific location. High-sensory areas may have bright flashing lights, whereas low-sensory areas have quiet areas. These maps communicate to people which areas of the museum to seek out or avoid, depending on their sensory preferences.

Sensory Processing Disorder: Condition that affects how sensory signals are processed in the brain, leading to misinterpretation of sensory information such as sounds, touch, or movement.

Sensory Seeking: See Sensory Diversity.

Social Model of Disability: This model looks to remove environmental barriers and create access through universal design, accommodations, and inclusive environments. The social model changes the role of the person with a disability from the patient, object of intervention, or a research subject, to a community member, customer, patron, partner, and museum guest.

Social Story: Visual and written guides which describe various social interactions, situations, behaviors, skills, or concepts.

Tactile Map: Raised-line maps that contain basic information on where walls, stairs, doors, and large obstructions are located.

Tokenism: Making a symbolic effort to do something, only to give the appearance of equality and inclusion.

Universal Design: A design process that aims to create products and environments that simplify life and are usable by as many people as possible.

Visual Schedule: A series of pictures or icons used to communicate a series of activities or the steps of a specific activity.

Visual Supports: Visual tools that help communicate with individuals who have difficulty understanding or using language. Visual supports can include drawings, photographs, lists, objects, and even written words.

Bibliography

The Accessible Icon Project. "Notes on Design Activism." Accessed October 13, 2019. http://accessibleicon.org/.

ADA Coordinator Training Certification Program. "About." Accessed November 6, 2019. https://www.adacoordinator.org/page/About.

ADA National Network. "ADA Publications and Videos." Resources. Accessed February 18, 2019. https://adata.org/national-product-search?keys=&type=All&tid=All

———. "Contact Your Region/ADA Center." Accessed October 27, 2019. https://adata.org/find-your-region.

———. "Opening Doors to Everyone." Fact Sheets. Accessed May 8, 2019. https://adata.org/factsheet/opening-doors-everyone.

———. "Public Accommodations." Accessed February 8, 2019. https://adata.org/publication/ADA-faq-booklet#Public%20Accommodations.

———. "What is the Americans with Disabilities Act (ADA)?" What is the ADA. Accessed February 8, 2019. https://adata.org/learn-about-ada.

———. "What is the definition of disability under the ADA?" Accessed February 10, 2019. https://adata.org/faq/what-definition-disability-under-ada.

Adobe. "Accessibility Products." Accessed July 14, 2019. https://www.adobe.com/accessibility/products/illustrator.html.

American Alliance of Museums. **Facing Change: Insights from the American Alliance of Museums' Diversity, Equity, Accessibility, and Inclusion Working Group.** Arlington, VA: American Alliance of Museums, 2018.

———. "Museum Facts & Data." Accessed September 7, 2019. https://www.aam-us.org/programs/about-museums/museum-facts-data/#_edn23.

American Council for the Blind. **The Audio Description Project**. Accessed March 6, 2019. http://www.acb.org/adp/about.html#contactus.

American Federation for the Blind. "Helen Keller: 'Alone We Can Do So Little. Together We Can Do So Much.' Accessed October 21, 2019. https://www.afb.org/blog/entry/happy-birthday-helen.

American Society on Aging. "Aging in America Conference." Accessed November 6, 2019. https://www.asaging.org/aging-in-america.

Americans with Disabilities Act of 1990 (ADA). Pub. L. No. 101-336, § 2, 104 Stat. 328 (1991).

Anapol, Avery. "Emoji Representing People with Disabilities Approved for 2019." **The Hill**, February 6, 2019. https://thehill.com/policy/technology/428880-emoji -representing-people-with-disabilities-approved-for-2019.

Anderson, Monica and Andrew Perrin. "Disabled Americans Are Less Likely to Use Technology." **Pew Research Center**, April 7, 2017. https://www.pewresearch.org /fact-tank/2017/04/07/disabled-americans-are-less-likely-to-use-technology/.

Anti-Defamation League. "A Brief History of the Disability Rights Movement." Accessed September 28, 2020. https://www.adl.org/education/resources/back grounders/disability-rights-movement.

The Arc. "Employment, Training, and Wages." Accessed July 5, 2019. https://www .thearc.org/what-we-do/public-policy/policy-issues/employment.

ARTabilityAZ. "About." Accessed March 5, 2019. http://www.artabilityaz.org /about/.

Art Beyond Sight. "Mining the Dimensions of Accessibility." Disability and Inclusion: Resources for Museum Studies Programs. Accessed June 18, 2019. http:// www.artbeyondsight.org/dic/module-5-museum-access-multimodal-engagement /mining-the-dimensions-of-accessibility/#Multimodal.

———. "Social and Medical Models of Disability: Paradigm Change." Accessed March 15, 2019. http://www.artbeyondsight.org/dic/definition-of-disability-para digm-change-and-ongoing-conversation/.

———. "Verbal Description Training." Accessed October 1, 2019. http://www.art beyondsight.org/mei/verbal-description-training/.

Art of Access Alliance Denver. "About." Accessed March 5, 2019. https://artof accessdenver.com/about-us/.

Arts Access for All. "About us." Accessed March 5, 2019. http://www.artsafa.org /content/our-history.

Assistive Technology Industry Association. "What is AT?" Accessed July 14, 2019. https://www.atia.org/at-resources/what-is-at/.

Association of Children's Museums. "Museums for All." Accessed July 7, 2019. https://childrensmuseums.org/about/acm-initiatives/museums-for-all.

Association of Registered Graphic Designers of Ontario. **AccessAbility: A Practical Handbook on Accessible Graphic Design**. Toronto: RGD Ontario, 2010. https:// www.rgd.ca/database/files/library/RGD_AccessAbility_Handbook.pdf.

Autism Society. "Autism 101 Online Course." Accessed November 17, 2019. https:// www.autism-society.org/autism-101-online-course/.

———. "Autism Facts and Statistics." Accessed June 22, 2019. https://www.autism -society.org/what-is/facts-and-statistics/.

Autism Speaks. "What is Autism?" Accessed June 7, 2019. https://www.autism speaks.org/what-autism.

Autistic Self Advocacy Network. "Identity-First Language." Accessed October 1, 2019. https://autisticadvocacy.org/about-asan/identity-first-language/.

Bay Area Arts Access Collective. "About." Accessed March 5, 2019. https://www
.bayareaartsaccess.org/about.html.

Berger, Craig. **Wayfinding: Designing and Implementing Graphic Navigational Systems**. Brighton: Rotovision, 2005.

Berger, Rob. "Top 100 Money Quotes of All Time." **Forbes,** April 30, 2014. https://www.forbes.com/sites/robertberger/2014/04/30/top-100-money-quotes-of -all-time.

Brindle, David. "Mike Oliver Obituary." **The Guardian**, March 19, 2019. https:// www.theguardian.com/society/2019/mar/19/mike-oliver-obituary.

Bureau of Labor. "Table A-6. Employment status of the civilian population by sex, age, and disability status, not seasonally adjusted." Accessed July 5, 2019. https:// www.bls.gov/news.release/empsit.t06.htm.

Canfield, Julie. "Where Have All The Old Words Gone." **Medium**, May 5, 2019. https://medium.com/@juliecanfield_41917/where-have-all-the-old-words-gone -ba665ba9265d.

CAST. "Homepage." Accessed October 1, 2019. http://www.cast.org/.

———. "The UDL Guidelines." Accessed October 1, 2019. http://udlguidelines.cast .org/.

Center for Disability Rights. "#Ableism." Accessed September 25, 2019. http:// cdrnys.org/blog/uncategorized/ableism/.

Centers for Disease Control and Prevention. "CDC: 1 in 4 US adults live with a disability." Last modified August 16, 2018. https://www.cdc.gov/media/releases /2018/p0816-disability.html.

———. "Understanding Literacy & Numeracy." Accessed September 27, 2019. https://www.cdc.gov/healthliteracy/learn/UnderstandingLiteracy.html.

Centre for Excellence in Universal Design. "What is Universal Design." Accessed April 20, 2019 http://universaldesign.ie/What-is-Universal-Design/.

Chang, Y. S., J. P. Owen, S. S. Desai, S. S. Hill, A. B. Arnett, J. Harris, E. J. Marco, and P. Mukherjee. 2014. "Autism and Sensory Processing Disorders: Shared White Matter Disruption in Sensory Pathways but Divergent Connectivity in Social-Emotional Pathways." **PLoS One** 9 (7): e103038. doi: 10.1371/journal.pone .0103038.

Charlton, James I. **Nothing About Us Without Us: Disability Oppression and Empowerment**. 1st ed., Berkeley: University of California Press, 1998. **JSTOR**, www.jstor.org/stable/10.1525/j.ctt1pnqn9.

Chicago Cultural Accessibility Consortium. "About." Accessed March 2, 2019. https://www.chicagoculturalaccess.org/about-us.

Child Mind Institute. "Sensory Processing FAQ." Accessed June 7, 2019. https:// childmind.org/article/sensory-processing-faq/.

Christidou, Dimitra. "Social Interaction in the Art Museum: Performing Etiquette While Connecting to Each Other and the Exhibits." **The International Journal of Social, Political and Community Agendas in the Arts** 11 (2016): 27–38. https:// doi.org/10.18848/2326-9960/CGP/v11i04/27-38.

City and County of Denver. "Human Rights and Community Partnerships." Accessed February 19, 2019. https://www.denvergov.org/content/denvergov/en /human-rights-and-community-partnerships.html.

Click-Away Pound. "Click-Away Pound Survey 2016 Final Report." Accessed July 27, 2019. http://www.clickawaypound.com/cap16finalreport.html

Cohen-Rottenberg, Rachel. "Doing Social Justice: 10 Reasons to Give Up Ableist Language." **HuffPost**, August 10, 2014. https://www.huffpost.com/entry/doing -social-justice-thou_b_5476271?guccounter=1.

Colorado Department of Labor and Employment, State of Colorado. "About Us." Accessed February 19, 2019. https://www.colorado.gov/dvr/about-dvr.

Cooper Hewitt, Smithsonian Design Museum. "The Senses: Descriptive Audio Tour." Accessed October 2, 2019. https://www.cooperhewitt.org/2018/05/24/the -senses-descriptive-audio-tour/.

Culture Track. "Culture + Community in a Time of Crisis." Accessed November 2, 2020. https://s28475.pcdn.co/wp-content/uploads/2020/09/CCTC-Key-Findings -from-Wave-1_9.29.pdf.

Dallman, Philip. "Access in Action #1." **Access Champions**. Podcast audio, May, 15, 2018. http://www.philipdallmann.com/accesschampionspodcast-853761/archives /05-2018.

DC Arts & Access Network. "Mission Statement & Overview." Accessed March 6, 2019. http://www.dcaan.org/mission-statement/.

Denver Public Library. "Services for Persons with Disabilities." Accessed February 20, 2019. https://www.denverlibrary.org/content/services-persons-disabilities.

Design for Accessibility: A Cultural Administrators Handbook. Washington, DC: National Assembly of State Arts Agencies, 1994.

Digital A11y. "Accessibility Forums Roundup." Accessed March 6, 2019. https:// www.digitala11y.com/accessibility-forums-roundup/.

Dupere, Katie. "The Incredible Ways People with Disabilities Customize Their Tech to Thrive." **Mashable**, May 16, 2017. https://mashable.com/2017/05/17/apple -accessibility-videos-disability/.

Durant-Kenrick House and Gardens. "Accessibility at the Durant-Kenrick House and Grounds." Accessed September 10, 2019. http://www.newtonma.gov/gov/historic /visit/durant_kenrick_house_and_grounds/accessdk.asp.

Federal Communications Commission. "Telecommunications Relay Service– TRS." Accessed November 12, 2019. https://www.fcc.gov/consumers/guides/tele communications-relay-service-trs.

Federal Communications Commission. "21st Century Communications and Video Accessibility Act (CVAA)." Accessed October 20, 2020. https://www.fcc.gov /consumers/guides/21st-century-communications-and-video-accessibility-act -cvaa.

Flanagan, Linda, "How Improv Can Open Up the Mind to Learning in the Classroom and Beyond." **KQED**, January 30, 2015. https://www.kqed.org/mindshift/39108 /how-improv-can-open-up-the-mind-to-learning-in-the-classroom-and-beyond.

Florida Access Coalition for the Arts. "Mission." Accessed March 5, 2019. http:// www.flaccess.org/mission.html.

FrameWorks Institute. "Gaining Momentum: A FrameWorks Communication Toolkit." Toolkits. Accessed September 25, 2019. https://frameworksinstitute.org /toolkits/aging/.

Fred Rogers Center. "About Fred." Accessed March 16, 2019. http://www.fredrogers center.org/about-us/about-fred/.

Gilman, Benjamin. "Museum Fatigue." **The Scientific Monthly** 2, no. 1 (1916).

Greater Pittsburgh Arts Council. "Accessibility." Accessed March 9, 2019. http:// www.pittsburghartscouncil.org/accessibility.

Hamraie, Aimi. **Building Access: Universal Design and the Politics of Disability.** Minneapolis: University of Minnesota Press, 2017.

Harris, Elizabeth. "Galleries from A to Z Sued Over Websites the Blind Can't Use." **New York Times**, February 18, 2019. https://www.nytimes.com/2019/02/18/arts /design/blind-lawsuits-art-galleries.html.

The Highly Sensitive Person. "FAQ: Is Sensory Processing (or Integration) Disorder (SPD) the same as Sensory Processing Sensitivity (SPS)?" Accessed October 04, 2020. http://hsperson.com/faq/spd-vs-sps/.

Hughes, Karen. "Museum and Gallery Wayfinding: Tips for Signage, Maps and Apps." **The Guardian**, August 25, 2015. https://www.theguardian.com/culture-pro fessionals-network/2015/aug/25/museum-gallery-wayfinding-tips-signage-maps -apps.

Institute for Human Centered Design. "History." Accessed April 23, 2019. https:// www.humancentereddesign.org/inclusive-design/history.

———. "Mission." Accessed May 8, 2019. https://www.humancentereddesign.org /about-us/mission.

———. "Principles." Accessed April 23, 2019. https://www.humancentereddesign .org/inclusive-design/principles.

Invisible Disabilities Association. "What is an Invisible Disability?" Accessed May 29, 2019. https://invisibledisabilities.org/what-is-an-invisible-disability/.

Jameson, Robert C. "Be Careful of Your Thoughts: They Control Your Destiny." **HuffPost**, April 28, 2014. https://www.huffpost.com/entry/be-careful-of-your -though_b_5214689.

Job Accommodation Network. "Multimedia Training Microsite." Accessed November 12, 2019. https://askjan.org/events/Multimedia-Training-Microsite.cfm.

John F. Kennedy Center for Performing Arts. "VSA Affiliates Worldwide." Accessed March 14, 2019. http://education.kennedy-center.org/education/vsa/affiliates/.

The Kennedy Center. "Leadership Exchange in Arts and Disability (LEAD)." Accessed October 30, 2019. https://education.kennedy-center.org/education/access ibility/lead/conference.html.

Kotecki, Emily. "'Access' with Seattle Art Museum's Regan Pro," August 12, 2019, in Museum Buzz, produced by Emily Kotecki, podcast, MP3 audio, http://emily -kotecki.com/podcast.

Lave, Jean and Wenger, Etienne. **Situated Learning: Legitimate Peripheral Par- ticipation.** Cambridge: Cambridge University Press, 1991.

Leahy, Helen Rees. **Museum Bodies: The Politics and Practices of Visiting and Viewing**. Farnham: Ashgate publishing, 2012.

Levine, Danise, ed. **The NYC Guidebook to Accessibility and Universal Design** (Buffalo: University at Buffalo, The State University of New York, Center for Inclusive Design and Environmental Access, 2003). http://www.nyc.gov/html/ddc /downloads/pdf/udny/udny2.pdf.

Lime Connect. "Leading Perspectives on Disability: A Q&A with Dr. Stephen Shore." Accessed June 6, 2019. https://www.limeconnect.com/opportunities_news/detail /leading-perspectives-on-disability-a-qa-with-dr-stephen-shore.

Louisville Cultural Accessibility Association. Accessed March 5, 2019. https://louis villeculturalaccessibility.yolasite.com/.

Luhby, Tami. "Internet Becomes a Lifeline for the Deaf." **New York Times**, February 12, 1998. https://archive.nytimes.com/www.nytimes.com/library/cyber /week/021398deaf.html.

Lundebjerg, Nancy E., Daniel E. Trucil, Emily C. Hammond, and William B. Applegate. "When It Comes to Older Adults, Language Matters: Journal of the American Geriatrics Society Adopts Modified American Medical Association Style." **Journal of the American Geriatrics Society** 65, no. 7 (July 2017): 1386–88, https:// onlinelibrary.wiley.com/doi/pdf/10.1111/jgs.14941.

Majewski, Janice. **Smithsonian Guidelines for Accessible Exhibition Design**. Washington, DC: Smithsonian Accessibility Program, n.d.

Martin, Colin. "The Evolution of Universally Accessible Building Design." **The Lancet Neurology** 18, no. 1 (2019): 34.

Martin, Jenni and Marilee Jennings. "Tomorrow's Museum: Multilingual Audiences and the Learning Institution." **Museums & Social Issues** 10, no. 1 (2015): 83–94. http://dx.doi.org/10.1179/1559689314Z.00000000034.

MCN. "About." Accessed November 17, 2019. https://conference.mcn.edu/2019 /about.cfm.

Memory Café Directory. "What is a Memory Café?" Accessed February 10, 2019. https://www.memorycafedirectory.com/what-is-a-memory-cafe/.

Merriam-Webster. "Disability." Accessed February 2, 2019. https://www.merriam -webster.com/dictionary/disability.

Michaels, Samantha. "The Americans with Disabilities Act Is Turning 25. Watch the Dramatic Protest That Made It Happen." **Mother Jones**, July 25, 2015. https:// www.motherjones.com/politics/2015/07/americans-disabilities-act-capitol-crawl -anniversary/.

Michigan Alliance for Cultural Accessibility. "What We Do." Accessed March 6, 2019. https://www.culturesource.org/.

Microsoft. "Inclusive Design." Accessed July 27, 2019. https://www.microsoft.com /design/inclusive/.

Miller, Max. Speech, in support of Denver's Scientific and Cultural Facilities District, Denver, CO, April 2016.

Minneapolis Institute of Art. "Inclusion, Diversity, Accessibility and Inclusion Policy." Accessed January 31, 2019. https://new.artsmia.org/about/diversity-and -inclusion-policy/.

Minnesota Access Alliance. "About Us." Accessed March 6, 2019. https://mnaccess .org/about-the-team/.

Moore, Kristi. "Welcoming Service Dogs to Your Museum." **American Alliance of Museums**. August 26, 2019. https://www.aam-us.org/2019/08/26/welcoming-service-dogs-to-your-museum/.

Museum, Arts and Culture Access Consortium. "About." Accessed March 6, 2019. https://macaccess.org/about-new/.

———. "Supporting Transitions." Accessed April 30, 2019. https://macaccess.org/rescources/supporting-transitions-cultural-connections-for-adults-with-autism/.

Museum Computer Network. "About." Accessed November 17, 2019. https://conference.mcn.edu/2019/about.cfm.

———. "Code of Conduct." Accessed November 17, 2019. https://mcn.edu/conferences/code-of-conduct/.

Museums for All. "About." Accessed October 16, 2020. https://museums4all.org/about/.

Museum of Modern Art. "The MoMA's Alzheimer's Project." Accessed June 18, 2019. https://www.moma.org/visit/accessibility/meetme/.

———. "Sensory Map of the Museum of Modern Art." Accessed October 9, 2020. https://www.moma.org/momaorg/shared/pdfs/docs/visit/MoMA_Sensory_Map.pdf.

Museums for All. "About Museums for All." Accessed July 9, 2019. https://museums4all.org/about/.

Museum of Science, Boston. "Universal Design for Museum Learning Experiences." Accessed September 9, 2019. https://www.mos.org/UniversalDesign.

Museum of Science, Boston. **Universal Design Plan: Exhibit Design & Development**. Accessed September 9, 2019. https://www.mos.org/sites/dev-elvis.mos.org/files/docs/misc/MOS_UD_Plan.pdf.

National ADA Symposium. "National ADA Symposium." Accessed November 7, 2019. http://www.adasymposium.org/.

National Association of the Deaf. "Community and Culture - Frequently Asked Questions." Accessed October 7, 2019. https://www.nad.org/resources/american-sign-language/community-and-culture-frequently-asked-questions/.

National Captioning Institute. "History of Closed Captioning." Accessed September 29, 2019. https://www.ncicap.org/about-us/history-of-closed-captioning/.

National Center for Civil and Human Rights. "American Civil Rights Movement." Exhibits. Accessed June 19, 2019. https://www.civilandhumanrights.org/exhibit/american-civil-rights/.

National Council of Nonprofits. "Community of Practice." Accessed February 10, 2019. https://www.councilofnonprofits.org/tools-resources/community-of-practice.

National Federation of the Blind. "National Convention." Accessed November 6, 2019. https://www.nfb.org/get-involved/national-convention.

National Institutes on Health. "American Sign Language." National Institute on Deafness and Other Communication Disorders (NIDCD). Accessed October 3, 2019. https://www.nidcd.nih.gov/health/american-sign-language.

National Organization on Disability. "About." Accessed April 29, 2019. https://www.nod.org/about/.

———. "Services." Accessed April 29, 2019. https://www.nod.org/services/.

Nedelman, Michael. "Autism Prevalence Now 1 in 40 US Kids, Study Estimates." **CNN,** November 26, 2018. https://www.cnn.com/2018/11/26/health/autism -prevalence-study/index.html.

New England ADA Center. "ADA Checklist for Existing Facilities." Accessed May 8, 2019. https://www.adachecklist.org/checklist.html.

———. "ADA Title II Requirements." ADA Title II Action Guide for State and Local Governments. Accessed February 26, 2020, https://www.adaactionguide .org/ada-title-ii-requirements.

———. "Self-Evaluation Forms." Resources. ADA Title II Action Guide for State and Local Governments. Accessed February 15, 2020, https://www.adaaction guide.org/resources#.

Nielsen, Kim E. **A Disability History of the United States**. Boston: Beacon Press, 2012.

The NYU Ability Project. "Home." Accessed July 27, 2019. http://ability.nyu.edu /index.

OF/BY/FOR ALL. "Vision." Accessed April 3, 2019. https://www.ofbyforall.org /vision.

Oliver, Mike. "The Social Model in Action: If I Had a Hammer." In **Implementing the Social Model of Disability: Theory and Research,** edited by Colin Barnes and Geof Mercer, 18–31. Leeds: The Disability Press, 2004.

Rakoska, Burgandi. "Disability and Tokenism: Why No One Can Speak On Behalf of Everyone." **Rooted in Rights**, December 21, 2016. https://rootedinrights.org /disability-and-tokenism-why-no-one-can-speak-on-behalf-of-everyone/.

Rehabilitation International. "International Symbol of Accessibility." Accessed October 13, 2019. http://www.riglobal.org/about/intl-symbol-of-access/.

Salmen, John P. S. **Everyone's Welcome: The Americans with Disabilities Act and Museums.** Washington, DC: American Alliance of Museums, 1998.

Salmen, John. "U.S. Accessibility Codes and Standards: Challenges for Universal Design." In **Universal Design Handbook**, 2nd ed., edited by Wolfang F.E. Preiser and Korydon H. Smith, 6.1. New York: McGraw-Hill, 2011.

Schencker, Lisa. "Libraries Hire Social Workers to Help Homeless Patrons." **Los Angeles Times**, October 27, 2018. https://www.latimes.com/nation/la-na-chicago -library-homeless-20181027-story.html.

Scientific Cultural Facilities District. "Why was SCFD created?" Accessed July 29, 2019. http://scfd.org/blog-entry/49/2014-05-22-Why-was-SCFD-Created.html.

Seiter, Courtney. "14 Quotes that Celebrate a More Accessible World." **Chicago Tribune**, May 26, 2016. https://www.chicagotribune.com/business/blue-sky/ct -buffer-14-quotes-that-celebrate-accessible-world-bsi-hub-20160526-story.html.

Senior Living. "How Ageism in Health Care is Affecting Society." Accessed September 25, 2019. https://www.seniorliving.org/health/ageism/.

Seo, Jinsil Hwaryoung. "Toys, Plants Provide Alternative Digital Interface for Kids, Elderly." **Arch One**, March 10, 2015. https://one.arch.tamu.edu/news/2015/3/10 /interactive-toys/.

Serrell, Beverly. **Exhibit Labels: An Interpretive Approach.** Lanham, MD: Rowman AltaMira, 1996.

Siegel, Betty. Keynote Address. Art of Access Symposium. Denver, July 12, 2017.

Smithsonian. "Project SEARCH." Access Smithsonian. Accessed April 30, 2019. https://www.si.edu/Accessibility/Access-opportunities.

Smithsonian Accessibility Program. "Smithsonian Guidelines for Accessible Exhibition Design." Accessed June 18, 2019. https://www.si.edu/Accessibility/SGAED.

Snapes, Laura. "Beyoncé's Parkwood Entertainment Sued over Website Accessibility." **The Guardian**, January 4, 2019. https://www.theguardian.com/music/2019/jan/04/beyonce-parkwood-entertainment-sued-over-website-accessibility.

Span, Paula. "Ageism: A 'Prevalent and Insidious' Health Threat." **New York Times**, April 26, 2019. https://www.nytimes.com/2019/04/26/health/ageism-elderly-health.html.

SPARK! "Our History." Accessed March 6, 2019. http://www.sparkprograms.org/history/.

Special Olympics. **Ten Commandments of Communicating about People with Intellectual Disabilities**, 2012. http://www.specialolympicsarkansas.org/uploads/1/6/6/8/16687598/tencommandments_2012.pdf.

Special Olympics. "The 'R'-Word Remains Prevalent Across Social Media." Press Releases. Accessed September 5, 2019. https://www.specialolympics.org/discriminatory-language-about-people-with-intellectual-disabilities-particularly-the-r-word-remains-prevalent-across-social-media.

Star Institute. "Understanding Sensory Processing Disorder." Accessed October 20, 2020. https://www.spdstar.org/basic/understanding-sensory-processing-disorder.

Steele, Carmen. "The Impacts of Digital Divide." **Digital Divide Council**, September 20, 2018. http://www.digitaldividecouncil.com/the-impacts-of-digital-divide/.

Sustaining Places. "State & Regional Museum Associations." Accessed November 13, 2019. https://sustainingplaces.com/about/museum-associations/.

Temple Grandin. "About Temple Grandin." Accessed November 25, 2019. http://www.templegrandin.com/.

Top Nonprofits. "Top 100 Nonprofits on the Web." Accessed July 27, 2019. https://topnonprofits.com/lists/best-nonprofits-on-the-web/.

United States Access Board. "Access Board Issues Guidance on Use of the International Symbol of Accessibility Under the Americans with Disabilities Act and the Architectural Barriers Act." Accessed October 13, 2019. https://www.access-board.gov/news/1899-access-board-issues-guidance-on-the-international-symbol-of-accessibility.

United States Department of Justice. **2010 ADA Standards for Accessible Design**. Washington, DC: Dept. of Justice, 2010.

United States Department of Justice. "Frequently Asked Questions about Service Animals and the ADA." Accessed September 2, 2019. https://www.ada.gov/regs2010/service_animal_qa.html#def.

———. "Service Animals." Accessed September 5, 2019. https://www.ada.gov/service_animals_2010.htm.

United States Department of Labor. **Inclusive Internship Programs: A How-To Guide for Employers**. Office of Disability Employment Policy. Accessed April 30, 2019. https://www.dol.gov/odep/pdf/InclusiveInternshipPrograms.pdf.

United States Department of Labor. "Section 504, Rehabilitation Act of 1973." Statues, Executive Orders and Federal Regulations and Policies, Office of the Assistant Secretary for Administration & Management. Accessed August 26, 2020. https://www.dol.gov/agencies/oasam/centers-offices/civil-rights-center/statutes/section-504-rehabilitation-act-of-1973.

University of Colorado. "H.I. = Having InterDependence." School of Medicine JFK Partners. Accessed April 28, 2019. http://www.ucdenver.edu/academics/colleges/medicalschool/programs/JFKPartners/educationtraining/fellowships/hi/Pages/default.aspx.

———. "Leadership Education in Neurodevelopmental and Related Disabilities (LEND)." School of Medicine JFK Partners. Accessed April 28, 2019. http://www.ucdenver.edu/academics/colleges/medicalschool/programs/JFKPartners/projects/Pages/LEND.aspx.

U.S. Department of Education. "Rehabilitation Act of 1973." Accessed January 16, 2020. https://www2.ed.gov/policy/speced/leg/rehab/rehabilitation-act-of-1973-amended-by-wioa.pdf.

U.S. Department of Justice. **2010 ADA Standards for Accessible Design.** Washington, DC: Department of Justice, 2010.

———. "A Guide to Disability Rights Laws." Accessed March 8, 2020. https://www.ada.gov/cguide.htm#anchor65610.

U.S. Department of Labor. Office of Disability Employment Policy. **Inclusive Internship Programs: A How-To Guide for Employers.** Accessed April 30, 2019. https://www.dol.gov/odep/pdf/InclusiveInternshipPrograms.pdf.

———. "Section 504, Rehabilitation Act of 1973." Accessed March 8, 2020. https://www.dol.gov/agencies/oasam/centers-offices/civil-rights-center/statutes/section-504-rehabilitation-act-of-1973.

U.S. Equal Employment Opportunity Commission. "The Americans with Disabilities Act Amendments Act of 2008." Accessed February 15, 2019. https://www.eeoc.gov/laws/statutes/adaaa_info.cfm.

U.S. General Services Administration. "IT Accessibility Laws and Policies." Accessed October 20, 2020. https://www.section508.gov/manage/laws-and-policies.

———. "User-Centered Design Basics." Accessed October 20, 2020. https://www.usability.gov/what-and-why/user-centered-design.html.

Vanderbilt Kennedy Center. "Community Engagement Program: Inclusion Network of Nashville." Accessed March 6, 2019. https://vkc.mc.vanderbilt.edu/vkc/triad/cei-INN/.

Vizcaya Museum & Gardens. "Director's Welcome." Accessed April 21, 2019. http://vizcaya.org/about-directors-welcome.asp.

Web Accessibility Initiative. "Generate an Accessibility Statement." Planning and Policies. Accessed September 5, 2019. https://www.w3.org/WAI/planning/statements/generator/#create.

———. "How to Make Your Presentations Accessible to All." Accessed November 1, 2020. https://www.w3.org/WAI/teach-advocate/accessible-presentations/.

Web Accessibility in Mind. "Introduction to Web Accessibility." Accessed July 7, 2019. https://webaim.org/intro/.

———. "The WebAIM Million." Accessed July 27, 2019. https://webaim.org /projects/million/.

———. "Web Accessibility Evaluation Tool." Accessed July 27, 2019. http://wave .webaim.org/.

Wilcher, Shirley. "The Rehabilitation Act of 1973: 45 Years of Activism and Progress." **Insight Into Diversity**, September 17, 2018. https://www.insightintodiversity .com/the-rehabilitation-act-of-1973-45-years-of-activism-and-progress/.

Williams, Bob. "The Rehabilitation Act of 1973: Independence Bound." Administration for Community Living. September 26, 2016. Accessed March 8, 2020. https:// acl.gov/news-and-events/acl-blog/rehabilitation-act-1973-independence-bound.

Williamson, Bess. **Accessible America**. New York: New York University Press, 2019.

Wright State University. "Crip Theory." Accessed October 1, 2019. https://www .wright.edu/event/sex-disability-conference/crip-theory/

World Health Organization. "Deafness and Hearing Loss." Accessed September 29, 2019. https://www.who.int/news-room/fact-sheets/detail/deafness-and-hearing -loss.

———. "Disabilities." Accessed March 8, 2019. https://www.who.int/topics /disabilities/en/.

———. "International Classification of Functioning, Disability and Health." Accessed March 8, 2020. https://www.who.int/classifications/icf/en/.

World Wide Web Consortium. "About W3C WAI." Accessed July 17, 2019. https:// www.w3.org/WAI/about/.

———. "Generate an Accessibility Statement." Planning and Policies. Accessed September 5, 2019, https://www.w3.org/WAI/planning/statements/generator/#create.

———. "Making Content Usable for People with Cognitive and Learning Disabilities." Accessed October 20, 2020. https://www.w3.org/TR/coga-usable/#how-to -use-this-document.

———. "Stories of Web Users." Accessed July 17, 2019. https://www.w3.org/WAI /people-use-web/user-stories/.

———. "Understanding the Four Principles of Accessibility." Accessed July 17, 2019. https://www.w3.org/WAI/WCAG21/Understanding/intro#understanding -the-four-principles-of-accessibility.

Yin, Michelle, Dahlia Shaewitz, Cynthia Overton, and Deeza-Mae Smith. "A Hidden Market: The Purchasing Power of Working-Age Adults With Disabilities." (Washington, DC: **American Institutes for Research**, 2018), April 17, 2018. https:// www.air.org/resource/hidden-market-purchasing-power-working-age-adults -disabilities.

Index

ableism, 126–28, 129, 189.
　See also language and identity
access consortiums, xvi, 25–27, 172–76
accessibility audit, 43, 46–53, 58, 138,
　177, 189; historic sites, 50–54,
　60n14; sensory audit, 81–85;
　transition plans, 10, 46, 49–51, 57, 81
accessibility, xiv, 189
accessibility web page, 120.
　See also digital accessibility
accessibility statement, 41–42, 120
accessible design. *See* inclusive design
accessible exhibition design, 10, 33,
　55, 72–73, 81–86, 121, 133–41;
　interactive elements, 53, 101, 135–
　37, 141, 146, 178–79; multimodal
　elements, 72–73, 145–46, 191;
　navigation and pathways, 66, 136
accessible web design, 102–107, 120.
　See also digital accessibility
ADA coordinator certification, 161–62.
　See also professional development
ADA Standards for Accessible Design,
　10, 46–48, 57–58
adaptive technologies. *See* assistive
　technologies
advisory committees or boards, 33–36,
　41, 47, 106, 151, 166, 172

alternative image text (alt text). *See*
　digital accessibility
American Sign Language (ASL), 123,
　145, 150–51.
　See also communication; language
　and identity
Americans with Disabilities Act (ADA),
　2–3, 7–10, 17, 45–47, 49, 55, 57–58,
　94, 95, 189
Americans with Disabilities Amendment
　Act (ADAA), 10
Architectural Barriers Act, 5, 8
assistive technology, 98, 100–101, 104,
　189–90.
　See also digital accessibility
audio description. *See* verbal description
auditory access, 142–45.
　See also communication

barrier removal, xiii, 1–5, 13–14, 24,
　35, 37, 45, 62–63, 97, 101, 103, 177,
　191; for historic sites, 35, 50–54,
　121–22.
　See also accessibility audit

captions, 96, 103, 142, 144–45;
　closed, 142, 144; open, 142, 144.
　See also communication

About the Authors

Heather Pressman is an educator with a passion for accessibility and inclusion. Her background includes work in museum education, development, and communications. She currently serves as the director of learning and engagement for the Molly Brown House Museum where she works to expand access, despite the physical challenges of a 130-year-old historic house. Heather got into this work because she saw through her friend's experience how much people with disabilities were missing out on in museums. She is a founding member of the organizing committee for the Art of Access Alliance in Denver, a consortium working to make Denver's arts and cultural attractions accessible to all. Heather holds a master's degree in museum studies from The Johns Hopkins University. There, her studies focused on education, accessibility, and developing online communities. She has presented at regional and national conferences including the American Alliance of Museums, Mountain-Plains Museum Association, Colorado-Wyoming Association of Museums, and the Kennedy Center's Leadership Exchange in Arts and Disability. Heather is also mom to a young boy on the autism spectrum.

Danielle Schulz is dedicated to an accessible and inclusive future. She currently serves as the senior manager of lifelong learning and accessibility at the Denver Art Museum, where she works with community members to promote inclusive practices that ensure visitors of all ages and abilities can enjoy and be inspired by their interaction with art. Danielle is a founding member of the organizing committee for the Art of Access Alliance Denver, a consortium working to make Denver-area arts and cultural attractions accessible to all. Her passion for promoting accessible and inclusive arts programming began at The Arc of the Arts community organization in Austin, Texas, where she worked while pursuing a master's degree in community-based arts education from the University of Texas at Austin. She has previously worked with accessibility at the Dallas Museum of Art and has presented on the topic of accessibility in the arts at numerous regional and national conferences, including American Alliance of Museums (AAM), the National Art Education Association (NAEA), and the Kennedy Center's Leadership Exchange in Arts and Disability (LEAD), and authored the 2012 publication, **Cultivating a Meaningful Experience: Art Education for Adults with Disabilities at a Community Based Art Center**.

CPSIA information can be obtained
at www.ICGtesting.com
Printed in the USA
BVHW042240130321
602253BV00003B/4